MONUMENTS OF THE INCAS

Watchman's hut and altar (Funerary Rock), Machu Picchu

MONUMENTS OF THE INCAS

TEXT BY JOHN HEMMING

PHOTOGRAPHS BY EDWARD RANNEY

UNIVERSITY OF NEW MEXICO PRESS

ALBUQUERQUE

LIBRARY OF CONGRESS CATALOGING-IN-PUBLICATION DATA

Hemming, John, 1935–
    Monuments of the Incas / text by John Hemming : photographs by Edward Ranney.
        p.   cm.
    Reprint. Originally published: Boston : Little, Brown, 1982.
    Includes bibliographical references.
    ISBN 0-8263-1216-0
    1. Incas—Architecture. 2. Incas—Antiquities. 3. Peru—
Antiquities. I. Ranney, Edward. II. Title.
[F3429.H38 1990]
985'.01—dc20   90-31705
                                                      CIP

Monuments of the Incas was originally published in 1982 by New York Graphic Society, Little, Brown and Company, Boston. ISBN 0-8212-1521-3. The University of New Mexico Press paperback edition published 1990 by arrangement with the authors.

Designed by Eleanor Morris Caponigro
Type set in Trump Mediaeval by The Stinehour Press, Lunenburg, Vermont
Printed by Litho Specialties, Inc., St. Paul, Minnesota

ACKNOWLEDGMENTS

Passages quoted from the following works are reprinted by permission of the publishers:

Hiram Bingham, *Lost City of the Incas*. E. P. Dutton, Inc., New York (for Duell, Sloan & Pearce); J. M. Dent & Sons Ltd., London, 1951.

Pedro de Cieza de León, *The Incas of Pedro de Cieza de León*. Translated by Harriet de Onis; edited and with an introduction by Victor W. von Hagen. University of Oklahoma Press, Norman, 1959.

Garcilaso de la Vega, *Royal Commentaries of the Incas*. Translated by Harold V. Livermore. Copyright © 1966 by the University of Texas Press, Austin.

The publisher is grateful for permission to reproduce the following plans:

The map on page 123 and the plan on pages 120–121 are adapted from *Machupijchu, enigmática ciudad Inka*, 1972; the plans on pages 91 and 93 are adapted from *P'isaq, metrópoli Inka*, 1970. Courtesy of Víctor Angles Vargas.

The site plans and reconstructions on pages 42 (right), 59, 69, 84, 85, 110, 111, 113, 183, 192, 193, and 205 are adapted from *Arquitectura Inka*, 1977. Courtesy of Graziano Gasparini and Luise Margolies.

The drawings on pages 15, 38, 42 (left), 49, and 64 are from Felipe Guaman Poma de Ayala, *Nueva corónica y buen gobierno* (?1580–1620).

The plan on page 196 is reproduced by the courtesy of Craig Morris and the American Museum of Natural History, New York.

CONTENTS

ILLUSTRATIONS

PHOTOGRAPHS

PREFACE

WHEN LIVING IN CUZCO in the 1960s I became convinced of the need for a comprehensive photographic study of Inca monuments. Archaeological documentation of Inca culture has consistently failed over the years to convey the intimate relation between the monuments and their surroundings— the shapes and spaces of the mountain landscape, which the Incas venerated. The unique setting of each major site, with the buildings erected upon it and the sculpture carved from the living rock, together embody the Incas' sense of visual space. It is the special capability of photography to apprehend that space, to see it differently from the way the unaided eye sees it, and to reveal meanings not apparent before. A group of photographs of each site, given their own logic and internal references, can make us aware of the Incas' spiritual intent as well as their practical planning, and can enable us to understand why, as well as how, they built as they did.

A number of the Incas' important religious sites are situated on ridges that overlook the surrounding area, yet their structures are effectively integrated with the landscape, and in some cases are even concealed by it. The temple-fortress of Sacsahuaman dominates the Cuzco valley, but its massive ramparts are related to the shapes of the hills behind it. The small site of Pisac is not visible from below, but it commands strategic and beautiful views of the sacred Vilcanota-Urubamba valley both to the east and the west. The sun temple of Ollantaytambo, set on a steep rock farther down the valley, faces a hill whose powerful shape is abstracted in the rising and falling step design carved on one of the temple monoliths.

The aspiration for the union of heaven and earth, of spiritual and physical forces, is most strongly felt at Machu Picchu. At this unique sanctuary the buildings are fused with granite outcrops in a way that is more sculptural in feeling than architectural. Steep stairways lead one up, into and around enclosed religious and residential compounds, onto small plazas with views precisely oriented to surrounding peaks, and to at least six major rock shrines. The altar on the highest pinnacle is open to the heavens and the movements of the sun, yet looks directly down to the Urubamba river two thousand feet below. The shapes of other altars clearly echo the forms of the landscape itself, and still others, like the awesome sacrificial condor stone, express the dark and terrifying forces of nature, which demanded continual attendance and propitiation.

The unique achievement of Inca sculpture, particularly the "in situ" carving of the rock outcrops, has in the past received little attention or serious study. To the Incas the rock outcrops were not an adjunct to the architecture. Rather their presence, along with other important landscape features such as sacred peaks, caves and rivers strongly influenced the choice of certain locations as temple sites, and to a large degree determined the planning of the religious compounds, as well as being the medium for religious worship itself.

The Incas also worshipped at many isolated rock shrines in the vicinity of Cuzco, and these, perhaps more than the major temple sites, or even the important landscape shrines of Huanacauri hill and Tambo-toqo, were the focus for religious worship by the general populace. The simple, though to us often obscure, carving which marked these rocks as special should be seen as part of a unique visual language. Like the patterns and concepts still evident in the best contemporary Quechua weaving, the forms of the carving are intimately related to the natural world, where they were first seen. Even though the rock sculpture may never lend itself to literal translation in terms of our own culture, it is my feeling that it represents an accomplishment as important as the architecture, and in fact provides the key to understanding both the architecture and the culture as a whole.

The religious intensity of the general population was a major force contributing to the Incas' architectural and sculptural achievements, but there was a definite split between the poetic vision that marked the Inca religion and the rigid utilitarian mentality which so efficiently organized and controlled the expanding empire. Ultimately the monuments came to serve two contrasting functions, and distinct types of sites speak to us in different ways, as a comparison of the desolate administrative settlement of Huánuco and the gardenlike sanctuary of Machu Picchu makes clear. Huánuco provides important answers to our desire to know what kind of political organization enabled the empire to flourish, while the unique achievements of Machu Picchu speak profoundly of the possibilities of art, religion, and culture.

I AM INDEBTED TO the Commission for Educational Exchange, Lima, Peru, for a year of study in Cuzco in 1964 and 1965, during which the background for this book was established. A return to Peru in 1971 enabled me to produce initial work for publication, but the major part of the project was realized in 1975, with the support of a photographer's fellowship from the National Endowment for the Arts. After beginning collaboration with John Hemming in 1976, I made a final trip to fill out the material needed for the book.

It is an impossible task to thank everyone who aided me over the years in the work of photographing, but my gratitude, whether for hospitality and company, or directions and encouragement, is expressed here once again. I am particularly indebted to Manuel Chávez Ballón of Cuzco for guiding me to such isolated shrines as Huanacauri, Choquequilla, and Quillarumi. Without his personal interest and sharing of knowledge my own work would have been severely limited.

To Luis Lumbreras, director of the Museo Nacional de Antropología y Arqueología, Lima, and to archaeologist Alfredo Valencia of Cuzco, I extend my warm appreciation for advice and suggestions. John Rowe's personal thoughts and priorities for study proved to be most helpful in Cuzco, and the opportunity to become acquainted with R. T. Zuidema's investigation of the ceque system of Cuzco provided a stimulating counterpart to my own explorations of the shrines.

John Hemming and I are deeply indebted to Graziano Gasparini and Luise Margolies for allowing us to reproduce site plans and architectural drawings from their book, *Inca Architecture*. We are likewise grateful to Víctor Angles Vargas for permission to reprint his plans of Pisac, Machu Picchu, and the Machu Picchu archaeological park, and to Craig Morris for lending us his plans of Huánuco and for sharing his as yet unpublished work on that site.

Reproduction of an image from the Bingham archive is through the courtesy of the family of Hiram Bingham and the National Geographic Society. I am grateful to Víctor and Julia Chambi for their permission to reprint photographs by Martín Chambi, the early twentieth-century Cuzco photographer. The opportunity to collaborate with them in 1977 on the reorganization of their father's archive, aided by members of Earthwatch, proved to be a particularly meaningful conclusion to an extended period of intense personal work in Cuzco.

Without the interest and support of certain persons intimately concerned with the traditions and possibilities of photography, this book might not have achieved its present form. I am particularly appreciative of the interest John Szarkowski, director of the department of photography, the Museum of Modern Art, New York, has shown in this project, and pleased that a selection of it, curated by Betsy Jablow, was shown at the museum in a joint exhibition with the work of Martín Chambi. The early support of David Travis, curator of photography, the Art Institute of Chicago, of Peter Bunnell of Princeton University, and of Paul Caponigro has also been warmly appreciated over the years.

John Hemming and I are grateful to the editors of New York Graphic Society Books for their commitment to publish this work in its entirety, and we extend particular thanks to Janet Swan and Jean Whitnack for their thoroughness and care in seeing it through publication. The contributions made by Eleanor Caponigro to integrating text and photographs have gone far beyond the responsibility of design alone. For her personal involvement and dedication to the highest standards of bookmaking, I am deeply grateful.

Edward Ranney

The upper stone of Saihuite, carved with terraces, houses, animals and divination channels

Soccllacasa pass, near the rock shrines of Saihuite

INCA ARCHITECTURE

THE INCAS WERE AN AUSTERE MOUNTAIN TRIBE, one of many Andean peoples who flourished briefly during the millennia before the European conquest of the Americas. The name Inca would be known only to archaeologists but for two things: the accident of history by which Pizarro's Spaniards invaded Peru just as the Inca empire was at its zenith—and the architectural legacy left by this energetic society.

The Incas were the Romans of the Andean world—efficient administrators, excellent soldiers, fine engineers, but with little of the artistic brilliance of the more flamboyant, sybaritic civilizations that preceded them. Their ceramics, metalwork and textiles were very competent, but derivative and often stereotyped. Their only artistic triumph was in architecture, or more precisely in masonry. Inca buildings were simple in plan and design, but their stonework was technically and aesthetically astounding. It is a durable legacy and it impresses modern visitors just as it did the first conquistadores. Bernabé Cobo wrote, soon after the Conquest, that "the only remarkable part of these [Inca] buildings was the walls—but these were so amazing that it would be difficult for any who have not seen them to appreciate them."

We know that the military expansion and political ascendancy of the Inca empire was short-lived, a mere seventy or eighty years before its defeat by Spanish invaders. To modern observers, the *quantity* of building achieved during so brief a span is as impressive as its excellence. To appreciate this great achievement we must know the historical and geographical context of Inca architecture.

The Incas themselves recorded eleven rulers—called "Inca" like the tribe itself—in the history of their rise from obscure origins to control of the vast empire overthrown by Pizarro. Under the first seven of these chiefs they were an insignificant tribe, one of hundreds that farmed, hunted and fought one another along the length of the Andes. Inca origin legends indicated that the tribe migrated northward from the high, fertile plain near Lake Titicaca and settled in the rich vale of Cuzco. They built a town and temple. Their huts were simple structures of fieldstone set in clay mortar, roofed with thatch tied to a wooden trellis. Their town probably had no organized plan. Its streets were simple paths between the houses, all that was needed by a mountain people with no draft animals or vehicles. The tribe gradually established an ascendancy over the people already settled near Cuzco. The Incas expanded under their early rulers, often by intertribal skirmishes, by marriage alliances between chiefs' families, or by wealth generated by successful farming. The tribes they absorbed near Cuzco left remains that can now be excavated by archaeologists; and when the Spaniards interrogated survivors of these pre-Inca tribes they found surprising resentment of the Inca conquest that had occurred little more than a century before the arrival of the Spaniards themselves.

By the 1430s of our Christian era, the Incas were in control of the valleys around their town Cuzco. Their territory was hilly ground between the canyon of the Apurímac and the deep valley of the Vilcanota–Urubamba river, which flows north toward the main stream of the Amazon. To the north and east lay mountains, with the endless forests of the Amazon basin beyond; to the west, the main chain of the Andes separated Cuzco from the deserts along the Pacific coast of Peru. The chronicler Cabello de Balboa tells us that the event that transformed Inca history occurred in about 1438. Pizarro's official secretary Miguel de Estete confirmed this. He wrote during the Conquest of 1532 that "by the reckoning of the most ancient men, this land has been subject to a prince for only ninety years." The turning point was an attack or invasion by the powerful Chanca tribe from beyond the Apurímac.

TAWANTINSUYU
THE INCA EMPIRE

Inca towns   ○ Corongo
Inca ruins   ▲ **Sahuite**
Inca roads   ———
Modern cities   ● *LIMA*

(All modern names are in italics)

QUITO
Latacunga
Ambato
Riobamba
Alausí
Cañar ▲ **Ingapirca**
Tumibamba
(CUENCA)
Tumbes
Cusipampa
Sullana
Piura
Serrán
Huancabamba
Cajas
Motupe
Chachapoyas
Marañón
Huallaga
Amazon
CHICLAYO
Zaña **Cajamarca**
Cajabamba
Huamachuco
Antamarca
Conchucos
Chan Chan
TRUJILLO
Corongo
Huaylas
Piscobamba
Yungay ▲ **Tantamayo**
CHIMBOTE
Huari
Casma
Huaraz **Huánuco(Viejo)**
Recuay *HUÁNUCO*
Tonsucancha
Cajatambo
Paramonga
Oyón **Pumpu**
Huaura *Lake Junín* Chacamarca
Tarma **Tarmatambo**
Chancay **Jauja**
Wari Willka
LIMA
Pachacamac
Huarochiri
Yauyos
Ucayali
Urubamba
Apurímac
Vilcabamba
Machu Picchu
Vitcos **Ollantaytambo**
AYACUCHO **CUZCO** **Paucartambo**
Mala **Incahuasi** **Vilcashuamán** ▲ **Sahuite** **Pisac**
Huarco **Huaitará** Abancay Urcos
Tambo Colorado *Andahuaylas* **Raqchi**
Ica **Soras**
Mantaro
Cañete
Pisco
Nazca
Ayaviri
Pucará Azángaro
Lake Titicaca
Sillustani Island of the Sun
Hatuncolla + *Mt. Illampu*
Colca *PUNO* ▲ **Coati Island**
AREQUIPA **Chucuito** Chuquiabo
(LA PAZ)
Tiahuanaco + *Mt. Illimani*
Desaguadero *COCHABAMBA*
To Lake Poopó Pocona
Incallacta

N

0 50 100 200 300
KILOMETERS

The Chanca invaders advanced to the heights above Cuzco itself. On the point of collapse, the Inca army rallied under a younger son of the ruling Inca. The Chancas were defeated and pursued back across the Apurímac, across the territory of the Quechua and into their homeland near modern Andahuaylas. The Inca victory was complete and so unexpected that in the Inca legend the rocks of the battlefield transformed themselves into warriors to turn the tide of battle. Those rocks, known as *pururaucas*, were later venerated in gratitude for their timely help.

The prince who commanded the victory of 1438 soon established himself as Inca with the title Pachacuti.* In Quechua, the Incas' language, *pacha* means land or time, and *cuti* means to turn around; so that the title Pachacuti could mean reformer of the world. There is an increasing belief among modern authorities that this one man was the architect of the Inca civilization and social system. Flushed with success over the Chancas, Pachacuti embarked on a rush of conquests that transformed the Incas into an imperial power. He was one of those protean figures, like Alexander or Napoleon, who combined a mania for conquest with the ability to impose his will on every facet of government. Cobo wrote that it was Pachacuti "who instituted the state with a code of laws and statutes. . . . He set everything in order: he abolished some rites and ceremonies and added others. He expanded the official religion, instituting sacrifices and services by which the gods were to be worshipped. He embellished the temples with magnificent buildings. . . . In short, he overlooked nothing and organized everything efficiently."

If this interpretation is correct, Pachacuti galvanized the people of Cuzco into activity immediately after the Chanca war. He razed the town center and began to rebuild it on a monumental scale, with a plan worthy of the capital city of a budding empire. He drained marshes below Cuzco and chan-

* "Pachacuti" is the old Spanish spelling. More modern, phonetic spellings of this and other Inca titles, personal names and place names, and of Quechua words are given in the Glossary (page 222).

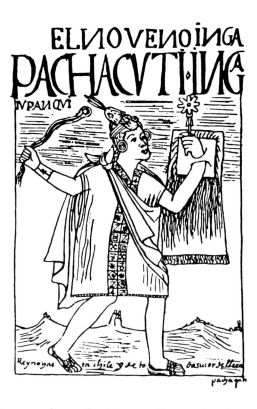

Pachacuti Inca, as drawn by Guaman Poma, the sixteenth-century Indian chronicler

neled the Saphi-Huatanay and Tullumayo streams that cross the city into stone-lined conduits.

Pachacuti conceived the center of Cuzco as the body of a puma, the mountain jaguar that had been the sacred animal of Chavín, Tiahuanaco and other pre-Inca civilizations. The hill above the city was deemed the puma's head, and the Inca started to build the fortress-temple of Sacsahuaman there with zigzag ramparts symbolizing the puma's teeth. The sloping ground between the two streams represented the feline's body, and the sharp triangle where the streams met was a district known as *pumachupan*, the puma's tail (page 42).

In reorganizing Inca religion, which had a number of interconnecting elements, Pachacuti established existing practices in a calendar of ceremonies and ritual. He ensured that the Inca, as spiritual head of the empire, had a leading part in each

A ceremonial stairway in a sacred outcrop near Chinchero, north of Cuzco, leads to the carved upper surface (see page 168)

element. There was an ancient agricultural tradition, with festivals marking the seasons of the farming year, puberty rites for Inca boys, and a veneration for the wonders of nature —rocks, caves, springs, mountain passes, or any plant or ani-

mal that "differed from others of its kind, through some extra-ordinary or exaggerated feature. . . . They reasoned that if nature had marked them out there must be something miracu-lous involved." The Inca himself directed many of these ceremonies, leading the chanting, or turning the first earth with a golden foot plow before plowing began throughout the empire.

Another canon of Inca religion venerated the sun, *inti*, and to a lesser extent the moon, stars, thunder and the rainbow. Pachacuti also claimed divine status for the Inca ruler—he himself was the son of the sun and his presence dazzled on-lookers with the brilliance of the sun itself. This was the same identity with the sun that Egyptian and Japanese em-perors claimed to enhance their majesty. A consequent ele-ment of the Inca religion was ancestor worship. Here again, traditional beliefs were elaborated and ritualized for the greater glory of the royal family. The body of each dead Inca was mummified and his spirit was represented by a *huauque* (totem). His lineage of male descendants, called *ayllu*, or more precisely *panaca*, was responsible for maintaining his possessions and for parading his mummy and huauque at frequent ceremonies. "When the king died, the prince did not inherit his palace and fortune: it was left, together with the body of the deceased, to the clan he had founded." Legends surrounding the start of the Inca tribe assumed religious im-portance. One tradition was that a godlike figure, Viracocha, had created the world and then disappeared westward over the Pacific toward the setting sun. Pachacuti's own father was called Viracocha, so that a cult of Viracocha worship was elaborated alongside the worship of the sun and celestial bodies. Viracocha was believed to have started his creation of the world at Lake Titicaca, and it was from here that the heroic founders of the Inca tribe had taken their people north to Cuzco. The exodus was led by the four mythical Ayar brothers and their sisters. Places involved in this migration became venerated shrines: the islands in Lake Titicaca; Tambo-toqo, the cave from which the brothers emerged; and Huanacauri, the hill near Cuzco on which one of them was

Lake Titicaca from the Island of the Sun

transformed to stone. Sites connected with the legendary first Inca, Manco Capac, were equally holy.

This sketch of Inca religion does not begin to embrace the complexity of its rituals, sacrifices, prayers and ceremonial. Andean Indians are highly spiritual and profoundly superstitious. Catholic priests who wrote many of the post-Conquest chronicles examined Inca religion in great depth: they were charged with the extirpation of this "idolatry"—as missionaries of a different faith, they had to understand the beliefs they wished to supplant and destroy. There is not space here to describe all the details they recorded. But a basic understanding of Inca religion is essential to an appreciation of Inca architecture. The Incas, like so many other peoples, built spectacular monuments in the name of their religion. Other triumphs of Inca masonry were built for the semidivine Inca and his government.

Anyone who contemplates imperial Inca architecture is awed by the devoted labor and thousands of man-hours it must have consumed. We have to remember that much of this labor was inspired by religious zeal. There was the same intensity of faith that has produced glorious religious architecture in all parts of the world. There was also patriotic devotion to a divine monarch: a desire that this venerated ruler should enjoy the very best available workmanship.

As their empire grew, the Incas harnessed and organized labor levies from all parts of the Andes. They exacted tribute in kind and in personal service. There was occasional reluctance or armed rebellion against these demands. But most of the labor levies went willingly, proud to serve their religion and their ruler. After the Spaniards had conquered Peru, they held official inquiries into taxation and tribute under their predecessors. One such inquiry has survived from the town of Acora on the shore of Lake Titicaca. Aged chiefs were asked about the tribute they had paid to the Inca, and "they replied that they gave him many Indians for warfare and to build his houses and chacaras [agricultural terracing] in Cuzco; male and female Indians to serve in his house and daughters of chiefs as handmaidens; they gave him Indian men and women to kill in sacrifice to the idols and shrines, and Indians to settle as mitimaes colonists in many places; they took him chuño [dehydrated potatoes] and other food from here to Cuzco, and chasqui [postal] runners took fish very quickly so that it would arrive fresh in Cuzco. They made agricultural chacaras for him in this province and gave him fine cumbi and abasca cloth—he sent Inca officials to collect it. They also gave him llamas for tribute, and Indians to mine gold for him in Chuquiabo [La Paz] and silver in the mines of Porco. They gave him Indians assigned to making featherwork. They gave him sandals and charqui, which is meat dried in the sun, and wool from communally owned llamas. They gave him llautus [woolen braids] as head ornaments and slings for battle, and copper battle-axes, and copper bars for his buildings, and everything else that the Inca requested of them, for they were very obedient to him."

After the defeat of the Chancas in 1438, the Incas' conquests moved steadily north and south from Cuzco. They advanced beyond the Chancas into the highland valleys of central Peru. Another campaign swept southward, up to the plateau of the altiplano around Lake Titicaca, to conquer the region of the tribe's legendary origins. Being a mountain people, the Incas were more at ease fighting along the ranges of the Andes. But with the Peruvian highlands secure, they were able to encircle and descend upon the rich kingdoms of the coastal deserts. Their most powerful opponent was the artistic, sophisticated and by then somewhat decadent kingdom of Chimor on the north coast. This was the region that had built the largest structures of South America in the pyramids of Moche and the vast city of Chan Chan—one of the world's largest urban complexes of its period. Under Pachacuti and his equally brilliant and belligerent son Topa Inca Yupanqui, Inca armies were well drilled and equipped. They had little difficulty in defeating Chimor, and then conquered southward along the Pacific coast. They took the ancient shrine of Pachacamac near modern Lima, a place so venerable and venerated that they incorporated its god into their own Viracocha cult.

Adobe retaining walls below the temple dedicated to Viracocha at Pachacamac, overlooking the Pacific ocean

The Incas were effective empire builders. They preferred to absorb tribes into their empire by negotiation than by force. Many Andean peoples chose to join the Inca hegemony, attracted by the obvious efficiency of Inca rule. But the Incas fought hard against any who offered resistance. There was a long campaign against the Chuquimanco people of the southern coastal valley of Lunahuaná. Another fierce campaign against the Cañari of southern Ecuador ended with the slaughter of most of the adult males of that tribe. A revolt by the Colla of Lake Titicaca was ruthlessly suppressed by Topa Inca Yupanqui. Campaigns into the Amazon forests were always failures, for the phalanxes of Inca warriors with their slings and battle-axes could not maneuver in the confines of the forests and were defeated by the archers of more primitive jungle tribes. But by the time the Spaniards began to explore the Pacific coast of South America in the 1520s, the armies of the eleventh Inca, Huayna Capac, were fighting on the distant marches of a vast empire, against the tribes of what is now southern Colombia, the Guarani of eastern Bolivia, and the Araucanians of southern Chile.

The Incas instinctively adopted many practices of other successful imperialist powers. They left pliant local chiefs with a measure of pomp and prestige, but reserved real power for their own centrally appointed officials. They brought the sons of subject chiefs for education at the court of Cuzco. They were reasonably tolerant of the deities of conquered tribes: such idols were transported to Cuzco, partly for the honor of inclusion in the empire's central pantheon, but also as hostages for the subject tribe's good behavior.

As the Inca empire expanded outward from the nucleus, Cuzco, the Incas secured its communications with a magnificent network of roads. They relied entirely on the mobility of their armies for military control of their federation of tribes. Subject regions were governed from administrative centers built at regular intervals along these roads. The main imperial highway, the *capac-ñan* (beautiful road), ran westward from Cuzco, across the Apurímac on a great suspension bridge, past the territory of the Chancas, and on toward the coast. At Vilcashuamán the main highway turned north and ran in intramontane valleys for over a thousand miles along the length of the Andes to Quito and the northern marches. Another important road ran along the coastal deserts beside the Pacific ocean. There were feeder roads through the mountains and down the main coastal valleys. The southern part of the empire was served by a road past Lake Titicaca, across the altiplano and into Chile.

The history and geography of Inca expansion are of fundamental importance in understanding Inca architecture. Historically, we have to keep reminding ourselves of the relative speed of the conquest. Allowing for consolidation after the Chanca war and for time lost in civil wars, there were only about eighty years between the start of the expansion and the arrival of the Spaniards. This was not long enough for significant chronological change of architectural style or technique. There was some evolution in detail—the adoption of new ideas in roof gables, more elaborate niches and lintels, the use of pillars and false domes. The chronicles tell us that certain buildings were built by each of the last three Inca

The royal highway, here seen winding through the uplands toward Huánuco

rulers. But the important differences in Inca buildings are due to differing function or geographical location rather than stylistic evolution. Nineteenth-century observers of Inca architecture used to compare the huge stones of the temple-fortress of Sacsahuaman (see plate, page 71) or of Hatun Rumiyoc palace with the walls of Mycenaean Greece. They wrongly concluded that there was a megalithic culture, perhaps built by a race of giants, far older than the Incas'. We now know that all Inca building was done during the burst of creative activity during the empire's expansion. Different styles of stonework were used to denote the relative importance of a building. Temples and royal lodgings naturally deserved the finest masonry. Freestanding or load-bearing walls were built in a different style from retaining or terrace walls. Surfaces that were going to be plastered and painted might be built with less care than those where the stone itself was exposed. There were obvious regional variations in architectural needs: for the rainy, humid foothills of eastern Peru, the cold Andean plateau, and the hot coastal desert. Although essentially uniform, Inca architecture did admit some local variation by regional craftsmen and to allow for the availability of different building materials.

Any observer will notice at least four types of wall construction in Inca buildings. There were sun-dried adobe bricks that are still so common throughout South America. When building Cuzco, Topa Inca Yupanqui "ordered adobes to be made of mud and sticky earth. A great quantity of straw was mixed into these adobes—a straw like Spanish esparto grass. The earth and straw were kneaded in such a way that the adobe bricks would be well made and compacted. These adobes were to be used above masonry, for buildings to reach the desired height and appearance." The American archaeologist John Rowe found some Inca adobes in one of the palaces in Cuzco. He noted that they did have a high straw content, and that they were generally long and flat, measuring some 20 centimeters (8 inches) across by 80 centimeters (32 inches) long. He also observed that they were of different shapes and evidently not made in standard molds. The Incas did not dis-

The fortified town of Incahuasi, built by Inca armies during their conquest of the Cañete valley, south of Lima

parage adobes or regard them as inferior to stone. They used them in some of their most holy buildings, including the sun temple Coricancha in Cuzco (where they were used on top of walls of incomparably fine masonry), the Viracocha temple at Raqchi (see plate, page 189), and the temple that is now the parish church of Huaitará. Adobes have survived quite well where they are protected by some form of roof. But where stone ruins are now bare, we must often appreciate that they were once higher, topped by courses of adobe that melted when the roof protecting them collapsed. Adobes were the obvious and normal building material on the rainless coastal desert plain. Adobe structures of Inca date can be seen at Puruchucu near Lima, at Pachacamac, at Tambo Colorado in the Pisco valley, and at Incahuasi in the Cañete valley.

The vast majority of Andean buildings were built of *pirca*: roughly shaped fieldstones set in clay mortar. This is a natural building method in the stony, rather treeless Andes. It was used in the very earliest buildings in Peru, thousands of years before the ascendancy of the Incas. Pirca differs according to the nature of the local stone—limestone breaks more neatly than granite; shale and mica form long, thin stones. Some

Adobe and pirca construction in the post-Conquest palace of Sayri Tupac at Yucay

builders worked their stones with more care, chipping or cutting them to interlock tidily or making the visible outer surfaces less rough. The majority of houses in any Inca town were built of pirca. These rough stones are the basic material of most of the ruins of Huánuco, Machu Picchu or even the capital city Cuzco itself. Anyone walking around the side streets of central Cuzco can observe the foundations of former Inca houses, with rounded stones that fit together snugly but without the uncanny precision of the masonry of important buildings. These wall bases had upper walls of adobe. There are regular breaks in these wall foundations, marking cross streets of the Inca grid that have since been blocked in. Pizarro's secretary Pedro Sancho wrote to the King that "most of the houses [of Cuzco] are of stone or faced with stone, but there are also many adobe houses, very well built and arranged in straight streets on a rectilinear grid. All the streets are paved and have running water in a stone-lined culvert down the middle. The only drawback is that these streets are narrow and allow only one mounted man to pass on either side of the gutter." Agricultural terraces, one of the glories of Inca engineering, were invariably made of fieldstone set in clay.

The most famous Inca buildings were of tightly fitting masonry of two types: either "polygonal" or "coursed." Blocks of stone were cut, ground and polished until their outer surfaces interlocked with absolute precision. In polygonal masonry, the stones interlock at random, with the convex of one fitting into another's concave. Every visitor to Cuzco is shown the famous stone of Hatun Rumiyoc with no less than twelve corners on its outer face; and at Machu Picchu there is a huge block with thirty-two fitted corners in three dimensions. To modern onlookers accustomed to rectangular sawn masonry, polygonal is baffling. It seems impossible to explain how the Incas could shape heavy stones into these irregular but highly accurate shapes. Polygonal masonry is strong, and was always used for containing walls holding back earth platforms or terraces. The style evidently derived from agricultural terrace walls. But instead of using roughly shaped fieldstones, Inca masons demonstrated their virtuosity by creating a stone jigsaw puzzle.

The chronicler Bernabé Cobo marveled at the size and brilliant fit of some Inca stone blocks: "These clearly show the human effort that must have been required, to transport and erect them in their present positions. Even though these are so extraordinarily large, they are cut with amazing skill. They are elegant, and so finely positioned against one another, without mortar, that the joints are scarcely visible. With the rusticated, polygonal walls, I can assure you that although they may appear rougher than walls of [coursed] ashlars, they seem to me to have been far more difficult to make. For, not being cut straight (apart from the outer face which was as smooth as on ashlars), and yet being so tightly joined to one another, one can well appreciate the amount of work involved in having them interlock in the way we see. Some are large and others small and both sorts are irregular in shape and structure; but they are still positioned with joints as delicate as those of coursed ashlars. Thus, if the top of one stone makes a curve or point there is a corresponding groove or cavity in the stone above that fits exactly into the other. Some stones have many angles and indentations all round their sides; but

The famous twelve-cornered stone in Hatun Rumiyoc, a palace built by the Inca Roca in Cuzco

Coursed masonry, with tightly sunken joints and a drainage outlet, of the acllahuasi on Loreto Street, Cuzco

the stones they meet are cut in such a way that they interlock perfectly. Such a work must have been immensely laborious! To interlock the stones against each other, it must have been necessary to remove and replace them repeatedly to test them. And being of such great size, it is obvious how many workers and how much suffering must have been involved!"

Every modern observer shares Cobo's awe at the sight of polygonal masonry. But the chronicler was right to stress that it was the product of days of patient human effort. There was no secret formula, no magic chemical that could shape stones, nothing but cutting with stone axes, abrasion with sand and water, and the skill and dedication of Inca masons. The Inca state efficiently mobilized the levies needed to perform this labor. The official religion and the mystique of the Inca monarchy inspired the workers. Subject regions of the empire were proud to send tribute labor "and everything else that the Inca requested of them, for they were very obedient to him."

The incomparable Cobo inquired about this problem, and observed native builders at work in post-Conquest Peru. He

wrote: "The thing that impresses me most when I study one of these buildings, is the question: what tools or machines can have brought these stones from the quarries, cut them, and placed them in their present positions? For the Indians had no iron tools or wheeled vehicles. . . . This consideration really does cause one to be justifiably amazed. It gives some idea of the vast number of people needed [to build] these structures. We see stones of such prodigious size that a hundred men working for a month would have been inadequate to cut one of them. By this standard, the Indian claim that it was normal for thirty thousand men to work during the construction of the fortress of Cuzco becomes plausible . . . for a lack of tools or clever devices necessarily increases the volume of labor, and the Indians had to do it all by brute force.

"The tools that they did use for cutting and working stones were hard black [obsidian] pebbles from the streams. They employed these more by pounding than cutting. They transported stones to where they were needed, by pulling them. Having no cranes, wheels or lifting devices, they made a

Polygonal masonry in the foundation terrace wall of Hatun Rumiyoc

Loreto Street, Cuzco. Photograph by Martín Chambi, 1925

sloping ramp up against the building and lifted the stones by rolling them up this. As the building rose, they raised the ramp proportionately. I saw this system being used in the building of Cuzco cathedral. Since the laborers engaged in the work were Indians, the Spanish architects and foremen let them organize their work using traditional methods. They made these ramps to raise stone blocks, piling earth up against the wall until it was level with the top."

The other great masonry style was "coursed," in which rectangular ashlars are laid in even horizontal courses. The Incas themselves probably valued this coursed system more highly than the polygonal that so impresses modern observers. They used coursed masonry for the walls of their palaces and temples. The most famous surviving stretches are the side of the *acllahuasi*, the home of the Inca's chosen women and now the convent of Santa Catalina, and the superb east wall of the sun temple Coricancha (see plate, page 83). Coursed masonry was used for freestanding walls. For aesthetic and technical reasons the stones became smaller higher on the wall. The walls themselves taper at the top and slope inward, so that the top of the inner surface overhangs its base. The respective uses of polygonal and coursed masonry are demonstrated on the ruin of the *usnu*, a stepped platform, at Vilcashuamán. The visible part of each tier is faced in coursed masonry; but the buried section of these same walls was polygonal.

The idea for coursed masonry may have evolved from rows of adobes or from peat blocks used in some parts of the Andes. This could also explain the bulge on the surface of Inca ashlars. When they dry, adobe and peat bricks bulge slightly, and Inca masons reproduced this in their famous rustication. The degree of bulge varies from building to building. In the splendid walls of Coricancha it is very subtle and slight. In the great blocks of the fortress-temple of Sacsahuaman or the famous polygonal terrace of Tarahuasi (see plate, page 179) the bulge is more pronounced. It is almost too prominent in the late-Inca or post-Conquest walls of Colcampata palace in Cuzco.

The surface of each ashlar was allowed to bulge so that the joints were slightly countersunk. The effect of this rustication is magnificent, with each stone outlined in a frame of sharp shadow in the clear Andean air. There is a ripple of chiaroscuro over the gray or tawny beauty of the stone. It is thrilling to see the accuracy of the masonry joints. Heavy blocks of stone interlock like putty, but with the strength to resist successive earthquakes.

The high skills of Inca masons cannot have been developed during the century or less of Inca ascendancy. Architecture anywhere in the world evolves from precursors. The Incas borrowed techniques or actual skilled artisans from all parts of their great empire. Their brilliant stonecutting clearly came from the region of Lake Titicaca—home of the Inca tribe in its original myths. Rectangular ashlars, huge stone blocks, tight polygonal joints and beveling of junctions are all found in the buildings of the Tiahuanaco civilization that swept across Peru from its cult center south of Lake Titicaca in the tenth century of the Christian era, five centuries before the rise of the Incas. Masonry skills were kept alive in this region, whose Colla and Lupaca tribes were conquered by Pachacuti and his son. Stone burial towers at Sillustani near Puno and at other places near the lake show many of the hallmarks adopted by Inca masons. A familiar Tiahuanaco motif was a zigzag step design, and this is found on doorways of the Inca palace on Coati island in Lake Titicaca itself. A similar design is carved in relief on the central usnu of the temple in Ollantaytambo (see plate, page 109). Sarmiento de Gamboa tells us that Topa Inca Yupanqui took captives from the Colla tribe to labor on the magnificent buildings he built at Ollantaytambo.

We know from post-Conquest interrogations that districts in the Colla had to provide labor for "the houses of the Inca in Cuzco" whereas other parts of the empire provided labor for other purposes. And Bernabé Cobo made it clear that "the Indians themselves tell that the Incas used [the temples of Tiahuanaco] as a model and design for the great structures of Cuzco and other parts of their empire."

*The Incas learned masonry from the Tiahuanacans of the Titicaca region. In a chullpa (burial tower)
at Sillustani near Puno, the sides of the perfectly fitted stones were hollowed to take mortar*

The Incas learned some bonding systems from Tiahuanaco. They occasionally held stones together with copper clamps: they cut a T-shaped groove in each stone, so that the clamp holding them was H-shaped. They also copied the Tiahuanaco device of cutting blocks to turn at the corners of buildings. This prevented the structural weakness of having a line of joints at the angle of a wall.

As efficient engineers and disciplined planners, the Incas liked rectangular plans for their buildings, streets and courtyards. These right-angle plans were a sharp departure from the round houses of most of the pre-Inca cultures around Cuzco and of the Incas' contemporaries the Chancas and the Huancas of the central highlands around Jauja. The inspiration for rectilinear plans may have come from the huge coastal cities of the Chimu kingdom, which had a complex grid of adobe enclosures. They might otherwise have been inspired by sites of the Tiahuanaco horizon period—Huamachuco in the northern Andes, Huari near Ayacucho in the central Andes, or the mysterious Pikillacta, an extensive ruin with rectangular and often doorless enclosures and little archaeological evidence of habitation, a few miles from Cuzco itself.

Whatever its origin, a square or trapezoidal enclosure (*cancha*) became the favorite planning unit of official Inca architecture. It formed a convenient corral in communities that raised llamas and alpacas. It was an assembly place for a people who spent little time inside their dark thatched houses. In Inca temples, much of the daily ritual took place in the courtyard. Inca houses had few internal compartments: their doors opened only outward. As Cobo said, "Each room or apartment was a separate entity—they did not intercommunicate or follow one another." But he stressed that courtyards were a sign of rank. Ordinary peasant houses "are so narrow and humble that they should be called huts or cabins rather than houses. There is nothing elaborate about them. . . . They have no windows to let in light, nor chimneys or outlets for the smoke. They have no compartments, courtyards or variety of rooms or chambers. Only the chiefs' houses have large courtyards—in which the people gather to drink at their parties and celebrations—or a greater number of rooms."

Large Inca houses might have several doors, but these were placed symmetrically along the façade and did not relate to internal divisions. With vast *kallankas* (assembly halls) there were many doors in the long walls. If there was an internal division, it was along the long axis with entrances from opposite sides of the building. Pizarro's men made deadly use of the kallankas that lined the great square of Cajamarca. When they prepared their ambush for the Inca Atahualpa on 16 November 1532, the cavalry were hidden in the kallankas. These buildings each had twenty openings onto the square "almost as if they had been built for that purpose." Pizarro's instructions were that "all were to charge out of their lodgings, with the horsemen [already] mounted on their horses." The resulting surprise attack was horribly effective: Atahualpa's men were taken wholly unawares by the horsemen charging into their ranks, and within a few hours seven thousand unarmed Peruvians were massacred and their Inca ruler was captured by the strange invaders.

Although the vast majority of Inca buildings were rectangular, there were a few round plans, generally for sacred structures. Some funerary towers (chullpas) continued to be round. Walls surrounding altars or sacred outcrops might be round, like the famous "torreón" at Machu Picchu, and the curving walls of sun temples, such as Coricancha in Cuzco (see plate, page 81), Pisac, and Ingapirca in Ecuador. There was also a round tower called Muyuc Marca in the fortress of Sacsahuaman, whose circular foundations were excavated in the 1930s (see plate, page 73), and there were round towers at Runcu Raccay on the road to Machu Picchu or outside the Amarucancha palace on the main square of Cuzco. Hundreds of qollqas (storehouses) in Inca provincial capitals were round; and the domestic huts of many subject tribes continued to be built on the traditional round plan throughout the Inca era.

One element of Inca architecture was the Incas' own invention. It was so common and so peculiarly Inca that it became their hallmark, the sure sign that a structure was built during the Inca era. This hallmark was the trapezoidal shape for doorways, niches, alcoves and even ground plans. In a trapezoidal opening, the lintel is shorter than the sill and the jambs slope inward toward the top. The structural advantage is obvious. The weight supported by the lintel stone is minimized and its thrust is spread on either side of the opening. The trapezoidal opening is aesthetically satisfying. Rows of tapering doors or niches relieve the austere simplicity of Inca buildings, and the sloping sides of these openings balance a slight inward lean of the walls themselves. In coastal buildings with adobe walls and flat cane roofs, the trapezoidal shape of doors and windows is often the only proof that the structure was of Inca date.

For all their brilliance in masonry, in mobilizing huge contingents of labor, and often building on recklessly steep locations, the Incas were conservative architects. Their structural solutions were repetitive. Their empire expanded so rapidly and they wanted to impose Inca rule so fast that there was no time for architectural innovation. They preferred simple designs and proved techniques. This is most evident in their cautious approach to woodworking and roofing. It is remarkable that a people who could shape stone with such virtuosity did not develop carpentry beyond the rough shaping of roof beams. The Incas had no specialized carpentry tools and did not use nails, although they did use wood effectively in making beakers (*keros*) and vessels.

We know little about Inca doors. The Spanish conquistadores regarded them as insubstantial—chroniclers marveled at the honesty of a society that possessed no locks and in which a man leaving his house simply placed a bar across the opening to indicate that he was away. In strategically important walls there was something more solid. We see stone sockets beside the bases of doorways at Machu Picchu and other sites: these evidently held swiveling upright beams. Such doors in defensive walls or important enclosures had stone pegs sunk into the masonry of either jamb. A stone ring was often fixed above the lintel on the inner side. The side pegs probably secured a defensive crossbeam, and the top ring may have been used to support a hanging doorframe. Normal

Defensive devices in a gateway at Machu Picchu: a stone ring above the lintel and side pegs were used to secure a door

doors were of cloth or hide on a wooden frame—as were the battle shields carried by Inca warriors. Whatever their construction, the doorways of fortresses were effective. During the siege of Cuzco in 1536, Francisco Pizarro's youngest brother Juan was killed in an unsuccessful attempt to force a gate into Sacsahuaman; the fortress finally fell to an attack by siege ladders. A similar attack on the terraces of Ollantaytambo, by Hernando Pizarro during the same campaign, also failed to penetrate any gates into that temple-fortress.

Inca conservatism was most marked when it came to roofing. A modern observer is struck by the incongruity of having magnificent masonry topped by thatch roofs. Although pre-Columbian Peru had a long tradition of pottery there was no attempt to use ceramic tiles for roofing. No pre-Conquest American culture discovered the Romans' great achievement, the arch. There were corbeled roofs in Peru, in the temple of Chavín de Huantar, dating from several centuries before the Christian era or almost two millennia before the Incas. The chullpas (tomb towers) of Lake Titicaca had corbeled false domes over the central burial chamber, and the Incas used a similar technique to roof small rooms in their temple on the Island of the Sun in Lake Titicaca. Storehouses for perishable goods were roofed with stone in this way. Flat stones were used extensively to make flights of projecting steps between agricultural terraces, and corbeled flat stones were used to support the ends of short bridges. Although slates exist in Peru, they were not used for roofing. Most Inca buildings, however important, were therefore roofed in thatch on a wooden frame.

The idea that thatch roofs were too humble and demeaning for royal palaces or the most venerated temples is misleading. Inca thatch could be very elaborate. The American traveler George Squier saw a surviving Inca thatch during his travels north of Lake Titicaca in the 1870s. He remarked that "the thin, long, and tough ichu grass of this mountain region is admirably adapted for thatch, lying smoothly, besides being readily worked." He then described and illustrated the Suntur-huasi, a circular Inca building, sixteen feet in diameter, in the town of Azángaro. In Squier's drawing the damaged thatch looks like a steep conical haystack. But his description showed its vanished splendor: "The dome of the Suntur-huasi is perfect, and is formed of a series of bamboos of equal size and taper, their larger ends resting on the top of the walls; bent evenly to a central point, over a series of hoops of the same material and of graduated sizes. At the points where the vertical and horizontal supports cross each other, they are bound together by fine cords of delicately braided grass, which

cross and recross each other with admirable skill and taste. Over the skeleton dome is a fine mat of the braided epidermis of the bamboo or rattan, which, as it exposes no seams, almost induces the belief that it was braided on the spot. However that may be, it was worked in different colors, and in panelings conforming in size with the diminishing spaces between the framework, that framework itself being also painted. . . . Over this inner matting is another, open, coarse, and strong, in which was fastened a fleece of finest ichu, which depends like a heavy fringe outside the walls. Next comes a transverse layer of coarser grass or reeds, to which succeeds ichu, and so on, the whole rising in the centre so as to form a slightly flattened cone. The projecting ends of the ichu layers were cut off sharply and regularly, producing the effect of overlapping tiles."

Azángaro's magnificent Inca thatch has now gone—I myself once searched in vain for it—but the roof seen by Squier is confirmed by descriptions in the chroniclers. Garcilaso de la Vega recalled seeing a remarkable building in the Yucay valley (the name for the canyon of the Vilcanota river northeast of Cuzco). It was a hall, seventy feet square in plan, with walls three times the height of a man. Above this towered a conical thatch roof, twelve times the height of a man (twelve estados or over sixty feet). As with other royal buildings, this thatch was over six feet thick and half its width projected as eaves to keep the walls dry.

Pedro de Cieza de León said that Inca thatch roofs were so densely woven that they lasted for many years unless destroyed by fire. It was such a fire that consumed the roofs of pre-Conquest Cuzco. In May 1536 the young Manco Inca led a desperate attempt to drive the Spanish invaders from the imperial capital. His men fired stones wrapped in burning cotton from their slings. "There was a strong wind that day, and as the roofs of the houses were thatch it seemed at one moment as if the city was one great sheet of flame." "They set fire to the whole of Cuzco simultaneously and it all burned in one day, for the roofs were thatch. The smoke was so dense that the Spaniards almost suffocated." Only one thatch survived the conflagration: that of a great hall, called Suntur-huasi like Squier's in Azángaro (see plate, page 42). The beleaguered Spaniards huddled inside this hall. When its thatch failed to ignite, they attributed their escape to a miraculous intervention by the Virgin Mary or by Santiago (Saint James) of Spain on his white charger.

The buildings of Cuzco all had flat-topped walls, for the roofs were built on frames without benefit of gables. This style is known as a hip roof. A frame of wooden beams sloped inward from the four flat walls and supported a central roof beam along the building's axis. "The timber that served as roof beams was laid on top of the walls and lashed down with strong ropes made of a long, soft grass . . . instead of being nailed. Over these main timbers they placed those which served as joists and rafters, binding them together in the same fashion." The royal palaces of Cuzco and even the most holy sun temple of Coricancha were covered with thatched hip roofs—the surviving chambers of Coricancha show no sign of gables. When the roofs of Cuzco burned in the siege of 1536, Manco Inca's attackers ran along the tops of the exposed flat walls, firing missiles down at the dreaded Spanish horsemen in the streets below. For once the native warriors had the advantage of height in the unequal battles of the Conquest.

By contrast, most buildings of Machu Picchu—in a wetter climate than Cuzco's—have roofs resting on gable ends. Inca gables were invariably at the shorter ends of buildings, but they might be built of stone or adobe. (A few Inca adobe gables survive: at Huaitará and at the Viracocha temple at Raqchi in the Vilcanota valley.) The main roof beam rested on these gables or, in longer halls, on a series of roof beams running the length of the building and supported by wooden pillars. A variation was for the roof to rest on a solid wall which divided the house into two long units without internal communication. Another variation was for the gables to have slopes of unequal length. This device meant that the rear wall of the house had to be higher; or the building might be on steep ground—common enough in the vertical world of the Andes —so that the front slope of the roof needed to be longer than

A house at Machu Picchu has bosses along the gables for tying down the thatch

that at the rear. Gables almost always had a straight slope, but a stepped variety is known at the ruins of Patallacta near Cuzco.

In the hot Urubamba valley, in Inca sites near Machu Picchu, some buildings have open sides. One side wall is

*A masma (open-sided building) at the northern end of Machu Picchu. To provide support
for the roof on the open side, a beam was passed into the slots in the gables*

omitted and the roof rests on a beam at the crest of the roof. In long buildings of this type there might be stone or wooden piers along the missing wall. Such structures were presumably for assembly or administrative purposes: their interiors are sufficiently light for daytime use. The Peruvian architect Emilio Harth-Terré calls these open-sided buildings *masmas*. There are fine examples at Machu Picchu, notably the famous "temple of the three windows," the "watchman's hut" near the cemetery, and the house whose thatch has been reconstructed on the path toward Huayna Picchu.

The space within the beams of a pitched roof was an obvious storage area. Any native hut had objects stored on the rafters or hanging from them. A natural development was to floor this attic area. Two-storied houses thus evolved among the Incas, with access to the upper story invariably from the outside: there might be a flight of external projecting stone steps or, on steep slopes, doors to the upper story at a higher level. There are various examples of this in Machu Picchu: the famous "house of the ñusta" (house of the princess) in the Torreón Group, or the imposing three-storied house with a commanding view over the Urubamba and with entrances to its three levels cunningly fitted into rock outcrops of the "Prison" Group. There are curious two-storied houses on the steep slopes of Pinkuylluna opposite Ollantaytambo—curious because the door levels of the upper floors do not correspond to the walls of the lower floors on the opposite sides of the buildings.

As Garcilaso de la Vega remarked, the Incas did not use nails. Their thatched roofs were therefore tied down with fiber or osier cords to bosses projecting from gables or to stone loops, "eye-bonders," sunk into the tops of walls. Other bosses or pegs were fixed along internal walls, often between storage niches. The same boss that secured the thatch could also be used for hanging household articles or fixing the ends of body looms. One of the many triumphs of Inca stonemasons was the skill with which they sculpted these utilitarian pegs and sank them into their fine stone walls. At Choquequirau, a rarely visited, overgrown Inca town on a mountain spur of the forested north bank of the Apurímac canyon, there is a row of full-length niches in a terrace with massive stone rings fixed between them: the first modern visitors to find this site wondered what could have been tethered there—possibly pumas, the only dangerous wild animal in the Andes.

There is another type of boss in Inca architecture. Some stones in walls of the finest masonry have one or a pair of low bosses protruding from their surfaces. There is no obvious explanation for these projections. The bosses may have been used to pull or lever the block into position. But masons as

Bosses on the wall of niches on the uppermost terrace at Ollantaytambo (see pages 106–107)

skillful as the Incas could easily have removed them. They serve no purpose. We can only conclude that they were left for aesthetic reasons. One of the most famous Zen Buddhist gardens in Kyoto in Japan is decorated only by a pair of low cones of gravel. The Inca projections are aesthetically just as satisfying. They provide sharp points of shadow to relieve the pattern of smooth surfaces and tight sunken joints of the best Inca stonework.

The other favorite device for decorating Inca walls is a line of niches. These niches must have had a strong appeal to the disciplined minds of the Incas. They were functional, useful and decorative—breaking the monotony of a bare wall with the symmetry of a row of classical columns. Inca niches come in many patterns, but almost all are of the standard trapezoidal shape, tapering upward toward the lintel. Domestic or temple buildings have simple niches (*phutu*) at chest height around their inside walls. These were obviously useful for storage or display. Most are simple openings with rectangular plans and trapezoidal façades, but Inca masons occasionally

The church of Huaitará was built on an Inca temple with elaborate double niches and trapezoidal windows

allowed themselves variations on this standard type. At Huaitará, in the Andes between Ica on the coast and Ayacucho, an important Inca building has survived as part of the town church. One interior wall has ten large niches with triangular plans—the side walls converge to form angles in the interiors of the niches; other niches in this same building are of conventional plan, but some have small window openings set into their back walls. A few Inca buildings have two rows of niches, set either directly above one another or in a diagonal arrangement. Such double rows are found at Incahuasi, a large coastal site in the Cañete valley south of Lima thought to have been a camp used by Inca armies when they subdued this region in about 1470 at the end of Pachacuti's reign; more elaborate and presumably later double rows of niches are at Choquequilla in the Anta valley west of Cuzco (see plate, page 159); and there are diagonal arrangements in some houses at Pisac, Ollantaytambo, the coastal Tambo Colorado, and at Incallacta on the eastern edge of the empire in Bolivia. The British archaeologist Ann Kendall has sought to demonstrate that these are architectural evolutions that can be dated from the reigns of Pachacuti's successors.

Terrace or retaining walls of important Inca buildings are sometimes decorated with lines of tall trapezoidal niches. It is easy to imagine a row of brilliantly uniformed attendants standing guard in these "sentry-box" alcoves. My favorite row of full-length niches is on the platform at Tarahuasi (see plate, page 179), the remains of the great way station Rimac-tampu (Limatambo), where the road from Cuzco dropped toward the Apurímac canyon. There are fine examples at Vilcashuaman, and in the late, possibly post-Conquest, buildings of Chinchero near Cuzco and Paullu Inca's palace of Colcampata above Cuzco itself. An elaboration in these tall niches was to sink one niche inside the outer frame of a larger niche, so that there were double or even triple jambs and lintels. The Colcampata niches are double in this way, and so are those of the Pilco Caima palace built by Topa Inca Yupanqui on the Island of the Sun, in Lake Titicaca. This palace or temple marked the supposed place of origin of the founders of the Inca dynasty. On the nearby Island of the Moon, Coati, is a building where the inner niches have stepped lintels reminiscent of a favorite Tiahuanaco motif—a decoration that makes the buildings look decidedly Moorish to Western eyes.

An architectural device used sparingly by the Incas was the pillar or column. It was sometimes necessary to use pillars to support the roofs of open-sided masma buildings. These were generally wooden piers, but some were monoliths—notably that of the temple of the three windows in Machu Picchu. There were adobe pillars under the flat roofs of coastal build-

ings. But the main use of columns was to support the roofs of huge ceremonial halls. The kallankas of Cuzco, Tumibamba and Cajamarca have disappeared; but where kallankas survive—at Incallacta near Cochabamba in Bolivia, at Chinchero near Cuzco, and most impressively at Huánuco in the central Andes—there are circles of stones at regular intervals that once secured the bases of great wooden piers. The most famous Inca columns are in the empire's greatest temple, the extraordinary Viracocha shrine of Raqchi midway between Cuzco and Lake Titicaca. The temple there has a high central wall that runs along its axis and supports the slopes of its enormous roof. Halfway between that central wall and the side walls are lines of columns that evidently helped the girders support this roof to cover the largest building in the Inca empire. These columns, eleven of them on either side, have round stone bases rising 3.3 meters (11 feet), above which they are made of adobe (see plate, page 191).

Modern archaeologists are concerned to identify the *function* of Inca buildings. There is a paradox about Inca ruins. On the one hand they are very obvious. The Incas tended to build in new locations, so that their provincial capitals are uncomplicated by earlier occupation. Inca ruins are relatively recent —only five centuries before the present—and, being solidly built, they survive well unless destroyed by later human abuse. There is also a reasonable fund of written information about the Incas by the Spaniards who conquered and destroyed their civilization. Spanish chroniclers tell us much about Inca daily life and about certain famous buildings. Interrogations of aged natives during the sixteenth century add useful details, particularly about the administrative and taxation systems. But despite all this evidence, surprisingly many mysteries remain. It is often impossible to assign precise function to individual buildings in an Inca site. We might know that an Inca city contains certain standard elements—royal lodgings, "convent" for *mamaconas* (holy women), sun temple, barracks, storehouses, kallankas (assembly halls), usnu (administrative platform), main square, water system—but it is difficult to identify which surviving ruin served which of these functions. Within the ruined buildings themselves, there are baffling details that defy explanation. There are important sites such as Pisac and Machu Picchu that were never mentioned by the Spanish chroniclers. There is still much debate about the purpose of either of these cities. All these unanswered questions add to the fascination of Inca ruins and architecture.

Two important structures that occur in most provincial centers are kallankas and usnus. Garcilaso mentioned the kallankas he had known as a boy in Cuzco: "In many of the Inca's palaces there were large halls some two hundred paces long and fifty to sixty wide. They were unpartitioned and served as places of assembly for festivals and dances when the weather was too rainy to permit them to hold these in the open air. In the city of Cuzco I saw four of these halls; which were still standing when I was a boy. . . . The largest was that of Cassana, which was capable of holding three thousand persons. It seems incredible that timber could have been found to cover such vast halls." The name Cassana meant "something to freeze." As Garcilaso explained, "The name was given to it out of wonder, implying that the buildings in it were so large and splendid that anyone who gazed on them attentively would be frozen with astonishment." This passage of Garcilaso's used to be dismissed as hyperbole, but recent excavations have revealed a number of enormous kallankas in provincial Inca cities. There were other kallankas in Cuzco: two more on the main square—Amarucancha (serpent's enclosure) on the site now occupied by the Jesuit Compañía, and Cora Cora, a place much fought over during Manco Inca's rebellion and now close to the cathedral—and Colcampata, occupied by the post-Conquest puppet, Paullu Inca.

We know the crucial role played by the kallankas at Cajamarca during the capture of Atahualpa. Pedro de Cieza de León described similar halls at Huamachuco, a couple of days' march south of Cajamarca: "There is a great square where the tambos or royal palaces stood, among which are two that are twenty-two feet wide and about one hundred feet long, all of stone and trimmed with long, thick beams covered with straw, which they employ very skillfully." The vast, undisturbed ruin of Huánuco contains the remains of two great kallankas, each about 70 meters (230 feet) long and standing in line along one side of the enormous square. There are remains of such halls moving south along the royal road, at Pumpu (Bombón) on Lake Junín, Tarma, and Vilcashuamán, and they doubtless existed at vanished sites such as Cajas, Tumibamba and Quito. But the largest of all surviving kallankas is far away on the southeastern marches of the empire, at Incallacta. The hall there measures 78 by 26 meters (256 by 85 feet) in plan, with twelve narrow doors onto the square. Inside, on the opposite wall, is a long line of forty-four niches, with more niches surmounted by windows in the end walls. There may well have been three rows of pillars supporting the roof, each sloping pitch of which was no less than 16 meters (52 feet) wide.

We know from Garcilaso that these great halls were built to hold assemblies that sheltered in them if it rained during festivals. But it is worth noting that kallankas are more common in "colonial" towns along the imperial roads and in Cuzco itself, but not in places near the capital city. This was because they served to accommodate the masses of people who were moving along the roads on official service: soldiers, artisans, laborers, or colonists being transplanted to settle newly conquered regions. The young priest Cristóbal de Molina, who was in Peru soon after the Conquest, wrote that when travelers finished a day's journey "they spent the night at the town they reached, in halls or large houses that had been made for this purpose. Some of these were over 150 paces long and very broad and spacious. A great quantity of people could be housed in each of these, which were very well covered, clean and well appointed, with many doors so that they should be very light and agreeable. Each person there was provided with his daily ration, for him and his wife, each in turn and without any bustle just as if they had been monks: for the common people of this land were the most obedient, humble and disciplined that I believe could be found anywhere on earth."

This same priest also noted that in every town along the main highways, the Incas had "a great royal plaza, in the middle of which was a tall rectangular platform [usnu] with a high stairway leading up to it. The Inca and three lords would ascend this to address the people and to review the fighting men when they held parades or assemblies." There was an usnu in the square of Cajamarca. On the fateful 16 November 1532, when Pizarro's surprise attack captured the Inca Atahualpa, the Spaniards had stationed the Cretan gunner Pedro de Candia on this usnu with his small cannon. Francisco de Jerez described it as "a stone fortress incorporated into the square, with a masonry staircase up which one climbs to it from the square." Pizarro waited until the Inca and his followers filled the square. He decided that his reckless plan to kidnap Atahualpa might succeed and alerted the gunner on the usnu. He "signaled the artilleryman to fire the cannon into their midst." At this the Spaniards rode out of the kallankas where they were hidden and charged into the mass of unarmed natives crowded into the square. "The Indians were thrown into confusion and panicked. The Spaniards fell upon them and began to kill." It was thus a cannon fired from an usnu that launched the terrible slaughter and the capture of the Inca ruler.

The largest surviving usnu in Peru is at Huánuco—an immense gray slab of masonry in the midst of a plaza over half a kilometer (550 yards) long. There was a less elaborate usnu in the square of Pumpu, the next important town south along the royal highway. But the most beautiful surviving usnu is that of Vilcashuamán (see plate, page 184). It is a stepped pyramid, all clad in the most perfect coursed masonry. Leading up to it is a flight of stone steps with a great trapezoidal portal at their foot. On top of the pyramid is a massive rectangular block of stone with two squared seats cut in its top. Cieza de León described it as "a bench where the Lord Inca sat to pray, all of a single stone so large that it was 11 feet long and 7 feet [3.3 by 2.1 meters] wide, with two seats cut for the aforesaid purpose. . . . In the middle of the great square was another bench, like that of a theater, where the Lord Inca sat

The usnu (administrative platform) at Huánuco

to watch dances and lay feasts." Felipe Guaman Poma de Ayala drew pictures of Atahualpa and Manco Inca seated on top of stepped usnus when they presided over ceremonial occasions.

Usnus were more than mere thrones or reviewing platforms. In a society as religious as that of the Incas, these platforms or pyramids also served spiritual purposes. The chronicler Cabello de Balboa said that when Huayna Capac visited his new northern city of Tumibamba, he "had erected in the square a structure called usnu or chinquin-pillaca, where sacrifices might be offered to the sun and its different phases, with chicha [maize beer] poured out in its honor." When this same Inca visited Vilcashuamán, "he went up to pray on an elegant and excellent terrace that had been built for that purpose. They sacrificed, in their blind ignorance, the things they usually sacrificed, killing many animals and birds." Guaman Poma confirmed this use: "The Incas had in their empire special places to make their sacrifices, called usno. These consisted of a stone fixed in the ground that served as a seat from which they invoked their god." And Cristóbal de Molina said that in the middle of the great square of Cuzco was "a golden usnu which was like a fountain into which they poured a sacrifice of chicha." Bernabé Cobo mentioned another usnu in Cuzco: a stone in the Aucaypata

An Inca ruler seated on an usnu

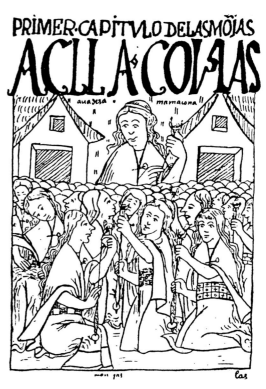

Holy women—mamaconas and acllas—making cloth for the state

square where young men being enrolled into the Inca nobility made their first sacrifices.

Archaeologists have no trouble identifying kallankas or usnus. But the identification of other standard Inca buildings is far harder. We know that every provincial capital was a microcosm of Cuzco itself. Each therefore had a replica of the sun temple, of the royal Inca palaces, and of the enclosure for the holy women dedicated to the service of the Inca and the official religion. The Incas chose beautiful girls from all parts of the empire to be acllas, serving the administration in weaving fine cumbi and other textiles, making quantities of chicha fermented from maize, attending religious services, and being awarded as wives or concubines to chiefs or officials whom the Inca wished to honor. Different chroniclers give different accounts of the relationship between acllas and mamaconas. The latter seemed to the Spaniards to correspond to their own

nuns—dedicated to religious service for life, vowed to remain chaste, cloistered against the attentions of men, and ruled by a form of mother superior. The young acllas seem to have been entrusted to the care of the more senior and holier mamaconas.

We know which building in Cuzco was the acllahuasi, or house of the acllas. It is on a site between the Jesuit Compañía and the Cathedral. Its superb, austere wall of coursed masonry runs along one side of Loreto Street, and the curved, heavily rusticated end of this wall juts into the arcade at the side of the Plaza de Armas. By a coincidence, although the Cuzco acllahuasi was allotted to two conquistadores immediately after the Conquest, the site soon came into the possession of the nuns of Santa Catalina. It has thus reverted to its role as a retreat of holy women, closed to archaeologists until the present.

In the finest coursed masonry, like this wall of the acllahuasi in Cuzco, the stones are perfectly rectangular, joints are deliberately beveled, courses diminish in size as they rise, corners are rounded, and walls taper and incline inward

Guaman Poma, the only chronicler who was a pure Indian, said that there were "virgins whom the Indians call acllaconas, chosen women, who were found ... in all places of this country and were confined in houses or retreats of nuns." Some of these women served in the various shrines and temples. Other acllas "belonged to the Incas: they were beautiful and were like maidens destined for the Inca's service." The most distinguished, the daughters of chiefs, sometimes slept with the ruler. "Their sole occupation was to weave cloth for the Inca, of a quality superior to taffeta or silk; they prepared a special rich chicha which was matured for a month . . . ; and they also prepared very agreeable meals for the Inca."

The problem in the ruins of provincial Inca cities is to try to identify which building can have been the acllahuasi. In the early days of the Conquest, when Pizarro's men were advancing down the northern coast of Peru, Hernando de Soto was sent to lead a reconnaissance into the mountains. His men entered the small northern town of Cajas. "There were in that town three houses of cloistered women whom they called mamaconas. When we entered, the women were brought out onto the square and there were over five hundred of them. And the captain [Soto] gave many of these women to the Spaniards"—to the outrage and fury of the Inca officials. A few weeks after this disgraceful rape of the holy women of Cajas, the Spaniards reached Cajamarca and kidnapped the Inca himself. When Atahualpa was in captivity he was closely attended by his female retainers. Pedro Pizarro and Juan Ruiz de Arce watched with amazement as the women dressed the Inca, held food for him to eat, removed any hairs from his person, and even held out their hands for him to spit into. There are many reports of the dispersal of mamaconas and acllas during the turbulent years of the Conquest. But, although we know that each town had such a "convent," it is very difficult to identify which was its building. One enclosure at Huánuco has been tentatively designated as the acllahuasi: it is enclosed by a high wall and has only one entrance. There are similar enclosures in the ruins of Machu Picchu. Hiram Bingham, the American discoverer of Machu Picchu, even speculated that the entire place might have been a retreat for holy women—he was impressed by the fact that most skeletons found at the site were those of women, and further assumed, by a flight of fanciful reasoning, that the other skeletons were those of "effeminate men" who attended the holy women.

The rock shrine of Quillarumi, near Anta, west of Cuzco

Other Inca buildings are equally difficult to identify from their ruins. Many Inca sites were occupied for only a few decades before the Conquest, so that their ruins contain few household goods that could assist identification. The utensils, decorations and wall hangings that distinguished important buildings vanished in the first Spanish onslaught. Fine masonry obviously indicates that a structure was for royal use; but it is hard to tell whether it served imperial officials or religious dignitaries, or was reserved for the Inca himself. The treatment of some shrines is more obvious. The Incas worshipped natural phenomena, and the most venerated of these might be enclosed in appropriate buildings. At Machu Picchu, for instance, there is no doubt about the religious significance of the rock outcrop surrounded by the curved wall of the "torreón" (see plates, pages 134–135) or of the elegant altar stone of the "inti-huatana" (hitching post of the sun). The same applies to the spring of Tambo Machay and the caves and rock outcrops of Kenko and other rock formations near Cuzco; of buildings surrounding the "inti-huatana" projections at Pisac; of cavern structures, such as the "Cave of the Moon" at Machu Picchu or Choquequilla in the Anta valley west of Cuzco (see plates, page 159); ornamental springs or fountains, on the Island of the Sun in Lake Titicaca, at Ollantaytambo, near Vilcashuamán, and at other places throughout the empire. We know the religious purpose of a few buildings from chronicle sources: the Viracocha temple at Raqchi, the coastal temple Pachacamac, and the sun temple Coricancha itself. But other temples may elude us. With no obvious sacred object within their walls and no clue in the written records, it is impossible to distinguish them from other fine Inca buildings.

The most sumptuous of all Inca buildings must have been the royal palaces of Cuzco. In Martín de Murúa's vision, an Inca's palace was as luxurious as the residence of an oriental potentate. "This great palace had two large main gates, one at the entrance to the vestibule and the other farther inside. From [the first] could be seen some of the finest of the celebrated stone masonry. There were two thousand Indian sol-

diers at this entrance gate, on guard with their captain. . . . Between this gate and the other inner gate there was a vast, extensive courtyard, to which all who accompanied the Inca would enter; but only the Inca himself and his chief noble lords—the four members of his privy council—would enter the second gate. This second gate also had a guard, of Indians native to the city [of Cuzco] and related to the Inca . . . and near it was the armory and arrow store of the Inca's royal palace. . . . Beyond was another great courtyard or patio for the palace officials and regular servants. They then entered further, to the rooms and chambers in which the Inca lived. All this was full of delights, for they had various arbors and gardens and the lodgings were very large and worked with marvelous skill." Garcilaso de la Vega confirmed that "all the royal palaces had gardens and orchards for the Inca's recreation. They were planted with all sorts of charming and beautiful trees, beds of flowers and . . . herbs found in Peru. They also made gold and silver replicas of many trees and lesser plants . . . done life size, with all their leaves, blossoms and fruits," as well as models of maize fields, animals, birds and reptiles. "In certain respects, their palaces surpassed those of all the kings and emperors that have ever existed. . . . The buildings of their palaces, temples, gardens and baths were extraordinarily even: they were of beautifully cut masonry, with each stone so perfectly fitted to its neighbors that there was no space for mortar."

Guaman Poma listed a variety of "royal courts, palaces, houses or lodgings that belonged to the Inca, as a dwelling place or for the functions and activities appropriate to his government." There was the *cuyus-manco*, the royal palace itself, within which were the private apartments, *quinco-huasi*. The *suntur-huasi* was "a round house, lodging of the Inca." There were ordinary circular houses, three-walled buildings, and buildings with two chambers. Special buildings, each with its own name, served as reception for visitors, as a dormitory, for storage, for chicha preparation, for servants, and for the poor.

The main square of Cuzco was surrounded by the palaces

Palaces of Cuzco with the "suntor uasi" (round house) in the foreground

of the Inca rulers. Even Pizarro's pedantic secretary Pedro Sancho was impressed. He wrote that "the city of Cuzco . . . is large and beautiful enough to be remarkable, even in Spain. It is full of the palaces of nobles, for no poor people live there. Each ruler builds himself a palace and so do all the chiefs. . . . The square is rectangular and is generally flat and paved with gravel. The palaces of four rulers lie around it and these are the most important buildings in the city, built of ashlars and painted. The finest is that of the former Inca Huayna-Capac. It has a gateway of red, white and multicolored marble, and has other flat-roofed structures that are also most remarkable." This was the palace of Amarucancha (enclosure of the snake). Garcilaso de la Vega, who grew up in Cuzco during the middle

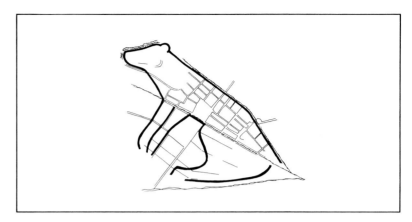

A modern drawing of Cuzco in the shape of the puma

decades of the sixteenth century, recalled seeing a fine round tower that stood in the square in front of Amarucancha. "I saw no other remains of this palace: all the rest was razed." The round tower's walls were four times the height of a man, "but its roof, made of the excellent timber they used for their royal palaces, was so high that I could say without exaggeration that it equaled in height any tower in Spain, apart from the [Giralda] in Seville. Its roof was rounded like the walls, and above it, in place of a weathervane . . . , it had a very tall, thick pole that enhanced its height and beauty. It was over sixty feet high inside and was known as Suntur-huasi, 'excellent house or lodging.'" This lovely isolated tower fell victim to a Spanish town planner, for it projected into the main square, and the Spaniards liked every one of their cities to have an unobstructed plaza as its heart.

Amarucancha, with its proud tower and great kallanka, lay on the south side of the square, on a site requisitioned by Hernando Pizarro and Hernando de Soto and later sold to the Jesuits. Facing it, at the northwestern side of the square near the channeled Saphi-Huatanay stream, was Cassana, the palace with the largest of all the kallankas. This was the palace built by the great conquering Inca Pachacuti, the Inca Napoleon, a dynamic genius who seems to have been responsible for planning Cuzco and for devising most elements of Inca administration, law and religion. The Spaniards' conquering

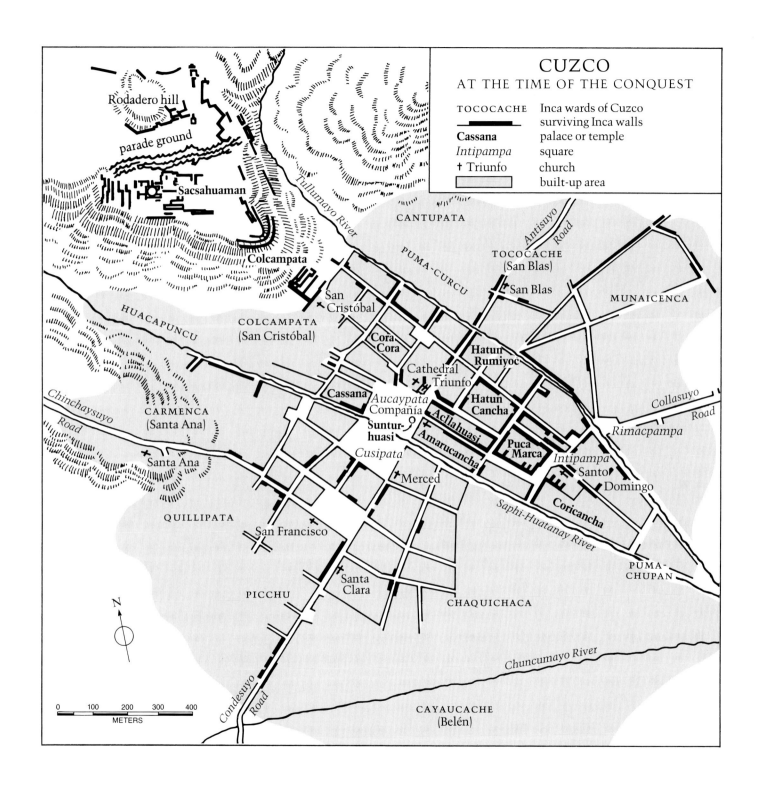

Rodadero hill

parade ground

Sacsahuaman

Colcampata

Tullumayo River

CANTUPATA

CUZCO
AT THE TIME OF THE CONQUEST

TOCOCACHE   Inca wards of Cuzco
━━━━━━   surviving Inca walls
Cassana   palace or temple
Intipampa   square
✝ Triunfo   church
▩   built-up area

PUMA-CURCU

Antisuyo Road

TOCOCACHE
(San Blas)

✝ San Blas

MUNAICENCA

San
Cristóbal

✝ San
Cristóbal

COLCAMPATA
(San Cristóbal)

HUACAPUNCU

**Cora
Cora**

**Hatun
Rumiyoc**

Cathedral
✝ Triunfo

Cassana

Aucaypata
Compañía

**Hatun
Cancha**

Collasuyo Road

Acllahuasi

Rimacpampa

*Chinchaysuyo
Road*

CARMENCA
(Santa Ana)

**Suntur-
huasi**

Amarucancha

**Puca
Marca**

Intipampa

✝ Santo
Domingo

✝ Santa Ana

Cusipata

✝ Merced

Coricancha

Saphi-Huatanay River

QUILLIPATA

PUMA-
CHUPAN

N

✝ San Francisco

PICCHU

✝ Santa
Clara

CHAQUICHACA

Chuncumayo River

0   100   200   300   400
METERS

Condesuyo Road

CAYAUCACHE
(Belén)

leader Francisco Pizarro took this palace for himself. His young cousin Pedro Pizarro later recalled that Cassana also had round towers like Amarucancha's. "This Cassana had two towers, one at each side of the gate, by which I mean that they were almost at the corners of that block. These towers were of finely worked and very strong masonry. They were round and roofed in thatch that was laid very skillfully—the eaves of the thatch projected from the wall for an arm's length so that when it rained they sheltered horsemen. . . . The Indian warriors set fire to these towers with burning arrows or stones when they besieged [Cuzco]. [The hall] contained so much thatch that it took eight days or more to burn—that is, until the timbers fell. Those towers were enclosed, with heavy beams placed above and earth on top of these, like flat-roofed adobe houses." Miguel de Estete, who was also present at the conquistadores' first entry into Cuzco, wrote that Cassana "has two towers of fine appearance, and a rich gateway faced with pieces of silver and other metals." Pedro Pizarro described the main kallanka of Cassana as being three-sided. It was "a great hall . . . , very long, with the entrance at one end, so that from it one could see everything inside: for this entrance was so large that it stretched from one wall to the other and was all open to the roof line. The Indians had these halls for holding their drinking celebrations. They had another type with the ends closed but with many doorways in one wall. These halls were very large and had no obstructions, but were level and clear." Cobo mentioned a sacred pool within the palace, which was demolished to make way for the shops and arcades of Spanish Cuzco. The earthquake of May 1950 revealed a stretch of its beautiful pale gray walls. One fragment is now exposed, and another stretch of its walls can be seen inside a modern restaurant.

Although each Inca ruler built himself a palace, his building was not occupied by his heirs. It was, instead, preserved as his spiritual resting-place. As Cobo explained, "When the king died, the prince did not inherit his palace and fortune: it was left, together with the body of the deceased, to the clan he had founded. The entire estate was dedicated to the cult of his body and the support of his family. The clan embalmed the body of its royal father and preserved it together with all its belongings and ornaments." Each Inca also had houses and fields in all parts of the empire, and these were also preserved intact after his death. Inca emperors "considered it to be a point of honor not to take over or use a woman, field or servant or anything else that had belonged to their parents: instead, these had to be provided in all the valleys [of the empire]. If the Christians had delayed [their invasion of Peru] all the fields and women and Indians would have belonged to the Sun [religion] and the Incas." Pedro Pizarro said that the last Inca, Atahualpa's brother Huascar, once became so angry at the way in which all the best parts of the country belonged to dead Incas, that he wished he could bury them all and remove their possessions. Cuzco itself was full of people, but "most of them served these dead rulers. Every day they brought them all out onto the square, seated in a circle, each according to his antiquity. All the male and female attendants ate and drank there," and offered food and chicha to the dead Incas. This ancestor worship meant that all the palaces of Cuzco were intact when the Spaniards arrived on 15 November 1533. The Incas were too confident in the security of their empire and the honesty of its citizens. There is thus no hope of a discovery in Peru of a Tutankhamen's tomb.

Other Incas had other palaces in Cuzco. One of the early rulers, Inca Roca, built Cora Cora at the northern corner of the square. During Manco Inca's siege of Cuzco, Cora Cora was a strategic bastion captured by the natives after a stiff resistance. Viracocha Inca may have used the Quishuar-cancha enclosure at the eastern end of the square; it later became a temple of the creator god, Viracocha, and was awarded to the Catholic Church after the Conquest as a site for the cathedral. One theory is that Quishuar-cancha was a palace occupied by successive living Incas. Pachacuti's son, the great conqueror Topa Inca Yupanqui, may have had the Pucamarca palace, a short distance to the southeast of the square. Huascar may have improved Amarucancha, but he also built Colcampata on the hillside below Sacsahuaman. This palace was later

The ruins of Huchuy Cosco, a royal retreat high above Calca in the Yucay valley

occupied by the post-Conquest puppet Paullu Inca, and something survives of its terrace and a short stretch of freestanding wall above. The Act of Foundation of Cuzco, which divided the city among its Spanish conquerors, also mentioned a palace that young Manco Inca was building for himself on the terraces above the main square.

The Inca rulers' palaces were not only in Cuzco. Each of them had a country retreat, lodgings near Cuzco to which he could retire for recreation. Each of the earliest, semimythical Incas was identified with a particular place where, in later times, his clan continued to tend his estates. Viracocha Inca retreated to a crag called Caquia Xaquixahuana when the

Chancas seemed about to capture Cuzco. He evidently had private property and a fortress-retreat at this place, for "he ordered palaces built for himself . . . where he could take his pleasure." It was here that his mummy was discovered by Spanish investigators a century later. This Caquia Xaquixahuana may be the place now known as Huchuy Cosco (little Cuzco) overlooking Calca in the Yucay valley.

Viracocha's son, the great Pachacuti, began his conquests by moving down the Vilcanota–Urubamba valley and capturing the lands of the Tampu tribe. This was one of his favorite places, and he decided to build a palace there. The result was Ollantaytambo, a place that remained with Pachacuti's clan until long after the Conquest. "He went down to the valley of Yucay to a place which is now called Tambo, eight leagues from Cuzco, where he erected some magnificent buildings." Tampu was the name of one of the four founding clans of Cuzco, which corresponded in the creation legends to the four Ayar brothers. Later in his life Pachacuti's sons pursued the campaigns of conquest, and the aged ruler "finished the edifices at Tambo, and constructed ponds and pleasure houses of Yucay. On a hill near Cuzco he erected some sumptuous houses called Patallacta, and many others in the neighborhood of the capital. He made water channels for use and for pleasure; and he ordered governors of provinces under his rule to build pleasure houses on the most appropriate sites, to be ready for him should he visit their jurisdictions." Cobo said that Patallacta was a place that Pachacuti assigned for sacrifices and in which he died. A few kilometers away, on the road to the Antisuyo—the eastern, forested quarter of the empire—was the fountain of Tambo Machay, a place now seen by all visitors to Cuzco. Cobo described this as a house of Pachacuti's "where he lodged when he went hunting." Pachacuti's son Topa Inca Yupanqui built himself country retreats at Calispuquio beyond the fortress of Sacsahuaman and at the town of Chinchero fifteen kilometers (nine miles) north of Cuzco, "where he had very rich arrangements for his recreation and ordered extensive gardens to be constructed to supply his household." The last Inca, Huayna Capac, had his private estate in the Yucay valley and after the Conquest Francisco Pizarro took this land as his own. It was thus normal, even in the regimented Inca state, for ruling Incas to own country estates and to build palaces on them.

There was one type of native building that was both functional and highly distinctive. Cobo noted that "great storehouses and granaries, which the Indians call qollqas, were built on the Inca's orders throughout the provinces of Peru. They stored and preserved the tribute and wealth of the crown and church in these. . . . They generally built these depots or stores outside populated areas, in high, cool and airy locations, near the royal road. We see their ruins today around towns, on the crests and slopes of mountains. They consisted of many square buildings as small as ordinary rooms, set in a line like little towers, very neatly and symmetrically and spaced two or three yards apart from one another. . . . The lines [of storehouses] sometimes consisted of twenty, thirty, fifty or more chambers. Since they were in high locations and arranged symmetrically they look admirable—for their walls are still visible today, and in some places they are standing in such perfect condition that only the roofs are missing." Cobo explained that the high, isolated locations were to protect stored goods from damp, and the spacing was to save a line of storehouses from burning if one caught fire.

These storehouses were the embodiment of the Incas' elaborate system of tribute; they were the key to their military triumphs; and they were the basis of a highly successful welfare state. Vast quantities of foodstuffs, weapons, cloth and manufactured goods were produced by the empire's tribute payers. Some storehouses were reserved for the state religion, for sacrifices, offerings and support of the temple attendants. Other stores held the Inca's personal tribute: cloth, precious objects, and fine chicha that the sovereign could give to deserving subjects or keep to enhance the luxury of his own estate. Other stores held food for distribution among the provinces and as insurance against bad harvests.

Bernabé Cobo explained that, apart from luxury goods, the Inca's storehouses "supported all the servants of the royal

The sacred spring of Tambo Machay, a shrine above Cuzco, was embellished with fine terraces and niches

palace and of the mummies of the dead Incas. They provided food for the Inca and his relatives and attendant lords. They also supplied the garrisons, patrols and fighting men, who received no pay apart from food and clothing—each soldier was paid with two sets of clothing each year. The Inca would also grant chiefs permission to distribute part of the cloth and food in the stores in their districts to keep their subjects contented. . . . Once a province had enough for its own needs [the Inca] provided for the requirements of other districts. Supplies were thus taken from one province to another—they often transported stores from the plains to the mountains and in the opposite direction. They took great care over this. It was done so systematically and efficiently that there was no lack in any area and none suffered want, even in lean years. . . . Whatever was left over or not needed was kept in storehouses for a time of need. There was always quite enough when such times occurred: for they sometimes stored food for ten or twelve years." There was careful control of stocks in the storehouses, for although the Incas had no writing, they had quipus, highly efficient mnemonic devices, knotted strings that functioned like abacuses to record units of measurement.

The vast complex of Inca storehouses may sound fanciful and utopian, but it was very real. The chronicles are full of accounts of the bulging storehouses found by the conquerors. Guaman Poma recorded some of the foods that could be kept: "In the region of the Collas [around Lake Titicaca] they stored *chuño* frozen, dried potatoes; *moraya* cooked and dried potatoes; *caya* cooked and frozen oca [a sorrel tuber]; dried meat; and wool for weaving. . . . In all parts of the kingdom they stored maize, sweet potatoes, chili peppers, cotton, *maxno* which was a fiber for dyeing wool, coca, and *rumo* which consisted of various foods specially treated for conservation and which could be eaten without prior cooking." Cobo said that the jerked meat was of llamas, vicuñas or deer, and he mentioned deposits of "different types of cloth—woolen, cotton and of plumage, sandals that they call *ojotas*, weapons of the types used in each different province."

The conquerors rapidly dissipated these treasures. "Our Spaniards found these storehouses packed with all these articles." But the system of tribute collection continued even after the first impact of foreign invasion. Sixteen years after the first conquest, when a royal army was suppressing a rebellion by Pizarro's youngest brother, it was quartered in the Jauja valley of central Peru. "Even though it waited there for seven months, supplies for the camp did not run out throughout this period. The reason was that there were many years of produce stored in the depots: over 500,000 hanegas [800,000 bushels] of foodstuffs."

Nothing had prepared the first Spaniards for the gigantic stores they found fully stocked at Cuzco. Pizarro's secretary Pedro Sancho described "storehouses full of cloaks, wool, weapons, metal, cloth and all the other goods that are grown or manufactured in this country. There are shields, leather bucklers, beams for roofing the houses, knives and other tools, sandals and breastplates to equip the soldiers. All was in such vast quantities that it is hard to imagine how the natives can ever have paid such immense tribute of so many items." The young Pedro Pizarro was equally amazed. "There were vast numbers of storehouses in Cuzco when we entered the city, filled with very delicate cloth and with other coarser cloths; and stores of tools, of foodstuffs, and of coca." But what struck Pedro Pizarro most were "deposits of iridescent feathers, some looking like fine gold and others of a shining golden-green color. . . . Quantities of them were threaded together on fine thread and were skillfully attached to agave fibers to form pieces of cloth over a span in length. These were all stored in leather chests."

The chroniclers' accounts have been amply corroborated in archaeological remains. There are rows of qollqas (storehouses) in many sites all over Peru. I can recall seeing a particularly fine row of them on a bare hillside below the remote pre-Inca ruins of Tantamayo near the canyon of the upper Marañón, another set on a hill above Jauja, and six uniform rectangular huts on a steep hillside southwest of the inti-huatana group at Pisac. Pedro de Cieza de León often described qollqas full of weapons, cloth and food, at such provincial cities as Tumibamba (the modern Cuenca in Ecuador), Jauja, and Vilcashuamán. "When the lord [Inca] was lodged in his dwellings and his soldiers garrisoned there, nothing, from the most important to the most trifling item, could not be provided." A sloping hillside near the flat expanse of ruins of Huánuco is covered in rows of huts that were clearly storage qollqas. The American archaeologist Craig Morris studied them in 1965 and counted 497 storehouses. He excavated 120 of them and noted that they were divided into "functionally specialized sets devoted to the storage of various products." Cieza de León said that there were seven hundred storehouses at Vilcashuamán. An isolated site called Cotapachi, near Cochabamba in Bolivia, has no less than twenty-four hundred qollqas; since there was no large town nearby, it was evidently a center for redistribution of tribute produce. All the thousands of qollqas at Cotapachi are round, all 3.0 meters (10 feet) in diameter, all 5.15 meters (17 feet) from one another in their rows and with the rows themselves 9.5 meters (31 feet) apart. Such accurate measurements were an impressive example of Inca engineering skill; and the military precision of the qollqas' formation was typical of Inca administrative efficiency. Guaman Poma has a fine drawing of rectangular qollqas with conical thatch roofs. We know from some ruins that these storehouses could have ingenious systems of ducting, under the floor and near the roof, to keep perishables like maize ventilated.

These tidy rows of storage huts are tangible evidence of the Incas' administrative brilliance. Hillsides neatly contoured with banks of agricultural terraces, stone-lined water culverts, roads, bridges, and posthouses all demonstrate the same organizational skill. The Inca empire was a network. A web of roads, *tambos* (posthouses or lodgings) and administrative centers radiated from the heartland near Cuzco. Inca architecture responded to this pattern of expansion and imperial government. There were different requirements and different solutions in each zone of the empire: the imperial court at Cuzco and its adjacent "pleasure houses"; the surrounding Inca heartland, specially geared to supplying luxuries for the court at Cuzco; and the thousands of miles of subject territory, ruled from provincial capitals at regular intervals along the imperial highways.

Qollqas (storehouses). Seated on the right is an administrator holding a quipu, the Inca abacus

Although the requirements might be different in the various parts of the empire, the architectural techniques were uniform. Alexander von Humboldt observed: "It is impossible to examine carefully a single Inca building without recognizing the same type in all the rest that exist in the length of the Andes. . . . It seems as if a single architect built this great quantity of monuments." Graziano Gasparini and Luise Margolies answered Humboldt in their splendid book *Arquitectura Inka*: "In effect, it was a single architect who chose and imposed the limited repertoire of technical and plastic solutions: it was the State."

We know that the Incas mobilized vast squads of laborers to build so much in so short a time. We also know that the astonishing Inca masonry was simply the product of innumerable man-days of patient labor. What we do not know is the spirit in which the labor was performed, the relationship between the Inca state and its subjects. The attitude of Inca stonemasons doubtless ranged from pride inspired by adulation of the emperor-deity to the sullenness of forced labor based on fear. The chronicles and the behavior of Inca subjects during the collapse of Inca rule leave no doubt about the worship of the Inca ruler. Even the highest officials trembled and humbled themselves in the presence of the Inca; every pronouncement by the Inca was obeyed as the word of a divine oracle; and every aspect of the Inca's daily life was of the highest conceivable standard of excellence—his food, clothing, ornaments, servants, women, and of course his buildings. Dedicated subjects worked on Inca palaces with religious devotion.

In contrast to the obedience of the most loyal subjects was the unenthusiastic performance of conquered tribes recently coerced into the Inca empire. There were major revolts during the reigns of the last pre-Conquest Incas. The tribes that had been defeated by Inca armies were understandably the first to side with the Spanish conquerors—the Cañari of southern Ecuador, Chachapoya of northeastern Peru, Huanca and Chanca of central Peru, and Colla of Titicaca. The Incas dominated such rebellious regions by the classic colonial stratagem of planting pockets of loyal settlers (called mitimaes) in their midst. A chief of Huancané on the north shore of Lake Titicaca testified, after the Conquest, that "the Inca Huayna Capac settled one thousand weavers . . . and one hundred potters . . . as mitimaes on our lands. Although their presence did us great damage, our ancestors did not dare resist the will of the Inca because they were so afraid of the tyrant."

Although we know that parts of the Inca empire were held down by force, there is remarkably little archaeological evidence of this. There were rudimentary defensive walls and a dry moat at Machu Picchu and to a lesser extent at Pisac; but most Inca towns had no defenses of any sort. Provincial capitals had no city walls and no fortresses. The great bastion of Sacsahuaman above Cuzco was a temple and storage area as well as a fortress; and, surprisingly, it was not reproduced in other parts of the empire. Military control relied on the rapid movement of armies and their supply from the network of storage depots. During excavations of the important provincial center Huánuco, almost nothing was found to indicate a military presence.

It is difficult to determine the Incas' attitude to landscape. They were an agricultural people, with monthly festivals closely related to the farming seasons. Each age group of Inca subjects had appointed tasks closely related to the land and its produce. Inca religion was intimately based on nature: celestial phenomena—the sun, moon, stars, thunder, lightning and rainbows—were all worshipped. Such humble natural features as rock outcrops, springs, caves, rivers or mountains had powerful superstitious or spiritual significance that infuriated Spanish priests in the sixteenth century and is almost beyond the comprehension of modern urban man. One Catholic priest explained that "this can be seen in the prayers they used to say when they knelt or prostrated themselves or stood still in some natural shrine. For they were not speaking to the hill, spring, river or cave, but to the great [creator god] Illa Tici Viracocha: they said that he existed in heaven and invisibly in that place. This was a very common practice among the Peruvians. They had different names for these natural shrines, calling passes *apachitas*, caves *huacas*, hills *urcos*, springs *pucyu*, and the heavens *huahua pacha*. They did not revere all hills and mountains, all springs and rivers, but only those which had some peculiarity worthy of special consideration, and these they held to be sacred places. . . . The Peruvians frequently used this type of natural temple without building any edifice; but they often made a stone altar, called *usno*, in such places for their sacrifices."

Inca architects were therefore in the closest possible spiritual harmony with the land. Does this mean that they admired natural beauty? To modern visitors, much of the thrill of Inca architecture derives from its setting in spectacular landscape. Chronicle sources give no clue whether the Incas

The lower city of Machu Picchu

themselves shared that aesthetic awareness—whether they chose to build in certain locations because they delighted in their breathtaking views or because their buildings would look better against a particular natural background.

There may possibly have been a connection between the purpose of an Inca site and its topographical setting. The ruins of Choquequirau, Pisac, Ollantaytambo and Machu Picchu are on saddle ridges projecting from mountainous slopes; such dramatic locations probably had religious significance. Some royal palaces—Vitcos or Caquia Xaquixahuana—were

The shape of the Sacred Rock, at the northern end of Machu Picchu, echoes that of the mountain beyond it

on similar mountain spurs. Most provincial towns were built in more familiar peasant locations: at the edges of fertile valleys. Quito, Tumibamba, Cajamarca, Huamachuco, Huánuco, Pumpu, Jauja, Chinchero, Chucuito and Cuzco itself all nestle against hillsides and open onto valleys. This was the natural site for an agricultural community: close to its pastures and fields, but consuming as little flat land as possible.

It is just as difficult to tell whether the Incas appreciated aesthetic detail in their buildings as to sense their awareness of beautiful landscape. They wasted no time on decorative embellishments such as pilasters, carvings, cornices and moldings. Pre-Inca civilizations on the Peruvian coast had covered their buildings with intricate frescoes, elaborate latticework and sculpted ornaments. The Incas were too restrained or too sophisticated for such obvious decoration. The few Inca buildings in Cuzco that have snakes or pumas carved in relief on their stonework probably date from the fall of the Inca empire, a time when Inca masons could indulge their fancies free of official restriction. It is clear that during the decades of imperial expansion, the Inca state imposed norms of simple, standardized plans and technology. Each new provincial town had its repertoire of official buildings, all on rectangular plans. Precise directives gave these state buildings a uniform character, and their construction was overseen by teams of the same government architects. The only permitted embellishments were trapezoidal gates and niches, with a little license about the number of jambs and the cut of the lintels.

The Inca decision to reject elaborate decoration was a conscious one. They borrowed freely from the more advanced, conquered regions of their empire. They adopted the stone-working techniques of the Colla of Lake Titicaca, and the enclosures and quadrangles of the Chimu of Chan Chan; and they filled their capital city of Cuzco with artisans, silversmiths, potters and weavers from subject tribes. They must therefore have decided that very ornate walls would be inappropriate for their own austere character and for their regimented and highly efficient empire.

Some unanswered questions remain. In an architecture so poor in decorative elements, why was such attention lavished on the shaping and fitting of stones? Why incorporate huge blocks into terrace walls, or devote so much labor to achieving perfect interlocking of masonry joints? There is a striking contrast between the perfection of Inca stone walls, which have survived successive earthquakes, and the far less durable adobes often used alongside fine stonework or the thatch roofs resting on frames of crudely worked logs. Inca masonry sometimes seems to adopt the most complex solutions and difficult methods. Was this an official aesthetic, intended to proclaim the state's success in mobilizing great reserves of manpower, or even a totalitarian attempt to employ excess labor? Was it an expression of the masons' own virtuosity— an outlet for their artistic expression in the face of official restriction? Or did it have a forgotten mystical significance? It could well have been a product of patriotic or pious devotion, a desire to build in the finest conceivable techniques for the most holy purposes.

Whatever the motives, there is no question about the beauty of Inca architecture. It impressed sixteenth-century soldiers and ecclesiastics, and it delights modern observers more conditioned to appreciate primitive art or simple and functional architecture. Some elements of Inca building can have been done only for aesthetic reasons. This must be an explanation for the countersinking of stone joints, ranging from the delicate indentations on the walls of Coricancha to the sharp rustication of the terracing of Colcampata or Tarahuasi. The pairs of projecting bosses, the subtle entasis on the curved wall of Coricancha, the perfectly graded coursing on the wall of the Cuzco acllahuasi, or the rounded ends of the ashlars where that wall reaches the main square, the angular sculpture of the holy caves or the inti-huatana at Machu Picchu, the dramatic location of so many Inca buildings—all these have beauty far beyond functional explanations. We can therefore enjoy the excellence of surviving Inca buildings, ponder the many questions they raise, and admire the vanished civilization that achieved so much in so short a time.

ISLAND OF THE SUN

IN THE INCA CREATION LEGEND, there was a flood similar to that of the Old Testament. The creator god, Viracocha, flooded the land in order to destroy the first iniquitous race of men. "When the flood had passed and the land was dry, Viracocha decided to people it again. To make it more perfect, he decided to create luminaries to give it light. With this purpose, he went with his servants to a great lake in the Collao in which there is an island called Titicaca, which means 'Rock of Lead.' Viracocha went to this island and duly ordered that the sun, moon and stars should emerge and be set in the heavens to give light to the world; and so it was." It was said that after the darkness of the flood "the sun rose one morning with extraordinary brilliance from a rock on the island of Titicaca; and those who lived there believed that that spur of rock was the true house or lodging of the sun. . . . They therefore built and dedicated a temple there that was sumptuous for that age."

Manco Capac, the legendary founder of the Inca tribe, claimed this sacred Island of the Sun as his own birthplace. He invented the "fable that he and his wife were children of the Sun, and that their father had placed them on that island so that they should go about the land teaching the people." The mysterious island in Lake Titicaca thus emerges, in different legends, as the place of origin of the sun, of all mankind, and of the Inca tribe in particular.

The sky above Lake Titicaca has the intense blue of high altitude, for at 3,810 meters (12,500 feet) above sea level Titicaca is the highest navigable lake in the world. Ships and hydrofoils now ply its 171-kilometer (106-mile) length. The blue sky of high altitude makes the deep water dark blue, and on a bright day the Island of the Sun looks Aegean, with its imported eucalyptuses and cypresses and its swifts and dung beetles. But it is too high to maintain this illusion for long.

Clouds race across from the surrounding Andes, a chill wind whips the lake waters in a dangerous squall, and the lake can suddenly become bleak and forbidding.

The Island of the Sun is almost ten kilometers (six miles) long, with its steep hills rising far above the waters of the lake. There is an Inca fountain at a wooded landing stage on the north shore, with a flight of steps and cascading water channels on the slope above. From the ridge along the bare spine of the island, a visitor looks down on fishing villages far below. There are llamas and alpacas on the terraced slopes, and Aymara shepherds play reed pipes. To the east, five kilometers (three miles) across the water, rises Coati, the smaller Island of the Moon.

The Jesuit chronicler Bernabé Cobo says that it was the tenth Inca, Topa Yupanqui, who decided to build on the islands of Lake Titicaca. Local Indians told him about the divinity of their shrine, which commemorated both the appearance of the sun after the flood and also the creation of the Inca tribe. The Inca was sufficiently impressed to take the shrine under his personal protection. "He went to [the Island of the Sun] and found the altar and temple dedicated to its gods. Knowing how greatly the natives worshipped this holy place . . . and that it was a shrine dedicated to the Sun, he was delighted to have found a place well suited to encourage worship and respect for the Sun among his subjects: for . . . the Incas greatly prided themselves on being descendants and worshippers of the Sun. Being well satisfied with the shrine, he determined to use all his energy, efforts and power to cause it to be venerated in all earnestness. He considered this an undertaking worthy of his great majesty." The Inca himself fasted and approached the sacred rock barefoot. All this was intended to enhance the sanctity of the shrine. "The Inca had many buildings built . . . to enlarge and add to the prestige of

Qollqas (storehouses) near the sun temple once held sacred idols in their niches

The finest cloth covered the convex side of the sacred rock

The concave face of the sacred rock was plated in gold

the shrine. He added magnificent new structures to the ancient temple, and ordered others built for other services—a nunnery of mamaconas, for instance; many splendid rooms and chambers for the lodgings of the priests and ministers; and a sumptuous tambo or hostel as accommodation for pilgrims, a quarter of a league before reaching the temple. He built great storehouses of food, clothing and other provisions for the pilgrims' route, around [the nearby peninsula of] Copacabana. The ruins of these survive today [c. 1620] and I [Cobo] have seen them."

The shrine itself was an outcrop of stratified rock, at the barren tip of the island farthest from Copacabana. Squier was awed by its wild location. "At almost the very northern end of the island, at its most repulsive and unpromising part, where there is neither inhabitant nor trace of culture, where the soil is rocky and bare and the cliffs ragged and broken—high up, where the fret of the waves of the lake is scarcely heard and where the eye ranges over the broad blue waters from one mountain barrier to the other . . . is the spot most celebrated and most sacred of Peru. Here is the rock on which it was believed no bird would light or animal venture, on which no

human being dared to place his foot; whence the sun rose to dispel the primal vapors and illume the world." Squier's observations tallied with Cobo's, made almost four centuries earlier: "The rock that was so greatly venerated lay in the open. . . . Its concave part, which is what was worshipped, is insignificant; the altar to the sun was inside it. The convex portion is a rock outcrop whose sides fall to the water in an inlet that the lake makes there. The rock's decoration consisted of covering its convex face in a curtain of the finest and most delicate cumbi cloth ever seen; while the concave part was covered in plates of gold. A round basin-shaped stone can be seen in front of the rock. It is admirably cut, the size of an average millstone, with an orifice—which now holds the foot of a cross!—into which chicha was poured for the sun to drink. The temple was to the east, some forty yards from the rock. Images of thunder and of the other gods of the Incas were worshipped here together with that of the sun. Many idols were placed in windows, recesses and niches along its walls: some of these had human shapes, some of llamas, others of birds or other animals, and all were made of copper, silver or gold, large and small in size. The ruins of the storehouses of

An altar near the sun temple

the sun can still be seen near the temple, with chambers resembling the labyrinth of Crete. From the walls and remains still standing today, one is struck by the excellence of the whole of the building of this idolatrous shrine."

The path leading to the holy promontory passed by another outcrop of rock. This contained eroded cavities, observed by Cobo, Squier and Ernst Middendorf, that looked like giant footprints. Before this, two hundred yards from the main temple, was a gate known as Intipuncu (gate of the sun). Cobo described great pilgrimages that the Incas organized to the shrine: the pilgrims advanced along the peninsula of Copacabana, where they were made to give offerings and suffer penances before being allowed to sail to the island on reed boats. They could not advance beyond the Intipuncu gate, but observed the sacred rock from it. Cobo's account was clearly colored by his memories of the great Christian pilgrimages to Santiago de Compostela. But Copacabana is now a Christian shrine that attracts thousands of Aymara and Quechua pilgrims, and a similar manifestation was entirely possible in Inca times. "To one side of the gateway can be seen buildings which the Indians say were the lodgings of the ministers and servants of the temple. On the other side are traces of a large building which was the convent of the mamaconas, the women dedicated to the sun, who served it by making the beverages and curious cloths that were consumed in the ministry of the shrine. This house of mamaconas was on the best location in the island."

Cobo described the elaborate rituals that took place on the holy islands. In one ceremony the priests of the Island of the Sun saluted those of nearby Coati, the Island of the Moon. "A great many rafts were employed in this service, going back and forth between the islands. To make the representation more living, the chief priest was prepared in one shrine to represent the person of the Sun, and an Indian girl in the other performed as the figure of the Moon. They drank to one another and the girl who represented the Moon caressed the man acting the Sun and begged him, with endearments, to shine out brightly and calmly every day, never hiding his rays,

so that the crops should grow until the time when rain was needed."

Little is left of the buildings of these great shrines. Treasure seekers have ransacked and pillaged the complex of buildings around the sacred rock. The most recent attempt to find the temple's treasure was a diving expedition led by the French oceanographer Jacques-Yves Cousteau: it found thousands of frogs but no Inca gold. Coati contains a remarkable ruin, rarely visited because of difficult currents and because the island has been used as a penal colony. The remains of Coati's convent of mamaconas consist of a rectangular court, roughly 53 by 25 meters, (174 by 82 feet), open to the lake on one long side and with the surrounding screen of chambers abutting against the hillside. It is very theatrical. Deeply recessed doorways and niches alternate along the ornamental façade. But the most striking feature of Coati is the frequent use of the Tiahuanaco step motif in an Inca building: local builders clearly drew their inspiration from the great pre-Inca ruin near the southern end of the lake. Doors and niches all have stepped arches above their lintels, and there are some windows with the step pattern arranged in a diamond—just as at Tiahuanaco and on the platform built by Colla masons at Ollantaytambo.

The best-preserved building on the Island of the Sun is the "palace" of Pilco Caima on its southeastern shore a few kilometers from the rock shrine. This was either the Inca's own lodging or a hostel for pilgrims. It is unusual in three respects: it is a freestanding complex of a dozen chambers and courtyards arranged in a rough square; it has two stories, unlike any other Inca building of this size; and the chambers of its lower floor have false domes of corbeled stones—the Mayas' favorite system of roofing, but unknown among other surviving Inca ruins.

Squier made a fine drawing of Pilco Caima, which shows that its upper floor has crumbled considerably during the century since his visit. He also produced tidy plans that made Pilco Caima look like a symmetrical renaissance palace; Gasparini and Margolies recently published the true plan, drawn

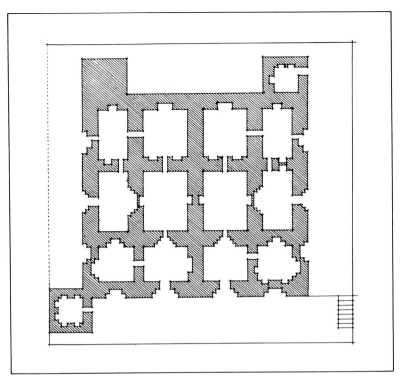

The palace of Pilco Caima on the Island of the Sun as drawn by George Squier in 1877

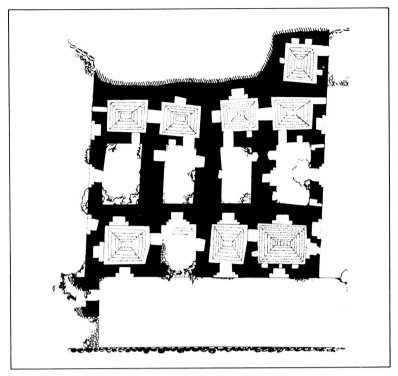

The true plan, as drawn by Bolivian architectural students a century later. Note the corbeled false domes

by architectural students from La Paz, which shows that the chambers, passages and niches of the Inca palace were far from regular or rectilinear.

Squier noticed that some of the walls of Pilco Caima still retained patches of stucco and deduced that "the building was originally yellow, while the inner parts and moldings of the doorways and niches were of different shades of red." But what impressed the American traveler most was a terrace or esplanade facing the lake in the center of the second story. Its rear wall had traces of niches, arranged as benches for anyone wishing to sit and admire the magnificent view. To Squier, this prospect is "one of the finest and most extensive in the world. The waves of the lake break at your very feet. To the right is the high and diversified peninsula of Copacabana; in the center of the view, the island of Coati, consecrated to the Moon . . . ; and to the left, the gleaming [mountain] Illampu, its white mantle reflected in the waters that spread out like a sea in front." This esplanade, so clearly built to enjoy the view, convinced Squier that the Incas "were not deficient in taste or insensible to the grand and beautiful in nature."

The top of Puma Orco, a hill thirty miles south of Cuzco. It was named for the small puma carved on its summit (see upper right plate, page 173)

TAMBO-TOQO AND HUANACAURI HILL

THE INCAS, WHO WERE RECENT ARRIVALS AMONG the powerful Andean tribes, adopted the places of origin of the Aymara of Lake Titicaca; but their tribe in fact flourished near Cuzco, 300 kilometers (180 miles) to the northwest. Inca origin legends explain this discrepancy by describing an underground migration by the four founding Ayar brothers and their three sisters. The precursors of the Inca tribe probably did migrate from Titicaca, over the Vilcanota hills and down the Vilcanota river valley to Cuzco. The legend was that the Ayar brothers and sisters emerged from a cave with three mouths, which was known as either Tambo-toqo or Paccari-tambo (*tambo* means way station; *toqo* means hole). A hill and a cave with these names still exist, fifty kilometers (thirty miles) south of Cuzco.

One Ayar brother was trapped in the cave, but the others marched north to approach Cuzco. At the hill of Huanacauri, just southeast of the city, the brothers and sisters rested and tried to examine a rainbow. Climbing the hill, they saw a rock in human shape near the rainbow's end. The brother called Ayar Uchu volunteered to investigate. "When Ayar Uchu reached the statue or shrine, he sat upon it with great courage, and asked what it was doing there. At these words the rock deity turned its head to see who spoke, but it could not see him as he was pressing down upon it with his weight. Ayar Uchu then tried to depart but could not: for he found that the soles of his feet were fastened to the shoulders of the rock deity. His six brothers and sisters, realizing that he was trapped, ran up to help him. But Ayar Uchu, seeing that he himself was transformed and that his brothers were unable to free him, said to them: 'O brothers and sisters, you have done

me an evil turn! It was for you that I came to the place where I shall remain, forever separated from your company. Go, my fortunate brothers; for I declare that you will become great lords! I beg you, however, . . . to honor and venerate me in all your festivals and ceremonies, so that I shall be the first to whom you make offerings.'" Ayar Uchu was thus transformed into a stone effigy; but Huanacauri hill became one of the most venerated shrines of the Incas. Felipe Guaman Poma de Ayala, the Indian artist-chronicler, made a vivid drawing of a bareheaded Inca ruler and his queen kneeling to worship the triple cave of Tambo-toqo and the hill of Huanacauri with its human-shaped rock shrine.

When the legendary Ayar Uchu was turned to stone on Huanacauri, he promised that he would "bestow the gifts of valor, nobility and knighthood" on the young nobles of Cuzco. Henceforth, the initiation rites of Inca boys were based on Huanacauri. This initiation was an elaborate annual ceremony called Capac Raymi, which was held during the month of November. Cristóbal de Molina, a Spanish priest resident in Cuzco in the 1570s, left a detailed description of the Capac Raymi ritual. The boys to be initiated were equipped with special rush sandals, llama-gut slings, fine black woollen tunics, mantles and headbands, and black feather plumes. The initiates and their families observed a strict fast. There were special sacrifices of llamas, prayers to the idol Huanacauri, flagellation of the adolescents and their arming with special slings and battle-axes, and processions of maidens in festive dress attending the youths with jugs of chicha. The ceremonies lasted for many days. At one stage the young men slept at the foot of Huanacauri and then climbed it to worship

The caves on the steep eastern side of Puma Orco, combined with building remains and ceremonial seats (see upper right plate, page 175), suggest that the Incas may have designated this site as Tambo-toqo, where the Ayar brothers and sisters emerged from underground

The holy hill of Huanacauri, looking south

Huanacauri hill and the cave of Tambo-toqo

The summit of Huanacauri hill

at their ancestor's shrine. They made offerings of wool, performed a ritual dance, and were again flagellated and admonished by their elders to be brave.

"The boys then arranged themselves in many rows, behind one another. Behind each of these rows of boys was another of older men who acted as their patrons—each was responsible for one knight, whom he was to help if he grew tired. A magnificently dressed Indian stood in front of all the rows. When he shouted, all of them started to run furiously. Some would be seriously injured. When they reached the bottom the girls gave them drink, first to the patrons and then to the foster sons." The culmination of the month of ceremonial, sacrifice, and initiation ordeals came when the young Inca nobles had their earlobes pierced to receive the golden disks that were the sign of their rank. During the Conquest the Spaniards easily recognized such Inca officials and called them *orejones* (large ears) because of these great ear pendants.

The Indian chronicler Joan de Santacruz Pachacuti Yamqui said that the shrine of Huanacauri contained a handsome stone idol shaped like a vulture. Pedro de Cieza de León said that Huanacauri was the second most important holy place of the Inca empire: "In olden days there was a shrine on this hill, and around it was buried a great wealth of treasure." The Indian author Guaman Poma wrote that "the shrine of Huanacauri, which was looted for the benefit of the Spaniards, contained incalculable quantities of gold and silver," and the great champion of the Indians Bartolomé de las Casas said that the buildings of Huanacauri were still extant in his day. Now all is gone. Huanacauri hill is a bare slope on the Cuzco skyline; and closer investigation reveals nothing more than vestiges of building foundations on its rocky, eroded flanks.

SACSAHUAMAN

WHEN THE INCAS IMAGINED THEIR CAPITAL CITY, Cuzco, as a crouching puma, they conceived the hill that towers steeply above the city, the source of the two streams Saphi-Huatanay and Tullumayo, as the feline's head. This hill of Sacsahuaman was a natural fortress, with cliffs falling toward the city below. All that was needed was to fortify the far side, to enclose the crown of the hill with zigzag ramparts that would be the teeth of the imaginary feline.

Sacsahuaman is the traditional Spanish spelling for the ruin; Saqsaywaman, the accepted Quechua spelling. Local Quechua-speaking Indians call it Sacsayhuaman. *Saqsay* means replete or full; *sacsa* means mottled or garlanded; *huaman* (*waman*) is a falcon; *uma* means a head. The name could mean garlanded head, which would tally with the notion of a puma's head; but it probably means replete falcon.

Sacsahuaman was far more than a fortress. It was primarily a shrine, an important temple to the sun to rival Coricancha in the city below. It was also the main storehouse for the ruling family and its army. Cieza de León attributed its construction to the great Pachacuti: "As the power of the Incas was increasing and Pachacuti had such great ambitions, . . . he decided to build a temple of the sun which would surpass everything done until then. It should house everything imaginable such as gold and silver, precious stones, fine garments, arms of all the types they used, materials of war, sandals, shields, feathers, skins of animals and birds, coca, sacks of wool and a thousand kinds of jewels; in a word, everything anyone had ever heard of was in it.

"The work was conceived on such a vast scale that even if the monarchy had lasted until now [1550] it would not have been completed. [Pachacuti] ordered that twenty thousand men be sent in from the provinces, and that the villages supply them with the necessary food." These great levies worked in relays so that the work was not too onerous. "Four thousand of them quarried and cut the stones; six thousand hauled these with great cables of leather and hemp; others dug the ditch and laid the foundations; while still others cut poles and beams for the timbers. . . . The living rock was excavated for the foundations, and for this reason it was so strong that it will last for as long as the world exists." Sarmiento de Gamboa also stressed that the Incas divided their laborers into parties, "each having its duties and officers: thus some brought stones, others worked them, others laid them." Garcilaso actually named the four successive master masons who planned and directed this vast enterprise. He explained how thousands of men were mobilized to drag immense rocks to their location in their fortress. "Learned Indians . . . affirm that over twenty thousand Indians brought up [the largest] stone, dragging it with great cables. Their progress was very slow, for the road up which they came is rough and has many steep slopes to climb and descend. Half the laborers pulled at the ropes from in front, while the rest kept the rock steady with other cables attached behind lest it should roll downhill."

The temple-fortress of Sacsahuaman rests on a natural hill of sedimentary rock with intrusions of diorite, particularly along the top of the cliff overlooking Cuzco. The Incas defended the far side with three mighty terrace walls. For 380 meters (415 yards) the hill is flanked by a magnificent zigzag of forty to fifty salient and reentering angles. The three terraces or ramparts are clad with the finest Inca polygonal masonry, with gigantic boulders interlocking perfectly and rusticated with smoothly polished surfaces. Each stone bulges in the traditional Inca fashion. One huge block is calculated to weigh ninety metric tons (88½ tons); another, 128 metric tons (126 tons). One single monolith measures 4.90 meters high by 4.75 wide by 2.60 thick (16 by 15½ by 8½ feet).

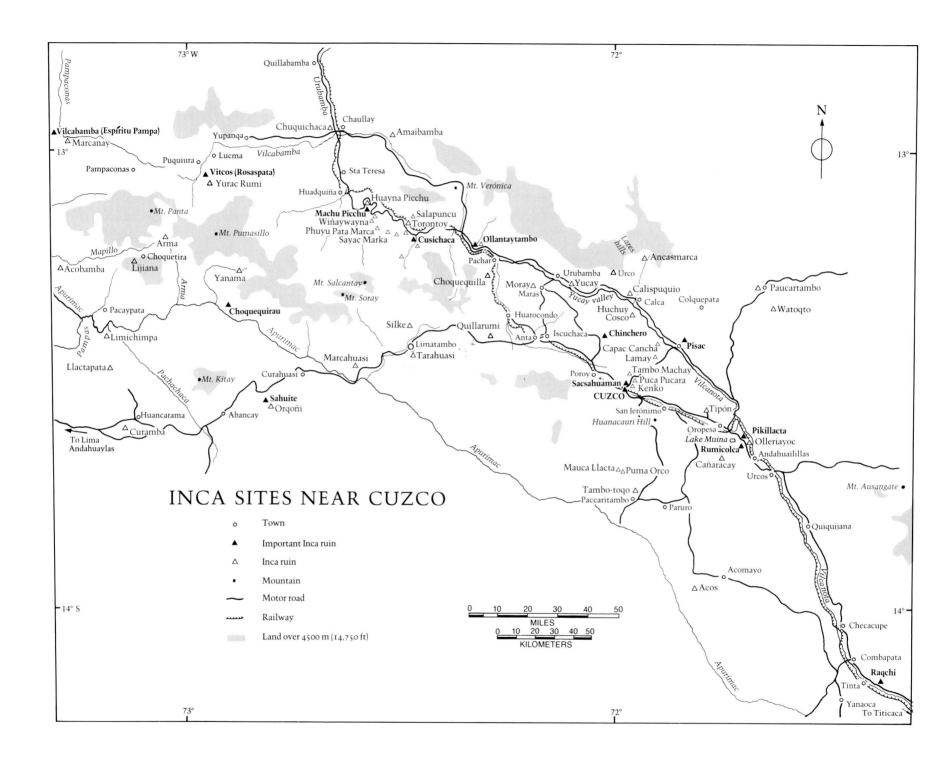

INCA SITES NEAR CUZCO

o	Town
▲	Important Inca ruin
△	Inca ruin
•	Mountain
—	Motor road
⌐⌐⌐	Railway
▨	Land over 4500 m (14,750 ft)

Map labels:

Quillabamba
Pampaconas
Urubamba
Chaullay
Chuquichaca
Amaibamba
Vilcabamba (Espíritu Pampa)
Marcanay
Yupanqa
Vilcabamba
Sta Teresa
Mt. Verónica
Lucma
Pampaconas
Puquiura
Vitcos (Rosaspata)
Yurac Rumi
Huadquiña
Huayna Picchu
Mt. Panta
Machu Picchu
Salapuncu
Torontoy
Wiñaywayna
Phuyu Pata Marca
Sayac Marka
Cusichaca
Ollantaytambo
Lares hills
Mt. Pumasillo
Arma
Pachar
Ancasmarca
Choquetira
Lijiana
Yanama
Choquequilla
Urubamba
Urco
Acobamba
Mt. Salcantay
Moray
Yucay
Calispuquio
Paucartambo
Mapillo
Maras
Yucay valley
Calca
Colquepata
Arma
Mt. Soray
Huarocondo
Huchuy
Cosco
Watoqto
Choquequirau
Pacaypata
Silke
Quillarumi
Anta
Iscuchaca
Chinchero
Pisac
Limichimpa
Limatambo
Capac Cancha
Lamay
Llactapata
Marcahuasi
Tarahuasi
Poroy
Tambo Machay
Vilcanota
Mt. Kitay
Curahuasi
Sacsahuaman
Puca Pucara
Kenko
Sahuite
CUZCO
Tipón
Huancarama
Orqoñi
San Jerónimo
Abancay
Oropesa
Pikillacta
Curamba
Huanacauri Hill
Lake Muina
Olleriayoc
To Lima
Andahuaylas
Rumicolca
Andahuailillas
Mauca Llacta
Puma Orco
Cañaracay
Urcos
Mt. Ausangate
Apurímac
Tambo-toqo
Paccaritambo
Paruro
Quiquijana
Acomayo
Acos
Checacupe
Combapata
Raqchi
Tinta
Yanaoca
To Titicaca

MILES
0 10 20 30 40 50

KILOMETERS
0 10 20 30 40 50

One of the first Spaniards to see this triumph of Inca masonry was Pizarro's secretary Pedro Sancho. He exclaimed that "these ramparts are the most beautiful thing to be seen among the buildings of that land. They are built of stones so large that anyone seeing them would say that they cannot have been placed there by human hands. They are as big as forest tree trunks. Some are thirty spans [over 6 meters or 20 feet] high, others are equally long, and others twenty-five or fifteen spans—three carts could not carry even the smallest of them. They are not straight-sided stones, but are extremely well joined and interlocking with one another. Spaniards who see them say that neither the [aqueduct] of Segovia nor any other structure built by Hercules or the Romans is as impressive a sight as this!"

The chronicler Garcilaso de la Vega echoed the wonder of every visitor who sees this triumph of Inca engineering: "The greatest and proudest work that [the Incas] ordered built to demonstrate their power and majesty was the fortress of Cuzco. To any who has not seen it, its dimensions sound incredible. But to any who has seen and studied [its stones] with care, they make him imagine and even believe that they were made by some form of magic—built by demons rather than men!" What amazed Garcilaso and other conquistadores was the means by which stones of such size could have been dragged from a quarry and then assembled into the complicated jigsaw that has survived so perfectly to the present day. Garcilaso felt that the Indians must have chosen natural blocks rather than quarried them. He said that the rocks were quarried at Muina and Rumicolca, over twenty kilometers (twelve and a half miles) southeast of Cuzco. Modern geologists reckon that most of the limestone or green diorite in Sacsahuaman was quarried a few hundred meters north of the site or from the hill itself. But the American authority on the Incas, John Rowe, agrees with Garcilaso: much of the rock *is* andesite from quarries at Huacoto or Rumicolca.

The effort of assembling stones of such size and grinding them to interlock so perfectly was stupendous. "It is indeed beyond the power of imagination to understand how these Indians, unacquainted with devices, engines or implements, could have cut, dressed, raised and lowered great rocks, more like lumps of mountains than building stones, and set them so exactly in their places." The Jesuit José de Acosta also marveled at the polygonal pattern, and correctly deduced that it had all been achieved by the deployment of vast levies of dedicated laborers: "The most remarkable thing is that, although the stones in the wall are . . . extremely irregular in size and shape, they nevertheless fit together with incredible precision without the use of mortar. All this was done with great masses of workers who patiently toiled to lay one stone on another, a task that required many trials since most of them were not level or uniform."

The zigzag arrangement of Sacsahuaman's three terrace walls may have represented the teeth of the head of Cuzco's puma, but they also provided obvious defensive strength. As Pedro Sancho remarked, "Anyone attacking them could not do so head-on, but would have to approach obliquely." Garcilaso said that there was only one gate in each rampart and he gave their names: Tiu-puncu (saturated gate or sandhill gate) in the lowest wall, Aqahuana-puncu in the middle (named after the architect Acahuana), and Viracocha-puncu in the upper (after the god or the Inca Viracocha). He said that these gates were closed by doors suspended from massive lintels. There is no evidence from surviving lintel stones here for such a system, but we know that it worked effectively against Spanish attacks during the siege of 1536. Garcilaso evidently referred only to the main gates, for there are in fact three gates and staircases in the lower rampart and a dozen in the upper ones. Far down at the eastern end of the walls was a great gate unearthed and scrupulously restored by Peruvian archaeologists in 1968.

Modern excavations of Sacsahuaman have also revealed an excellent system of drainage of the terrace ramparts. Thirty-six finely cut channels lead rainwater off the middle level rampart alone.

The original Sacsahuaman of the Incas consisted of far more than these three mighty terraces. Pedro Sancho, who saw it in all its glory, described it as "a magnificent stone and earth fortress, whose great embrasures overlook the city." He wrote that "there are many buildings inside the fortress and one principal tower in the middle. This is square, with four or five stories [stepped] above one another. The rooms and chambers inside it are small. The stones with which it is built are excellently cut, and so well fitted together that there is apparently no mortar. The blocks are so smooth that they look like polished slabs; and the courses are regular, as in Spain, with the joins alternating." Garcilaso said that there were three towers rising above the hill of Sacsahuaman. He named the largest as Muyuc Marca (round tower), and said that it contained a fount of water brought underground from a long distance. This was the Inca ruler's lodging, with its walls decorated with a tapestry of animals, birds and plants sculpted in gold and silver. The other towers, called Paucar Marca and Sallac Marca, were square and contained many chambers for the soldiers of the garrison. "The towers went as far below ground as they did above it. There were tunnels between them so that one could pass from one to the others below ground as well as above it."

The fortress-hill was covered with a labyrinth of chambers. Sancho viewed it with a soldier's eye, and was impressed. "The fortress has too many rooms and towers for a person to visit them all. Many Spaniards who have visited it, and who have traveled in Lombardy and other foreign countries, say that they have never seen a building to compare with this fortress nor a stronger castle. It could contain five thousand Spaniards. It could not be battered and it could not be mined, for it is situated at the top of a hill."

The beautiful buildings of Sacsahuaman did not long survive the Conquest. Its lovely rectangular polished ashlars were too tempting to the new masters of Cuzco. Sarmiento de Gamboa said that "the fortress was intact until the [1540s] after which they began to dismantle it to build the houses of Spaniards in Cuzco with its stones. Great regret is felt by those who see the ruins." The soldier-chronicler Cieza de León, who reached Cuzco at the end of that decade, exploded with fury over the wanton destruction: "The Spaniards have already done so much damage and left it in such a state that I hate to think of the responsibility of those governors who allowed so extraordinary a thing to have been destroyed and cast down, without giving thought to the future. . . . The remains of this fortress . . . should be preserved in memory of the greatness of this land!"

Garcilaso de la Vega, who was born in Cuzco in 1539, used to play as a boy among the ruins of Sacsahuaman. He recalled years later that "there were so many underground passages, large and small, twisting and turning in all directions, with so many doors, all of the same size but some opening to one side and some to the other, that anyone entering the maze soon lost his way. . . . When I was a boy, I often went up to the fortress with others of my own age. Although the stone part of the building was already ruined—I mean the part above ground and even a good deal of the part below the surface— we never dared enter certain parts of the remaining vaults, except as far as the light of the sun penetrated, lest we should get lost inside."

Even as he played in the temple-fortress, Garcilaso observed its destruction. He accused his compatriots of doing this almost out of envy of the achievements of the Incas. The Spaniards "pulled down all the smooth masonry in the walls, to save themselves the expense, effort and delay of having Indians work the stone. There is indeed not a house built by the Spaniards in the city that has not been made of this stone. The large slabs that formed the roofs of the underground passages were taken to serve as lintels and doorways. The smaller stones were used for foundations and walls. For the steps of staircases they sought slabs of stone of the size they needed, pulling down all the stones above the ones they wanted in the process. . . . In this way the majesty of the fortress was brought to the ground. [It was] a monument that deserved to be spared such devastation—which will cause everlasting regret to those who ponder what it was. It was pulled down in such haste that all that was left, in my own time, was the few relics I have mentioned."

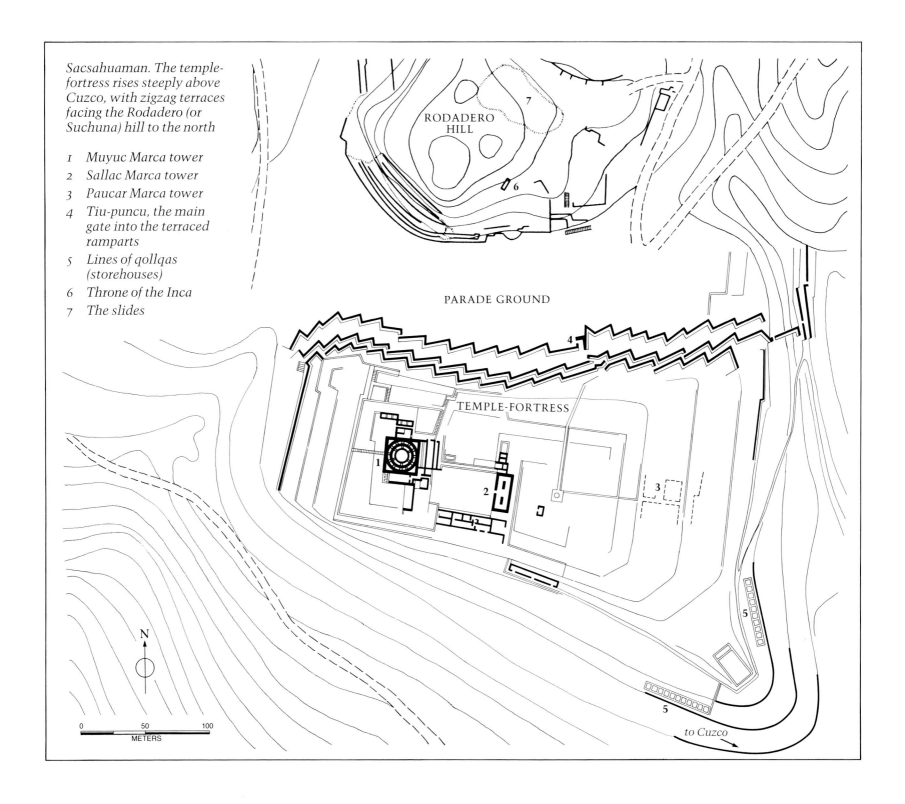

Sacsahuaman. The temple-fortress rises steeply above Cuzco, with zigzag terraces facing the Rodadero (or Suchuna) hill to the north

1 Muyuc Marca tower
2 Sallac Marca tower
3 Paucar Marca tower
4 Tiu-puncu, the main gate into the terraced ramparts
5 Lines of qollqas (storehouses)
6 Throne of the Inca
7 The slides

RODADERO HILL

PARADE GROUND

TEMPLE-FORTRESS

N

0   50   100
METERS

to Cuzco

Rodadero hill (Suchuna) from the ramparts of Sacsahuaman. The incised throne of the Inca is visible on the smooth upper surface of the outcrop. Temporary markings are made on the parade ground each year in June for the reenactment of Inti Raymi, the sun festival

The zigzags of Sacsahuaman's massive terraces, from the Throne of the Inca on Rodadero hill

When George Squier visited Cuzco in the 1860s, he observed the foundations of considerable structures on top of the hill of Sacsahuaman. He assumed that these were the bases of Garcilaso's towers but could not make out the plans. It was not until 1933, the fourth centenary of the Conquest, that there was a scientific excavation of the great ruin. Archaeologists led by Luis Valcárcel removed up to 4.5 meters (fifteen feet) of cover and revealed a series of fine chambers overlooking Cuzco. Their most thrilling achievement was to find the foundations of the three towers. Valcárcel wrote: "Only the bases of these magnificent monuments were discovered. The first tower [Muyuc Marca] was in the form of a cylinder, its base contained in a rectangle. The notable thing about it was that, in the central part, there was a deposit for water, from which the water was distributed by canals. The base of the tower has three concentric circumferences with the following diameters: 9.35, 15.0 and 22.2 meters (about 30, 50 and 75 feet). The base of the tower of Sallac Marca is a rectangle 21.8 by 10.2 meters (about 75 by 33 feet). There is evidence of several stories, and in the central part two platforms can still be seen. The tower of Paucar Marca has fallen into the worst ruin and only traces of it remain."

Facing the mighty ramparts of Sacsahuaman is another hill, the Rodadero (slide) or Suchuna. The hill's most famous feature is the Throne of the Inca or Kusilluj Hinkinan (monkey's lift). This is a series of low steps cut into the eastern slope of the diorite hill, a symmetrical sculpture of great beauty. It is easy to imagine the Inca and his court reviewing a ceremony or parade from this throne.

To the north of it, a part of the hill is covered with passages, stairways, niches and the Tiahuanacan step motif. The excavators of 1934 called this area Warmi Kajchana (meaning "where a woman is raped") because they found objects involved in a phallic cult here. This is the site of the famous slides that have delighted generations of Cuzqueño children and that now puzzle geologists. The slides look like glacial striations, but are not. They were caused by an intrusion of igneous diorite into limestone, with some form of faulting

before the igneous rocks had cooled. This part of the Rodadero has two tunnels resulting from karst erosion of the limestone, and a spring that has been carved by the Incas to form another of the many shrines on this plateau north of Cuzco. Below the slides is an amphitheater of niches surrounding a pool or altar. This was one of the many discoveries of the excavations started in 1968. Their other great surprise was to reveal a series of agricultural terraces and canals, all of fine Inca masonry, that rose to cover the entire western end of the hill.

Two hundred meters north of the amphitheater is the so-called Piedra Cansada, the Tired Stone, a great block of limestone that looks as though it never reached its intended destination (see plate, page 175). Cieza de León and Garcilaso both described their wonder at the size of this block. Their speculations were in fact misplaced, for the rock is a natural outcrop that had been squared off and embellished by the Incas. Beside it is yet another Throne of the Inca, with niches of superb precision like the alcoves of a baroque retable.

The maze of rocky outcrops of the Rodadero played an important role in the fighting of May 1536, the only occasion when the mighty fortress was attacked. Inca Cuzco had twice been captured without any resistance at Sacsahuaman—once to Atahualpa's general Quisquis and the northern Inca army, in the civil war between Atahualpa and Huascar (rival claimants to the Inca throne whose fighting weakened the empire on the eve of Pizarro's invasion); and then to Pizarro himself on 15 November 1533, when Quisquis abandoned the city. Two and a half years later, the Incas realized the full horror of European invasion, and rose in a valiant attempt to expel the Spaniards. Manco Inca, leader of this rebellion, made Sacsahuaman his advanced headquarters. Native levies secretly occupied the great fortress, without resistance since the Spaniards had failed to garrison it. It was from here that the chief priest, Villac Umu, directed the siege of Hernando Pizarro's Spaniards trapped in the city below.

At first the siege went well. Vast native contingents surrounded Cuzco on all sides. The attackers set fire to their city's thatch roofs. They advanced along its streets with mo-

The foundation and water supply of Muyuc Marca, the round tower

bile defenses against the Spaniards' horses and trapped the invaders in a couple of palace enclosures beside the main square. Manco Inca's son later exulted that the besieged "secretly feared that those were to be the last days of their lives. They could see no hope from any direction and did not know what to do." "The Spaniards were extremely frightened, because there were so many Indians and so few of them."

The beleaguered Spaniards now decided that their immediate survival depended on the recapture of Sacsahuaman on the cliff above them. It was determined that Juan Pizarro would lead fifty horsemen—the greater part of the Spaniards' cavalry—in a desperate attempt to break through the besiegers and attack their fortress. Observers from the Indian side remembered the scene as follows: "They spent the whole of that night on their knees and with their hands clasped [in prayer] at their mouths—for many Indians saw them. . . . On the following morning, very early, they all emerged from the church [Suntur-huasi] and mounted their horses as if they were going to fight. They started to look from side to side. While they were looking about in this way, they suddenly put spurs to their horses and at full gallop, despite the enemy, broke through the opening which had been sealed like a wall, and charged off up the hillside at breakneck speed."

Juan Pizarro's horsemen galloped up the Jauja road, climbing Carmenca hill. They somehow fought their way through the native barricades. Pedro Pizarro was in that contingent and later recalled the dangerous ride, zigzagging up the hillside under fire from above. Once on the plateau, the Spaniards pretended to be dashing down the road toward the coast; but at the village of Jicatica they left the road and wheeled around beyond the hills north of Sacsahuaman. Only by this broad flanking movement could they avoid the steep ascent and mass of obstacles between Cuzco and the fortress.

The natives had fortified the "parade ground" between Sacsahuaman and the Rodadero with earth barriers. It took repeated attacks and heavy fighting for the horsemen to force these barriers. The Spaniards then rode toward the mighty terraces. They were greeted with a withering fire of slingshots and javelins. It was late afternoon and the attackers were exhausted by the day's fierce fighting. But Juan Pizarro attempted one last charge, a frontal attack on the main gate into the fortress. This gate was defended by side walls projecting on either side, and the natives had dug a defensive pit between them. The passage leading to the gate was crowded with Indians defending the entrance or attempting to retreat from the barbican into the main fortress. Juan Pizarro had been struck on the jaw during the previous day's fighting in Cuzco and was unable to wear his steel helmet. As he charged toward the gate in the setting sun, he was struck on the head by a stone hurled from the salient walls. It was a mortal blow. The Governor's younger brother, a magistrate of Cuzco and one of the most dashing conquistadores, was carried down to Cuzco that night in great secrecy. Francisco de Pancorvo recalled that "they buried him by night so that the Indians should not know he was dead, for he was a very brave man and the Indians were very frightened of him. But although the death of Juan Pizarro was [supposed to be] a secret, the Indians used to say 'Now that Juan Pizarro is dead' just as one would say 'Now that the brave are dead.' And he was indeed brave."

On the following day the natives counterattacked repeatedly. Large numbers of warriors tried to dislodge Gonzalo Pizarro from the Rodadero. "There was terrible confusion. Everyone was shouting and they were all entangled together, fighting for the hilltop the Spaniards had won. It looked as though the whole world was up there grappling in close combat." Hernando Pizarro sent twelve of his remaining horsemen up to join the critical battle—to the dismay of the few Spaniards left in Cuzco. Manco Inca sent five thousand reinforcements, and "the Spaniards were in a very tight situation with their arrival, for the Indians were fresh and attacked with determination."

But the Spaniards were about to apply European methods of siege warfare: throughout the day they had been making scaling ladders. As night fell, Hernando Pizarro himself led an infantry force to the top of the hill. Using the scaling ladders in a night assault, the Spaniards succeeded in taking the

Retaining walls on the southwestern side of Rodadero hill

mighty terrace walls of the fortress. The natives retreated into the complex of buildings and the three towers.

There were two individual acts of great bravery during this final stage of the assault. On the Spanish side Hernán Sánchez of Badajoz performed feats of prodigious panache worthy of a silent-screen hero. He climbed one of the scaling ladders under a hail of stones which he parried with his buckler, and squeezed into a window of one of the buildings. He hurled himself at the Indians inside and sent them retreating up some stairs toward the roof. He now found himself at the foot of the highest tower. Fighting around its base he came upon a thick rope that had been left dangling from the top.

The Throne of the Inca on Rodadero hill

Commending himself to God, he sheathed his sword and started clambering up, heaving up the rope with his hands and stepping off from the smooth Inca ashlars with his feet. Halfway up the Indians threw a stone "as big as a wine jar" down on him, but it simply glanced off the buckler he was wearing on his back. He threw himself into one of the higher levels of the tower, suddenly appearing in the midst of its startled defenders, showed himself to the other Spaniards, and encouraged them to assault the other tower.

The battle for the terraces and buildings of Sacsahuaman

was hard fought. "When dawn came, we spent the whole of that day and the next fighting the Indians who had retreated into the two tall towers. These could only be taken through thirst, when their water supply became exhausted." "When the following day dawned, the Indians on the inside began to weaken, for they had used up their entire store of stones and arrows." The native commanders decided that there were too many defenders in Sacsahuaman, whose water supply was running out. Villac Umu broke through the Spanish lines with half his men and went to seek reinforcements. He left the defense of Sacsahuaman to an Inca noble, an orejón who had sworn to fight to the death against the Spaniards. This officer now rallied the defenders almost single-handed, performing feats of bravery that Pedro Pizarro described as worthy of any Roman. "The orejón strode about like a lion from side to side of the tower on its topmost level. He repulsed any Spaniards who tried to mount with scaling ladders. And he killed any Indians who tried to surrender. He smashed their heads with the battle-ax he was carrying and hurled them from the top of the tower." Alone of the defenders, he possessed European steel weapons that made him the match of the attackers in hand-to-hand fighting. "He carried a buckler on his arm, a sword in one hand and a battle-ax in the shield hand, and wore a Spanish morrión helmet on his head." "Whenever his men told him that a Spaniard was climbing up somewhere, he rushed upon him like a lion with the sword in his hand and the shield on his arm." "He received two arrow wounds but ignored them as if he had not been touched." Hernando Pizarro arranged for the towers to be attacked simultaneously by three or four scaling ladders. But he ordered that the brave orejón should be captured alive. The Spaniards pressed home their attack, assisted by large contingents of native auxiliaries. Manco's son wrote that the battle was a bloody affair for both sides. As the native resistance crumbled, the orejón hurled his weapons down onto the attackers in a frenzy of despair. He grabbed handfuls of earth, stuffed them into his mouth and scoured his face in anguish, then covered his head with his cloak and leaped to his death from the top of the fortress, in fulfillment of his pledge to the Inca.

"With his death the remainder of the Indians gave way, so that Hernando Pizarro and all his men were able to enter. They put all those inside the fortress to the sword—there were fifteen hundred of them." Many others flung themselves from the walls. "Since these were high the men who fell first died. But some of those who fell later survived because they landed on top of a great heap of dead men." The mass of corpses lay unburied, a prey for vultures and giant condors. The coat of arms of the city of Cuzco, granted in 1540, had "an orle of eight condors, which are great birds like vultures that exist in the province of Peru, in memory of the fact that when the castle was taken these birds descended to eat the natives who had died in it."

Hernando Pizarro immediately garrisoned Sacsahuaman with a force of fifty foot soldiers supported by auxiliaries. Pots of water and food were hurried up from the city. The high priest, Villac Umu, returned with reinforcements, just too late to save the citadel. He counterattacked vigorously, and the battle for Sacsahuaman continued fiercely for three more days, but the Spaniards were not dislodged, and the battle was won by the end of May 1536. This was the only record of fighting on the great temple-citadel of Sacsahuaman. Its recapture by the Spaniards proved to be the turning point of Manco's long rebellion—the battle that confirmed Spanish rule of Peru forevermore.

CORICANCHA

WHEN THE SPANIARDS KIDNAPPED the Inca Atahualpa in northern Peru, they kept hearing about the fabulous wealth of Cuzco and its sun temple, Coricancha. Atahualpa had offered to buy his freedom with a ransom of gold and silver, and he callously urged his captors to secure the treasures of the empire's holiest temple. Pizarro therefore sent three envoys for hundreds of miles into the unknown heart of the Inca empire, to the legendary Cuzco itself. He dispatched the three men in February 1533, "commending them to God. They took many natives to carry them in litters, and they were very well served." But when they finally reached Cuzco, the foreign envoys were given a frosty reception by Atahualpa's general Quisquis, the recent conqueror of the Inca capital. "He liked the Christians very little, although he marveled greatly at them."

The three Spaniards went straight to Coricancha. They found, as they had suspected, that it was still intact. "These buildings were sheathed in gold, in large plates, on the side where the sun rises; but the more [the buildings] were shaded from the sun, the baser the gold they had on them." Pizarro's men had to desecrate the temple by themselves. "The Christians decided to strip the ornament with some copper crowbars, without any help from the Indians—these refused to help because it was a sun temple and they said they would die if they did." The vandals loaded the gold onto llama trains for the long journey north. Pizarro's secretary recorded the arrival of 260 loads of gold and 25 of silver from Cuzco. The plates from the temple averaged two kilos (four and a half pounds) of gold each when melted down. There were 700 of these plates, looking "like boards from chests; they had been stripped from the temple's walls and had holes where they had evidently been secured."

The Jesuit Bernabé Cobo called Coricancha "the richest, most sumptuous and most important temple in the empire." He could compare it only to Rome: "It was considered the head and metropolitan temple of their false religion, and was the holiest sanctuary of these Indians. All the people of the Inca empire frequented it, coming on pilgrimages out of piety. It was called Coricancha, which means 'Enclosure of Gold,' because of the incomparable wealth of this metal that was buried among its chapels and on its walls, vaults and altars. It was dedicated to the Sun, although statues of Viracocha, the Thunder, Moon and other leading idols were placed in it, for it served the same purpose as the Pantheon in Rome."

Coricancha lay in the lower part of central Cuzco, in the district known as Pumachupan (the puma's tail) because it was in the triangle of land where the two streams joined and at the tail end of the imaginary feline whose head was Sacsahuaman. The temple buildings were deceptively simple. They stood on a platform enclosed by retaining walls of the finest masonry. There were five, or possibly six, single-story rectangular chambers opening onto a square courtyard. As so often with the Incas, the temple's beauty derived from excellence of workmanship and simplicity of plan. "The building of this great temple was of the finest craftsmanship to be found among these Indians. Inside and out it was made of amazing ashlars, extremely skillfully set, without mortar, and so finely adjusted that it would be impossible to improve on them." Cieza de León compared Coricancha with some of the most famous buildings in Spain, but acknowledged that it was "finer in terms of its walls and the cutting and laying of its stones; and its retaining wall was plumb and very well laid. The stone seems to me blackish and tough and of excellent quality."

All the chroniclers agreed that the temple was surrounded by a cornice of gold, "two handspans wide," nailed to the stone. The eyewitness accounts leave the impression that this band was halfway up the outer wall—where the retaining, terrace wall became the back wall of the temple chambers; but there is no trace of nail holes in the surviving masonry. Some accounts also said that the main gate and inner doors were clad in gold. Garcilaso said that the chapels dedicated to the Moon, Thunder and Stars were coated in silver.

The daily ritual at Coricancha revolved around an image of the sun. Juan de Betanzos, a conquistador who married an Inca princess and learned much from her family, said that this idol was of solid gold and shaped like a naked, year-old baby. It was dressed in a tunic of the finest brocade and wore a royal fringe, a gold paten on its head, and golden sandals. His description sounded suspiciously like that of a Catholic Christ Child. Pedro Pizarro, who actually saw one such idol, described it as "a small covered statue which they said was the sun." But by the time the young Pizarro saw it, the original effigy might already have been melted down. A Spanish horseman called Mancio Sierra de Leguízamo boasted that he had received this sun idol as part of the Inca's ransom at Cajamarca, but had lost it in a night of gambling. This story gave rise to a Spanish expression, "to gamble the sun before it rises"; but the story was improbable, since the Inca treasure was all crushed and melted down before being divided up among Pizarro's men. By the middle of the sixteenth century, the Spaniards became convinced that they had never found the true sun image. Cristóbal de Molina wrote that "the Indians hid this sun so well that it could never be found up to the present day." Cieza de León imagined the missing idol, called *punchao*, as "an image of the sun of great size, made of gold, beautifully wrought and set with many precious stones."

When Pizarro's invaders finally entered Cuzco in November 1533, five months after their cruel execution of Atahualpa, they immediately advanced on the sun temple, whose gold had been removed earlier that year. Diego de Trujillo recalled the scene. "We entered the houses of the Sun, and Villac Umu—who was a form of priest in their canon—said to us: 'How dare you enter here! Anyone who wishes to enter here must first fast for a year, and must enter carrying a symbolic load and barefoot!' But, paying no attention to what he said, we went in." Despite this insult, Villac Umu continued to perform his rituals for some months after the Spaniards' arrival. Pedro Pizarro described the daily ceremonial. The mummies of dead Incas were brought out to the main square and food and drink were offered to them. Villac Umu then carried the sun image from Coricancha to the square. He wore a long tasseled gown with other garments over it. Behind him came two priests holding long lances with golden ax heads sheathed in woolen sleeves. The sun idol was placed on a bench covered in a bright feather mantle. The mace bearers held their weapons upright and fed the punchao by burning food before it and pouring chicha into a ceremonial font. "While they were burning the food, an Indian arose and cried out so that all could hear; and when they heard his voice, everyone who was in the square and outside it, sat down and fell silent, without speaking, coughing or moving, until the food was consumed." After the ceremony, the sun idol was returned to Coricancha, where it rested during daylight on a gold-plated platform along one side of the courtyard. At night it was placed in a small chamber that was also clad in gold plates. Here, "many mamaconas slept in its company. These were daughters of the nobility and claimed to be the wives of the sun, pretending that the sun made love to them." Pedro Pizarro was more cynical about these two hundred temple women. He wrote that "they pretended to live chastely, but they lied, for they involved themselves with the male servants and guardians of the Sun, who were many."

These mamaconas were responsible for tending a famous garden of maize, which was almost certainly on terraces below the western wall of the temple and attached to it. "They irrigated [the garden] by hand with water that they carried up for the Sun. Whenever they celebrated their festivals—which was three times a year: when they sowed, when they harvested, and when orejones were initiated—they filled this garden with stalks of maize made of gold, with life-sized ears and leaves all of fine gold, which they kept stored to be planted on those occasions." The Spaniards were naturally excited by the thought of this golden garden. One of its golden stalks of maize was carried to Cajamarca and thence taken to Spain by Hernando Pizarro. He reached Seville in January 1534 with this and other masterpieces of Inca metalwork. Among them was "a golden effigy, the size of a four-year-old boy," which may possibly have been the sun idol of Coricancha. The Council of the Indies begged King Charles V to see Hernando Pizarro and his remarkable treasures. But the King—who is famous today as a patron of the arts—was callously indifferent: he ordered his officials to melt the objects down into coins, after first putting them on public display for a few weeks. One boy who saw this exhibition and was thrilled by its "magnificent specimens" was the future chronicler Pedro de Cieza de León. Albrecht Dürer witnessed similar treasures from Mexico that had been exhibited in Germany a few years earlier, and exclaimed: "Never in all my life have I seen things that delighted my heart as much as these. For I saw among them amazing artistic objects, and I marveled at the subtle ingenuity of the people of those distant lands."

Most chroniclers agree that it was the great Inca Pachacuti who decided to rebuild Coricancha. The early Incas had a primitive temple on the site; but it was Pachacuti who organized the teams of masons to build the homogeneous and superbly fitted buildings we see today. The temple clearly dates from the period of late Inca rule. The stones are finely polished and laid in even courses with very restrained countersinking of their joints.

Garcilaso said that Coricancha consisted of six chambers or chapels: two large, two medium-sized, and two small. The two large halls, which lay to the north and south of the courtyard, have been demolished, but all or part of the other four survive. The large halls were probably gabled, but the surviving chambers have walls that are flat on all sides. John H. Rowe measured the magnificent stretch of sixty meters (196 feet) of wall that is intact on the northeast side overlooking Ahuacpinta Street. This wall rises 4.5 meters (15 feet), of which the lower 1.5 meters (5 feet) are retaining wall for the temple platform and the upper 3 meters (10 feet) are the walls of the chambers. He found that the walls taper, from 91 centimeters at the base to 81 at the top (36 to 32 inches), and lean inward slightly, with the inner top overhanging its base by 4 centimeters (1½ inches). Because the tops of the chamber walls are perfectly level and they all have twelve courses of stones, Rowe concluded that the surviving masonry is complete and was never capped by adobes. Garcilaso said that these chapels were "covered in the form of a pyramid." He evidently meant the type of roof of four pitches, with the ichu-grass thatch tied to a wooden frame that rested on the four flat walls.

The most famous surviving feature of Coricancha is the magnificent curving wall beneath the western end of the church of Santo Domingo. This is in the shape of a half parabola, a lovely arc of dark-gray stone. It is 6 meters (20 feet) high, of which about half is terrace wall. Its stones are particularly brilliantly finished and fitted, and there is even a slight bulge halfway up, to correct any optical illusion about the wall's strength. The chronicles do not mention this famous wall, except to say that one of Cuzco's important shrines was "a stone called Subaraura, which was where the open gallery of Santo Domingo now stands: it was believed to have been the chief of the pururaucas [the gods who helped the Incas defeat the Chancas, and were later turned to stone]." Recent excavations have revealed an elaborate niche at the top of the curving wall. The pururauca stone evidently stood here before being removed by censorious Spanish priests.

Another interesting feature of Coricancha is the stone font in the center of its cloister. It is a sober porphyry basin, rectangular but with its corners angled to form an octagon. It could once have been clad in gold. The Dominican friar and chronicler Reginaldo de Lizárraga saw it in place in 1600 and said that there was a tradition that it had once been covered with a golden disk. He wondered whether this could have been the disk that the conquistadores thought was the image of the sun. The only doubt is whether it is truly Inca: its octagonal shape looks more colonial.

Coricancha's curving wall was photographed by Martín Chambi in 1925 before the church of Santo Domingo collapsed in an earthquake and was rebuilt with a different west end

At the Conquest, Coricancha fell to Juan Pizarro, the Governor's brother who was killed in the attack on Sacsahuaman in 1536. He bequeathed the sun temple to the Dominicans, the powerful religious order that administered the Inquisition. Friar Vicente de Valverde, the chaplain of Pizarro's invading force and later first bishop of Cuzco, accepted the gift and arranged for Dominican friars to come from Spain. The Dominicans have occupied the site ever since. They built a church where the great northern hall and main gate of Coricancha once stood. Fortunately, the temple cancha (courtyard) plan could easily be adapted to form a monastic cloister: the Spanish friars built a fine two-storied baroque colonnade above and around four of the Inca chambers. Thanks to this continued religious use, much of Coricancha has survived.

The Dominicans were well aware that their monastery occupied the holiest place in the Inca empire. Reginaldo de Lizárraga, for one, was proud of the Inca remains in his order's house. When in 1558 Manco Inca's son Sayri Tupac was lured back to Cuzco from his neo-Inca kingdom of Vilcabamba, he was instructed in the Christian faith and taken to Mass in Santo Domingo. He worshipped there with much devotion, although one Spaniard noted, "Malicious observers said . . . that he was doing it to worship his father the Sun and the bodies of his ancestors who had been kept in that place." When this Inca descendant died three years later, he provided for a chapel to be built in the church of Santo Domingo and asked to be buried there. Various witnesses said that Sayri Tupac was indeed buried in this church and was later joined there by his wife-sister and by his brother Tupac Amaru, who was executed by the Spaniards in 1572.

The first modern investigator to penetrate Coricancha was the tireless George Squier. He reported that "the few ignorant but amiable friars that remain of the once rich and renowned order of Santo Domingo in Cuzco admitted me as an honorary member of their brotherhood, gave me a cell to myself, and permitted me, during the week I spent with them, to ransack every portion of the church, and every nook and corner of the convent, and to measure and sketch and photograph to my fill. Here a long reach of massive wall, yonder a fragment, now a corner, next a doorway, and anon a terrace— through the aid of these I was able to make up a ground-plan of the ancient edifice." The result was a commendable plan of what remained of the Inca walls, and a charming sketch of the friars in their cloister.

In 1928 the German archaeologist Max Uhle reported that Inca walls lay beneath one of the side altars of Santo Domingo. The next important observation came in 1943, when the American archaeologist John H. Rowe—the foremost authority on the Incas—was allowed to explore the monastery and made brilliantly accurate measurements of its Inca remains. Rowe agreed with Uhle that the foundations of the original north wall and entrance gate could be revealed by excavation beneath the church and the triangular terrace in front of the monastery door.

The next important date for Coricancha was 21 May 1950, when a severe earthquake destroyed much of the church (itself built after an earthquake in 1650) and its churrigueresque late eighteenth century bell tower. The following year, UNESCO sent a mission led by the Yale art historian George Kubler to recommend a program to restore Cuzco's ruined monuments. This team resisted pleas to demolish Santo Domingo to reveal what remained of Coricancha. It argued that "the church and cloister are not irreparably damaged, and these colonial buildings are of outstanding importance and beauty. No new Inca walls were found beneath Santo Domingo during [our] excavations. Possibly Inca foundations underlie the church farther to the east in the nave, and beneath the tower. It is unnecessary, however, to dismantle any part of the Dominican establishment to get at these foundations. They may be traced and exposed by a system of underground passages."

During the 1960s and 1970s Coricancha–Santo Domingo has been restored by a team led by the architect Oscar Ladrón de Guevara Avilés. These restorers faced the difficult task of reconciling a damaged colonial building with the remains of

The three channels in the superb coursed masonry of the eastern wall along Ahuacpinta Street

the Inca temple hidden within it. They decided to ignore the recommendations of the UNESCO team and to give precedence to anything Inca. The result is that many colonial additions have been removed, and the baroque cloisters now rest uneasily on ugly scaffolding. The four Inca chambers to the east and west of the cloister are fully revealed. Where their original dimensions were obvious, the restorers adopted the dubious practice of building walls in the Inca manner to replace those that were missing. The result is that the baroque cloister is gone beyond repair, and the Inca chambers, supplemented with modern pastiche, lie roofless under a corrugated iron shelter held up by makeshift supports.

The Venezuelan architectural historians Graziano Gasparini and Luise Margolies have compared Rowe's plans of 1943 with the state of the ruins in 1974. The foundations of the large north and south buildings have since been revealed. A wall of the northern building, which Garcilaso described as the main temple, has emerged where Rowe surmised that it would: beneath the triangular platform in front of the monastery door. This stretch of foundation is directly in line with the northern end of the curved wall, and between them would have run the enclosure wall whose foundation was seen beneath the church by Max Uhle.

Garcilaso wrote that beside the main temple chamber there was "a cloister with four sides, one of which was the wall of the temple. . . . Around the cloister were five halls or large square rooms each built separately and not joined to one another . . . and forming the other three sides of the square." This description exactly fits the surviving chambers. The southern chamber (F on the plan), facing the temple, is gone, but excavations have revealed the foundations of its northeastern corner and part of its southern wall. The two eastern chambers (C and E), to the left on entering, are smaller than those facing them on the west. They may have been dedicated to the thunder, *illapa*, and to the rainbow, *cuichu*. Garcilaso said that the chapel for the thunder, thunderbolts and lightning was clad in gold, whereas that for the rainbow was decorated with a colored arc. The modern restorers have rebuilt

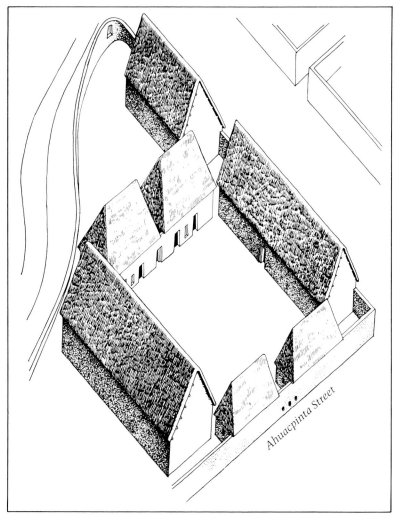

A reconstruction of Coricancha, showing its high thatched roofs and the simplicity of its seven temple chambers

the northern end of the northern of these two rooms, adding an Inca door to match one in the other chamber. Their work has also revealed a fine Inca floor, cobbled with neat round pebbles.

Between these two eastern rooms there is an open space (D) from which three small channels run through the wall to emerge above Ahuacpinta Street. These channels are symmetrical, cut cleanly into the top of a single ashlar. There are

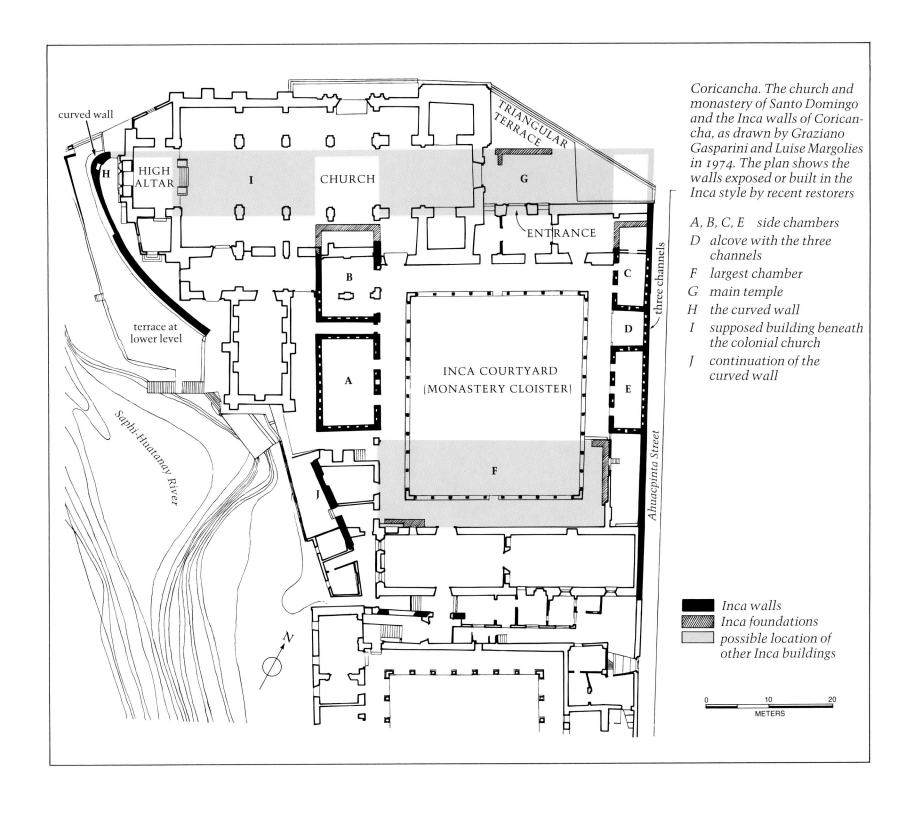

curved wall

TRIANGULAR TERRACE

HIGH ALTAR

H

I

CHURCH

G

ENTRANCE

B

C

D

terrace at lower level

A

Saphi-Huatanay River

INCA COURTYARD
(MONASTERY CLOISTER)

E

Ahuacpinta Street

three channels

J

F

N

Coricancha. The church and monastery of Santo Domingo and the Inca walls of Corican-cha, as drawn by Graziano Gasparini and Luise Margolies in 1974. The plan shows the walls exposed or built in the Inca style by recent restorers

A, B, C, E   side chambers
D   alcove with the three channels
F   largest chamber
G   main temple
H   the curved wall
I   supposed building beneath the colonial church
J   continuation of the curved wall

■ Inca walls
▨ Inca foundations
▨ possible location of other Inca buildings

0   10   20
METERS

A double-jambed trapezoidal door, between the two chambers on the west side of the courtyard

various theories about them. One is that they were drains for sacrificial blood or chicha; another that they were for water, either drinking water from the fountains inside the temple, or to carry off excess rainwater; lastly that they were for sound,

either for instructions from priests inside the temple to assistants without, or for musical effect—when struck the channels sound the notes re, la and mi. Whatever their purpose, the three holes give elegant, satisfying relief to the long stretch of Inca wall enclosing the temple from the east.

Across the courtyard were the two larger chambers (A and B). According to Garcilaso, chamber A was dedicated to the planet Venus, the Pleiades and other constellations; chamber B to the moon. The restorers have cleared colonial structures from chamber B, built its rear wall in Inca style, and extended it toward the church. They have opened a passage that once existed between the two chambers, and rebuilt the northern wall of chamber A to complete this passage. The walls of chamber A, which used to be the chapter house, are decorated with twenty-five handsome, equidistant niches (of which the northern five are modern reconstructions). Garcilaso wrote that its roof was once embellished with figures representing the stars, and its walls were clad with silver plates.

There was a large niche in the center of the eastern wall of the temple of Venus. Half of the niche has been destroyed to open a colonial doorway, but it has now been restored and is surrounded by stones apparently perforated to take golden cladding. Garcilaso said that three of Coricancha's chambers were still standing with their ancient walls and roofs in the 1560s. He also recalled four "tabernacles" hollowed out of the walls facing the courtyard. "They had moldings round the edges and in the hollows of the tabernacles. As these moldings were worked in the stone, they were inlaid with gold plates on the tops, sides and also the floors of the tabernacles. The edges of the moldings were encrusted with fine stones: emeralds and turquoises, for diamonds and rubies were unknown there. The Inca sat in these tabernacles when there were festivals in honor of the sun. He sat sometimes in one and sometimes in another, according to the festivity." When he did so, he was contemplating the temple that, to the Incas, was "the center of the center of the universe."

Niches in the western wall of the chamber of Venus (Hall A on the site plan)

The ruins of Pisac are perched on a spur above the Vilcanota valley:
the inti-huatana group on the right, and Pisacllacta below to the left

PISAC

GARCILASO WROTE THAT CORICANCHA was imitated in every important town of the Inca empire. The central group of buildings in Pisac could well have been such a replica: a sun temple and five rectangular chapels nearby. These chambers are preserved to their original roof line as are those that survive in Cuzco, and are built of the most magnificent coursed masonry. This central group at Pisac, displayed theatrically on three artificially leveled terraces and perched on the saddle of a mountain spur far above the Yucay valley, is one of the most spectacular achievements of Inca architects.

The great mystery about Pisac is its anonymity. Here is a stupendous ruin of the finest Inca stonework, with many attendant buildings, baths and storehouses, exceptional flights of terracing and quantities of tombs, all well defended by walls, gates and towers. It is the closest major ruin to Cuzco —a mere seventeen kilometers (ten and a half miles) to the northeast as the condor flies—and at the same altitude of 3,300 meters (10,800 feet) above sea level. And yet, apart from two passing references by Sarmiento de Gamboa to the valley of Pisac, the place is not mentioned in any chronicle, either in terms of Inca history, or as an important place in the Inca empire, or as the scene of any post-Conquest action. Nor was there a town in this location known by any other name. The only possible mention of Pisac is that Pachacuti used to go "for greater pleasure and enjoyment . . . to the town of the Cuyos," which may have been this ruin.

The central, dominant feature of the Pisac temple group is an outcrop of rock jutting above two levels of platform and surrounded by a D-shaped wall of the finest masonry. A tall trapezoidal gateway, with its lintel still in place, leads up to this shrine. The rock has two stone bosses or gnomons rising from its top surface, and there is another projecting horizontally from its wall. There are four more rock projections in the Pisac temple group, all with evident religious significance. These bosses are inti-huatanas, a word which, as Garcilaso explained, means hitching place of the sun (*inti*). They were clearly intended for solar observation or worship. The first modern visitor to record his impressions of Pisac was George Squier, and his Indian guides told him that the central group at Pisac was called inti-huatana. He was also told that the central boss had once been clad in a copper sheath. He recalled having seen similar rock bosses near Huaitará in the central Andes, overlooking Ollantaytambo, on the banks of the Tullumayo stream beside the ruined palace of Colcampata in Cuzco, and in front of the original temple of the sun on the Island of the Sun, in Lake Titicaca. Squier's visit was long before the discovery of Machu Picchu, which has the most famous of all inti-huatanas (see plate, page 151). Squier felt that these bosses were the same as the pillars near Cuzco by which the Incas observed the sun's passage and determined the dates of agricultural seasons and important festivals. They were "inti-huatanas or sun-fingers, where the sun might appear to be stopped, or tied up for a moment in his course; and on which, in his passage through the zenith, he might sit down in all his glory."

Beside the Pisac inti-huatana is a magnificent two-doored rectangular building. It has the lintel in place on each of its doors and is closely associated with a series of liturgical baths and watercourses. This may have been the temple of the moon. On the terrace above it, the northernmost of the five chambers has sharply cut stone pegs projecting from ashlars between its internal niches. Above the entire group is a great platform, presumably an usnu, with a stone throne (*tiana*) facing west toward the sunset.

The ruins of Pisac are spread out in clusters on the mountain spur. Immediately above the inti-huatana group is a

The uppermost gnomon of the sun temple, looking east

The trapezoidal gateway leads to the sacred rock of the sun temple

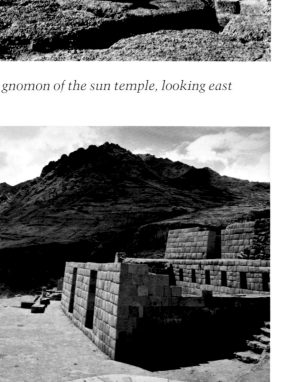

The chamber with two doors, west of the sun temple

The inti-huatana group, with the sacred outcrop (right center)

group of houses around a courtyard. This contains a rock sculpted into a sofa, with back and arms, for two people to sit facing toward the sunrise. A path from here climbs the mountain on its western flank. Squier described this route as "steep and devious, . . . skirting the faces of cliffs a thousand feet sheer down on one side, and five hundred feet straight up on the other; where the brain grows dizzy, and where it is impossible for two men to pass abreast. Along such narrow pathways, where the condor sails level with you above the abyss below, and where you lean inwards till your shoulder grazes the rock, along such paths as these, . . . the visitor to Pisac must make his perilous way." Beyond the frightening cliff is a flight of steps and a tower, with a cluster of buildings perched recklessly on the mountainside. One path descends, through a 16-meter (52-foot) tunnel in a rock fault, to the perfectly preserved foundations of an Inca bridge on either side of the Kitamayu ravine. Beyond is a hillside full of rows of rock tombs—the largest known Inca cemetery in Peru. The cliff of Tanqanamarca above the tombs may have been a place of execution, for persons sentenced to death in Inca law were thrown from such mountain precipices.

Another path climbs and, passing a short, low tunnel, reaches Kalla Qasa, the largest group of buildings in Pisac. Here, on the crest of the ridge, is a mass of chambers and towers protected by a magnificent limestone wall reminiscent of Sacsahuaman. Squier imagined this as a frontier outpost of the Inca army, protecting the Yucay valley from the wild Amazonian tribes to the east. "There are inner walls and forti-fied barracks with outlooks and portholes, all admirably situ-ated for defence, with covered parades and granaries, abodes for servants, and the material protection for a garrison of two thousand men. Quaint symbols cut on the rocks, needless stairways built up against them, *dilettante* elaboration of doorways, and a hundred other evidences exist here for an idle and *ennuyé* garrison."

There is no question about Pisac's military role. On the eastern side of the mountain every approach road is guarded by at least two stone gates and stretches of defensive wall. All

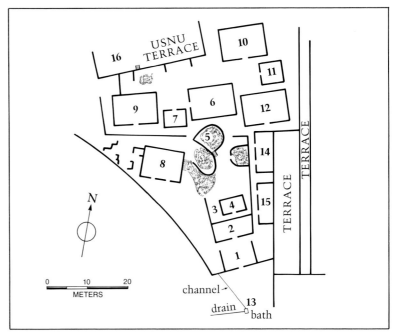

The inti-huatana group of Pisac occupies a triangular terrace. The main sacred outcrop (5) is surrounded by a D-shaped wall. Fine rectangular buildings (6–12) may have been the chapels of a temple complex. To the south is a liturgical bath (13) fed by a water channel. An usnu platform (16) overlooks the site. Build-ings (1–4 and 14–15) may have housed priests or mamaconas

the gates have stone pegs sunk into the inner sides of their jambs to secure their doors. This slope of Pisac has the famous agricultural terraces. Looking back down the Chongo ravine from the cluster of buildings called Qanchis Raqay, from out-side the northern approach to the first gate, these terraces make one of the most spectacular views in the Inca empire. The entire mountainside is disciplined with great flights of terracing that undulate majestically to fit its curving contours. Central irrigation channels plunge down the hill and fan out into each terrace. There are long flights of stairs, and flying steps projecting diagonally from the terrace walls. The mod-ern archaeological authorities have made great efforts to clear and restore these terraces. They would like to see them farmed by the local community; but Inca terraces were designed to be

A magnificent flight of terraces covers the entire eastern slope of Pisac.
Above it lies the Pisacllacta group; below it, the Chongo ravine

worked by hand and modern farmers prefer to plow with oxen or small motorized plows whose weight is too great for the old retaining walls.

As with many Inca sites along the Vilcanota–Urubamba valley, Pisac's tiers of agricultural terraces far exceed the needs of its dwellings. The place was clearly designed to grow surpluses for the court in Cuzco. Paradoxically, there are few obvious qollqas (storehouses): only one line of six rectangular huts, built of adobe, on a steep slope three hundred meters (almost a thousand feet) from the central inti-huatana group.

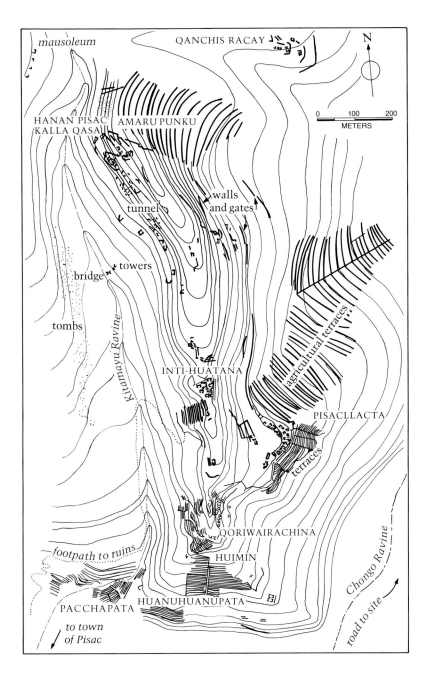

General plan of Pisac. The ruins occupy a mountain spur above the modern town. In the saddle of the ridge is the sacred inti-huatana precinct. Below it, to the east, lies the Pisacllacta group, overlooking the terraces sweeping down to the Chongo ravine

There are other interesting structures on the mountain spur above the modern town of Pisac. One is a fine two-story building at a hub of paths below the inti-huatana. Víctor Angles Vargas, the modern interpreter of Pisac, regards this as an administrative center as it is such an important building, on the narrowest part of the saddle with views to east and west over the enclosing ravines. Nearby, at the top of the largest group of terraces, is a curving group of twenty-three enclosures called Pisacllacta or Pisaqa by modern Indians. Some of the walls in this section are of the finest imperial coursed masonry. Others are of adobe, a building material well regarded by the Incas and much used in Pisac. The Inca builders used flat, rectangular adobe bricks, well packed with ichu grass for added strength. They laid their bricks in an "English" bond, alternating the long stretchers with the shorter ends or headers at the corners of buildings. Doors and niches had wooden or stone lintels and there were often wooden braces at the corners of adobe houses. The clays of the adobes varied from yellow to brown and there was mud plaster over many walls. Inca architects were always skillful in adapting their buildings to the steep terrain of the Andes. One device was to have gables sloping at different angles or with a longer pitch on the valley side of a roof. Close to the Pisacllacta group is a solitary building that John Rowe called the mirador (lookout) because its southern wall has large openings on to a spectacular view of the valley below. This is the finest adobe house in Pisac, with good bricks and bonding, niches and braces.

A final feature of Pisac is its towers, of which there are remains of some twenty throughout the ruins. The finest are on the steep slope, the snout of Pisac's spur, above the modern town. These towers are of distinct types. There are massive watchtowers with solid bases, equidistant from one another for shouted messages and admirably sited to repel attack from below. Other towers are more conical, with sharply tapering walls. These appear to have been water cisterns: their bases are chambers carefully sealed with plaster, and they are connected to irrigation channels.

The terraces of Moray near Maras follow the contours of the depressions in the limestone plateau

MORAY

IN THE VERTICAL WORLD OF THE ANDES, flat agricultural land is scarce and landslides are a constant threat. The Incas solved both these problems by building agricultural terraces. Entire hillsides were tamed by great flights of terraces that followed contours like the layers of an architect's model. The most magnificent terraces are at Pisac, but there are many at other Inca sites: in the Colca valley north of Arequipa, at Chinchero northwest of Cuzco, and particularly in the Vilcanota–Urubamba valley, at Ollantaytambo, Cusichaca, Phuyu Pata Marca, Inti Pata, and Machu Picchu.

A typical Inca agricultural terrace (*pata*) would be from 1.5 to 4.0 meters (5 to 13 feet) high, contained by a stone wall of fieldstones roughly shaped to fit one another. Such containing walls might be 60 to 75 centimeters (2 to 2½ feet) thick, and, as Garcilaso observed, "they slope back slightly so as to withstand the weight of earth with which they are filled." The inward lean of a terrace wall was fifteen to twenty degrees. Within this containing wall, Indian farmers carefully filled the cavity with larger stones at the base for drainage and with good soil at the surface.

Effective irrigation was essential for terraced agriculture, and the Incas used admirable ingenuity and engineering skill —as well as the customary prodigious labor—to channel water to their terraces. Banks of terraces were linked by a web of long flights of stairs; but individual terraces could also be climbed by occasional projecting steps—stone slabs protruding in diagonal flights from the face of the terrace wall.

The most enigmatic Inca terraces are at the Inca site of Moray, near Maras, on the limestone plateau thirty-eight kilometers (twenty-four miles) northwest of Cuzco. Here, three large circular depressions were carefully terraced, as if to form the seating for a giant circular arena—although the terraces are purely agricultural and far too high for seating. Slopes near the depressions were similarly terraced. The limestone may have subsided into sinkholes typical of karst topography, or deep gullies may have opened into dolines. But the Incas clearly expended much energy to sculpt these depressions into perfect circles and to fill the land between them. The lowest tier of terraces in the three depressions is from 40 to 45 meters (130 to 148 feet) in diameter, and the surface of each terrace is from 4 to 10 meters (13 to 33 feet) wide. The three depressions have six or seven layers of terracing around their sides, and these terraces were once level and filled with earth of good quality.

The Incas evidently used the natural cavities of Moray— which are near no large settlement—as a shrine and a place for special agriculture. The crop most prized by the Inca court was the bush coca, whose leaf looks like a bay leaf but is a mild narcotic when chewed and mixed with lime. Coca chewing is now an addiction of all Andean Indians; but it was once a privilege reserved for the ruling caste. Hernando de Santillán, a Spanish administrator who was particularly well informed about native ways, wrote about coca: "They considered it something very precious and of great nourishment and sustenance, because they say that someone taking it feels no hunger, thirst or fatigue. This coca grows in all the valleys and lowlands, and in very deep gullies in many parts of the mountains—anywhere that the wind does not disturb the land, where the sun shines intensely and the climate is hot and humid." The terraced depressions of Moray would admirably fulfill these requirements for growing coca.

A more ingenious interpretation has come from anthropologist John Earls of the United States. He discovered vertical stones in the Moray terraces that mark the limits of afternoon shadow at the equinoxes and solstices. Local people told him that these stones were called *ñustas* (princesses) and that

A natural flow of salt near Maras has been channeled since Inca times into a crystalline labyrinth of evaporating pans

they themselves used similar stones to mark shadow limits in their own fields. Earls concluded, by additional experiment, that each terrace at Moray reproduced climatic conditions in different ecological zones of the Inca empire. Because of their sheltered position, each of these terraces represented roughly a thousand meters of altitude in normal farming conditions, and the entire complex contained in miniature twenty or more ecological zones. The Moray site would thus have helped Inca officials to calculate yields from different parts of the empire in each year.

The Moray terraces may have been used for agricultural experiment, for making
moraya *(dehydrated cooked potato), or perhaps for ceremonial purposes*

The plateau at Maras, overlooking the Urubamba valley northwest of Cuzco, with the Lares hills in the distance

OLLANTAYTAMBO

FIFTY KILOMETERS (THIRTY MILES) DOWN THE Vilcanota–Urubamba river, northwest from Pisac, the mighty fortified temple of Ollantaytambo towers above the Yucay valley. The Spaniards first became aware of this temple during Manco Inca's great rebellion of 1536–1537. After Pizarro's men had recaptured Sacsahuaman there was stalemate in the siege of Cuzco. Manco's levies returned to their harvests and he apparently planned to mobilize them again the following year. The besieged Spaniards learned that the Inca had his headquarters at Ollantaytambo. They decided on a bold, desperate attack at this very center of native resistance.

Hernando Pizarro took all his best men for the strike: seventy horse, thirty foot and a large contingent of native auxiliaries. The march down the Vilcanota–Urubamba was difficult. The meandering river often ran against the steep rocky walls of its valley, and these narrows were defended by native forts and walls. The river "had to be crossed five or six times, and each ford was defended." When the Spaniards finally fought their way to Ollantaytambo, they were appalled by the sight of its massive terraces and ramparts. Pedro Pizarro recalled that "when we reached Tambo we found it so well fortified that it was a horrifying sight. For Tambo's location is naturally very strong, with very high terraces and fortified with great masses of masonry." The town was full of Inca soldiers and forest Indians who were deadly archers. Its defenses were excellent. "Its gate was tall, with great walls on either side made from compacted stone and clay: a very thick rampart, with only one small hole in it through which an Indian could pass on all fours." The attacking Spaniards occupied the small plain of the Patacancha stream below the temple-citadel. They found that they were in a trap. "The Indians were fighting them from three sides: some from the hillside, others from the far bank of the river, and the rest from the town. . . . The Inca was in the fortress itself with many well-armed warriors." "They amassed such a quantity of men against us that they could not crowd onto the hillsides and plains."

Two of the older conquistadores bravely rode their horses up against the walls of the town. They were repulsed, and "it was amazing to see the arrows that rained down on them as they returned, and to hear the shouting." Another group of horsemen tried to attack the terraces below the citadel. But the defenders "hurled down so many boulders and fired so many slingshots that, even had we been many more Spaniards than we were, we would all have been killed." A missile broke the haunch of the lead horse. The animal rolled over, kicking, rearing and falling down terraces, and dispersed the horsemen trying to follow. Hernando Pizarro sent a party of foot soldiers to try to seize the heights above the fortress; but these men were driven back by a hail of rocks.

As the Spaniards wavered, the natives attacked. They charged out onto the plain "with such a tremendous shout that it seemed as if the mountain were crashing down. So many men suddenly appeared on every side that every visible stretch of wall was covered with Indians. The enemy locked [Pizarro's men] in a fierce struggle, more savage than had ever been seen by either side." The natives had acquired many Spanish weapons and were learning to employ them effectively. They attempted to fire captured culverins and arquebuses, with powder prepared by Spanish prisoners. "It was impressive to see some of them emerge ferociously with Castilian swords, bucklers and morrión helmets. There was one Indian who, armed in this manner, dared to attack a horse: he prided himself on death from a lance to win fame as a hero. The Inca [Manco] himself appeared among his men, on horseback with a lance in his hand, keeping control of his army."

Manco now released his secret weapon. Unobserved by the Spaniards, native engineers diverted the Patacancha river along prepared channels to flood the plain. Spanish horsemen soon found themselves trying to maneuver in rising water that eventually reached the horses' girths. "The ground became so sodden that the horses could not skirmish." Hernando Pizarro realized that his position was untenable. He ordered a retreat to Cuzco, and his men tried to slip away under cover of darkness, abandoning their tents below Ollantaytambo's grim walls. But the column of retreating horsemen was observed "and the Indians came down upon them with a great cry . . . grabbing the horses' tails." Pedro Pizarro praised his adversaries: "They attacked us with great fury at a river crossing, carrying burning torches. . . . There is one thing about these Indians: when they are victorious they are demons in pressing it home, whereas when fleeing they are like wet hens. Since they were now following up a victory, seeing us retire, they pursued with great spirit." Manco's son Titu Cusi recalled how delighted his people had been by the defeat of this powerful force. A few of the attackers were killed, but "the Inca was extremely sad that Hernando Pizarro had gone, for he was sure that had he delayed another day no single Spaniard would have escaped. In truth, anyone who saw the appearance of the fortress could have believed nothing else."

Ollantaytambo was the scene of a very different assembly in the following year, 1537. The arrival of Spanish reinforcements had broken the siege of Cuzco. The Spaniards were regaining control of all Peru and Manco Inca decided that he was too exposed, even in the fortress-temple of Ollantaytambo. He determined to retreat into the fastnesses of the Vilcabamba hills, leaving the mass of his countrymen under foreign domination from which they have not escaped to this day. His departure was marked by poignant ceremonies and sacrifices. "Before leaving they armed themselves and, in a great square near their camp, in which an idol stood, they begged and prayed it not to desert them, with many tears, sobbing and sighs. Near this idol were others with insignia of the Sun and the Moon. In the presence of these, which they

regarded as gods, they offered sacrifices by killing many animals on their shrines and altars." Manco Inca then retreated to the northeast, never to return to the Yucay valley so beloved by his royal forebears.

Because the Spaniards were repulsed at Ollantaytambo and awed by its towering terraces, they always referred to it as a fortress. The ruins show clearly that the buildings on the spur of rock were in fact a temple; but the entire temple precinct and adjoining town were fortified. Such protection of a holy place was common—the temple of Viracocha at Raqchi, the inti-huatana at Pisac, and the temples of Machu Picchu were all protected by enclosing walls, gates, precipices and even dry moats.

At Ollantaytambo some of the most formidable defenses were *upstream* toward Cuzco, protecting the site from attack down the Vilcanota, as Hernando Pizarro's men found to their cost. Two kilometers (one and a quarter miles) upriver, on the left bank, just above the river waters, is a garrison fort called Chocana. Its houses, stores, irrigation system and narrow streets are remarkably well preserved. Some walls even retain their original red frescoes. Chocana has a fine view up the Vilcanota and its canyon, and is also clearly visible from Ollantaytambo. There is little doubt that it was a fortified outpost to control traffic along the valley and act as a lookout to the southeast. There is a massive terrace wall and another fort to block the valley where the river meanders against the hill nearly opposite Chocana. Parts of these outer defenses on either side of the river had to be dynamited earlier in this century to enable a road and a railway to pass downstream. Various nineteenth-century travelers—the Frenchman Wiener, the German Middendorf and the American Squier—all left drawings of these handsome forts crouching beneath the cliffs of the valley wall.

Ollantaytambo had a second, inner line of defense. There is another small fort, known as Choquekilla, also on the left bank not far upstream of the temple complex. To Squier, Choquekilla was "confined between heavy artificial walls, . . . a long building of two stories, with turrets and loopholes,

Ollantaytambo from across the Uru-bamba river. The fortified temple stands on a spur beneath the steep mountains, above the town and the Patacancha ravine

The "avenue of the hundred niches" may have been the inner walls of barracks-like kallankas

hanging against the mountain. . . . It more resembles the castles of the Rhine . . . than anything we have yet seen." Below Choquekilla, a wall with a double parapet—for defense in either direction—used to cut the flat plain between the temple and the river. And the temple itself is strongly defended by a wall, of schists covered in stucco, that climbs the mountain behind the site.

Anyone approaching Ollantaytambo from Cuzco crosses a bridge resting on supports of massive Inca masonry. The central pier is protected against the current by huge stone breakwaters, and the banks of the river itself are revetted and channeled with Inca masonry. Across the bridge, the modern road goes to the foot of the mountain before turning left toward Ollantaytambo. At this point can be seen the jambs of a huge stone gate, Punku Punku (gate of gates), which penetrated an inner defensive wall. Beside it are two guardhouses. They mark the start of the long "avenue of the hundred niches." The wall that gives this avenue its name is on the left, with fine terraces and irrigation channels on the right. The wall with the niches inclines toward the road and has the finish of an internal wall. It was also normal for Incas to build small niches only inside their houses. The wall might thus have been the inner wall of one or more long kallankas; or the road itself might even have been roofed. It would be interesting to excavate the outer, river side of this long wall.

Beyond the avenue of the hundred niches the hills open out in the deep ravine of the Patacancha stream. The town of Ollantaytambo lies at its mouth. Straight ahead, at the end of the western wall of the Patacancha ravine, is the terraced hill of the sun temple. It is a majestic sight, with the rocky spur buttressed to the east by a monumental flight of seventeen straight, broad terraces. They climb at a smooth angle of forty-five degrees, and both embellish and protect the sanctuary above. It was on these platforms that Manco Inca appeared, in Western armor and riding a horse, during Pizarro's attack. To the south, overlooking the river, the outcrop is flanked by tiers of undulating terraces. The temple must have looked inspiring when it was intact, with its entire mountain spur apparently converted into a gigantic stepped pyramid crowned by the gleaming enclosures of its sacred buildings.

Access to the temple is by a stairway that starts in the center of the terraces and continues up their left edge. Near the top another stair turns left up a flight of five superbly cut, tall terraces, 35 meters (115 feet) long, that protect the northern side of the spur. The fourth of these terraces has the same fine polygonal masonry as the others for the first 20 meters (66 feet), but its western end was once a roofed chamber or entrance passage. The terrace wall here slopes inward to the chamber and contains ten elegant niches. At the far end is a trapezoidal gate with its lintel in place; at its other end, one of the finest of all Inca niches or portals. It is double-jambed, fitted with supreme skill, and surrounded by enigmatic pairs of bosses protruding from otherwise smooth stones.

The sun temple of Ollantaytambo is now sadly ruined and fragmented. Spanish zealots probably destroyed it. They feared both its religious purpose and its potential as a fortress. Seekers of building blocks contributed to the sack. Many blocks were hurled down to build the Spanish town below. We can see stones of the temple's pale-pink porphyry in the foundations of the church and flanking the door of the curate's house. Ollantaytambo also fell victim to treasure hunters. Pedro de Cieza de León reported a rumor that "in a part of the royal palace or temple of the sun, molten gold was used in place of mortar. . . . They say that Governor don Francisco Pizarro collected a great deal of this before the Indians broke it up and carried it away."

Some gigantic blocks remain on the temple platform because they were too large to remove. Others, at the top of the main flight of terraces, appear never to have been used: it is possible that one part of the temple was being built when the Conquest occurred. Fortunately, the great end wall survives. It consists of six enormous monoliths of pink porphyry, quarried from a place called Cachicata high in the hills a few kilometers downstream. This monolithic screen stands to a height of 4 meters (13 feet) at the right-hand stone, but it is impossible to say what form of structure it once supported.

Terrace stairway to the sun temple

The sun temple was defended by seventeen terraces overlooking the square of Mañay Racay

The approach to the sun temple along the uppermost terrace, with the wall of niches at the far end. One of the remaining blocks of building stone can be seen at the top right

The portal of the sun temple, decorated with pairs of bosses

The trapezoidal gate at the far end of the wall of niches

Two of the niches; bosses were apparently left for aesthetic effect

Detail, the wall of niches

Six great monoliths flank the eastern wall of the sun temple

The German painter Moritz Rugendas sketched the monoliths in the 1840s and showed stones above them that have
since disappeared. There is also a mysterious passage running
for almost 8 meters (25 feet) behind the frieze of monoliths.
The thinner monoliths have been shored up with niched
walls of Inca masonry to form the corridor. One can imagine
priests using this passage during some now-forgotten ritual.

Anyone visiting Ollantaytambo must ponder the prodigious human effort expended in quarrying and cutting these
vast blocks and dragging them down to the valley and up to
the temple. One "tired stone" that never completed the journey lies half buried on an inclined plane below the promontory. Squier measured it and found that it was over 21 feet
long by 15 broad, and with 5 feet projecting above ground
(6.55 by 4.6 by 1.5 meters).

There are striking and fascinating similarities between
the central part of Ollantaytambo and the great pre-Inca ruin
of Tiahuanaco near Lake Titicaca. The square cut of the large
blocks and their rectangular projections are Tiahuanacan; so
also are the pairs of T-shaped grooves for the H-shaped copper
clamps that once joined them. But the most striking example
of Tiahuanacan work is on the wall of the six porphyry monoliths. The great blocks are separated by intricate vertical strips
of stone—a technique of great virtuosity, strongly reminiscent of the monoliths separated by smaller blocks in the sides
of the Calasasaya platform at Tiahuanaco. One of the central
blocks has three step-designs embossed on its surface—and
this symbol is a hallmark of the Tiahuanaco civilization.
These are now sadly weathered, but were sharper a century
ago in Squier's day. Another block has a large projection that
has been crudely chipped and may once have had a feline or
sun effigy, both of which were Tiahuanacan symbols.

There is remarkable written confirmation of the link between Ollantaytambo and Tiahuanaco in the chronicle of
Pedro Sarmiento de Gamboa. This historian conducted official interrogations of aged natives during the 1570s, in an
attempt to discredit Inca rule for propaganda purposes. The
inquiries did reveal surprisingly bitter hostility to the Incas,

Detail of the stepped motif and the jointing of the monoliths

even among subject tribes close to Cuzco itself, and they
described the Inca invasion of this region. Some informants
were Ollantay-tampus, and made it clear that *tampu* or *tambo*
in this context did not mean posthouse but was the name
of their tribe. They told how Pachacuti Inca had demanded
that their Tampu ancestors pay homage. When the ancestors

The canchas are still in use as farmyards

Entrances to canchas (enclosures) and a water channel on one of the four long streets in the Inca town of Ollantaytambo

One of the alleys, or transversal streets

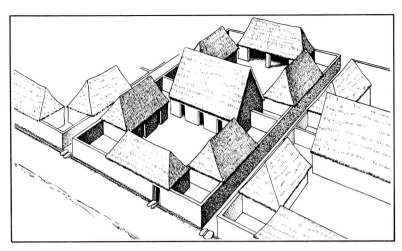

A reconstruction of the canchas

A stone footbridge on the eastern edge of Mañay Racay square

Each of Ollantaytambo's blocks contains two canchas. These are independent of one another, back to back, with gates on opposite sides of their blocks. Inside the monumental double-jambed portals the canchas are all alike. There is a gatehouse of open-sided masma design facing the main, three-doored house across the courtyard. The main house of one cancha backs onto that of another cancha, so that each house has its roof pitched down from the dividing wall. A pair of identical houses also faces inward on either side of the patio. All these buildings are liberally provided with storage niches on their inner walls; but the internal partition walls that we now see in them are recent additions. The four houses in each cancha are arranged with open spaces in the corners of the walled compound. Such openings would have made useful storage areas or corrals for domestic llamas. The elegance of Ollantaytambo's residential area is enhanced by stone-channeled culverts that bring mountain water pouring along its straight cobbled streets. By Andean Indian standards, Ollantaytambo's compounds were small palaces.

Between the town and its temple-citadel is the walled square attacked by the Spaniards in 1536. This has one monumental portal and many lesser entrances. It is called Mañay Raqay, which means hall of petitions in Quechua. A handsome two-storied building of masonry and adobe at the edge

of this square may at some time have served as a court for hearing petitions. East of the square, up the Patacancha valley, are a series of elaborate Inca shrines and watercourses. One such channel pours over a lovely stone font, now hidden in a private meadow between Mañay Raqay and Ollantaytambo town. This elegant stone has a carved façade that rises in a stepped pattern. It is known, romantically, as the bath of the ñusta (bath of the Inca princess).

The hills that tower over Ollantaytambo have a number of fascinating Inca remains on their steep slopes. There is a cluster of buildings above the sun temple, and beyond these, immediately overlooking the main flight of terraces, two-story houses that cling giddily to the mountain. Behind and above the houses runs a wall of quarried stone set in yellowish clay mortar. The wall climbs steeply up the mountain and seems superfluous for defensive purposes: it must have been built more for symbolic, religious seclusion than to repel attackers —in the manner of a similar wall on the hills around the Viracocha temple at Raqchi. The paths on this mountain are

A carved outcrop north of Mañay Racay square

narrow and the slopes precipitous. It is a place better suited to surefooted Indians impervious to vertigo than to foreign visitors. Above the enclosure wall, to the west, is a complex now known as Inca-huatana (hitching place of the Inca). This consists of a wall with tall niches whose sides have securing holes some 80 centimeters (2½ feet) above the ground; in front is a towerlike structure that overhangs the precipice. We know that Inca punishments included beatings and cord tortures and, for capital crimes, death by being hurled from cliffs. In popular imagination, therefore, this Inca-huatana was a place of torture and execution. But it could just as well have been some form of observatory or signal station.

The ceremonial pool known as the bath of the princess. Its fountain is carved with the Tiahuanacan stepped motif

Pinkuylluna hill from the sun temple

Opposite the Ollantaytambo sun temple, on the far side of the stream and town, is another steep hill that projects into the angle between the Patacancha and Vilcanota-Urubamba valleys. This hill is called Pinkuylluna (where the pinkuyllu [flute] is played). Two enigmatic groups of buildings are perched on the rocky slope facing Ollantaytambo. The group immediately opposite consists of three rectangular and identical buildings directly above one another. Each is two-storied, with gables that show that its roof once had a longer and steeper pitch on the valley than on the mountain side. Each long building has six tall windows on the valley wall of its lower story, and ten similar openings on the inner side of its upper story. There are also doors and windows in the gabled end walls. These halls must have been relatively light and airy by Inca standards. They are built of shaped stones set in yellowish clay, so that each tawny cluster of buildings stands out sharply against the gray hillside.

The popular local idea is that these buildings on Pinkuylluna were prisons—the group near the Urubamba for men and the more northern group for women. Another theory is that they were convents for acllas and mamaconas; or that they were schools for young Inca nobles. Víctor Angles Vargas has examined and rejected these various hypotheses. He argues that the Pinkuylluna buildings need not have been prisons just because they were in locations that seem inhospitable to modern eyes. Lengthy imprisonment was not an Inca punishment; and it would have been ludicrous to build prisons with so many doors and such magnificent views. The buildings were too exposed and distant from the temple to be places of seclusion for holy women. They were equally unsuitable for schools, which were rare in the Inca empire— being reserved for a small royal elite. Angles also points out that they were not alone on the mountain: many other houses existed on its sides overlooking the Urubamba valley. He therefore argues that they were places where the people who once lived on these hills could assemble for communal tasks or entertainments. But the buildings look to foreign eyes like barracks, and they might have been just that. They could have been built to house some of the thousands of soldiers who appeared on the hills when Hernando Pizarro tried to attack Manco Inca here. Their upper stories might have been used to store military rations and impedimenta. Ollantaytambo occupied a strategic location, a place where roads led from the Inca heartland toward the forests of the Antisuyo; and the royal town and temple were clearly worth defending. Ollantaytambo would therefore have needed temporary lodgings for its garrison, for passing armies, or for the many tributary laborers who were working on its unfinished monuments.

Machu Picchu lies on a saddle dominated by the pinnacle of Huayna Picchu

MACHU PICCHU

IT WAS ON 24 JULY 1911 that the young American Hiram Bingham discovered the ruins of Machu Picchu. He had had his first glimpse of Inca ruins on a trip to Peru two years earlier. After returning home, he had fired his classmates at a Yale reunion with his own excitement: the result was the Yale Peruvian Expedition of 1911. Hiram Bingham had all the necessary qualities for finding Inca ruins: he was full of enthusiasm and curiosity, he was brave and tough, and he was something of a mountaineer and historian. He was also phenomenally lucky. His expedition was the first to use a new trail blasted through the mighty granite gorges of the Urubamba below Ollantaytambo. The trail was rough, cut with great effort by government engineers to provide an outlet for coca and other produce from plantations on the lower river; but it opened a stretch of river that had been bypassed by all previous conquistadores and travelers. Ever since Inca times, the easiest route to the rich Vilcabamba valley was by a road behind mountains to the northeast, one that rejoined the river some forty kilometers (twenty-five miles) *downstream* of Machu Picchu, where it crossed into the Vilcabamba region on the Chuquichaca bridge. The stretch of river near Machu Picchu had thus been untraveled since Inca times.

When Bingham's mule train moved down the new Urubamba trail, it passed from the open highlands of the Incas into the edge of the Amazon rain forests. Below Ollantaytambo, trees seize the land and cover it without interruption as far as the Atlantic ocean, thousands of kilometers to the east. Bingham was struck by the soaring beauty and savage contrasts of the region he was penetrating. The seething water of the mountain rivers, the granite cliffs and sparkling snowy peaks reminded him of the grandeur of the Rockies. But the tropical vegetation that clings to the steep hillsides or cascades over the rocky outcrops, and the mists that shroud the sugarloaf hills were like the most stupendous views of Hawaii.

"Not only has it great snow peaks looming above the clouds more than two miles overhead; gigantic precipices of many-colored granite rising sheer for thousands of feet above the foaming, glistening, roaring rapids; it has also, in striking contrast, orchids and tree ferns, the delectable beauty of luxurious vegetation, and the mysterious witchery of the jungle. One is drawn irresistibly onward by ever-recurring surprises through a deep, winding gorge, turning and twisting past overhanging cliffs of incredible height."

Bingham had been directed toward Vilcabamba by Peruvian historians. An important chronicle had recently been discovered: an autobiographical report by Manco Inca's son Titu Cusi Yupanqui, who had ruled the neo-Inca state of Vilcabamba for twelve years before the Spaniards finally conquered the area in 1572. This chronicle and other contemporary documents mentioned various places in this last remote refuge of the Incas. Bingham hoped to find their ruins. He had also heard the name Machu Picchu. When the French traveler Charles Wiener was at Ollantaytambo in 1875, he was told to seek the ruins of Choquequirau (which he had already visited) and Vilcabamba. "They also spoke to me of other towns, of Huaina-Picchu and of Matcho-Picchu, and I resolved to make a final excursion towards the east." But Wiener's excursion took him by the standard road that bypassed Machu Picchu— he located the two hills correctly in his sketch map of the region, but never managed to reach them. Bingham was only three days out of Cuzco, along the new trail, when his party camped by the edge of the Urubamba. A local farmer called Melchor Arteaga asked their purpose. When they told him it was to find Inca ruins, he said that there were excellent ones on top of the opposite mountain. He then said that the mountain and its ridge were called Huayna Picchu and Machu Picchu. Bingham recalled the reference in Wiener and decided that he must investigate.

MACHU PICCHU

AGRICULTURAL SECTOR
1 houses of the agricultural guardians
2 main flight of terraces
3 dry moat
4 main gate and inner city wall
5 staircase

FUNERARY ROCK
6 Upper Cemetery
7 watchman's hut
8 tambo or barracks

TORREÓN
9 royal mausoleum
10 house of the ñusta
11 stone baths
12 serpent gate

KING'S GROUP
13 Hanged Man's rock

SACRED PLAZA
14 temple of the three windows
15 principal temple
16 high priest's house
17 ornament chamber

INTI-HUATANA

SACRED ROCK
18 masmas facing plaza

MAIN SQUARE

MAIN RESIDENTIAL SECTOR
19 Upper Group
20 Three-Doors Group
21 kallanka
22 rock shrine

INDUSTRIAL SECTOR
23 double masma
24 Mortar Group

PRISON GROUP
25 condor stone

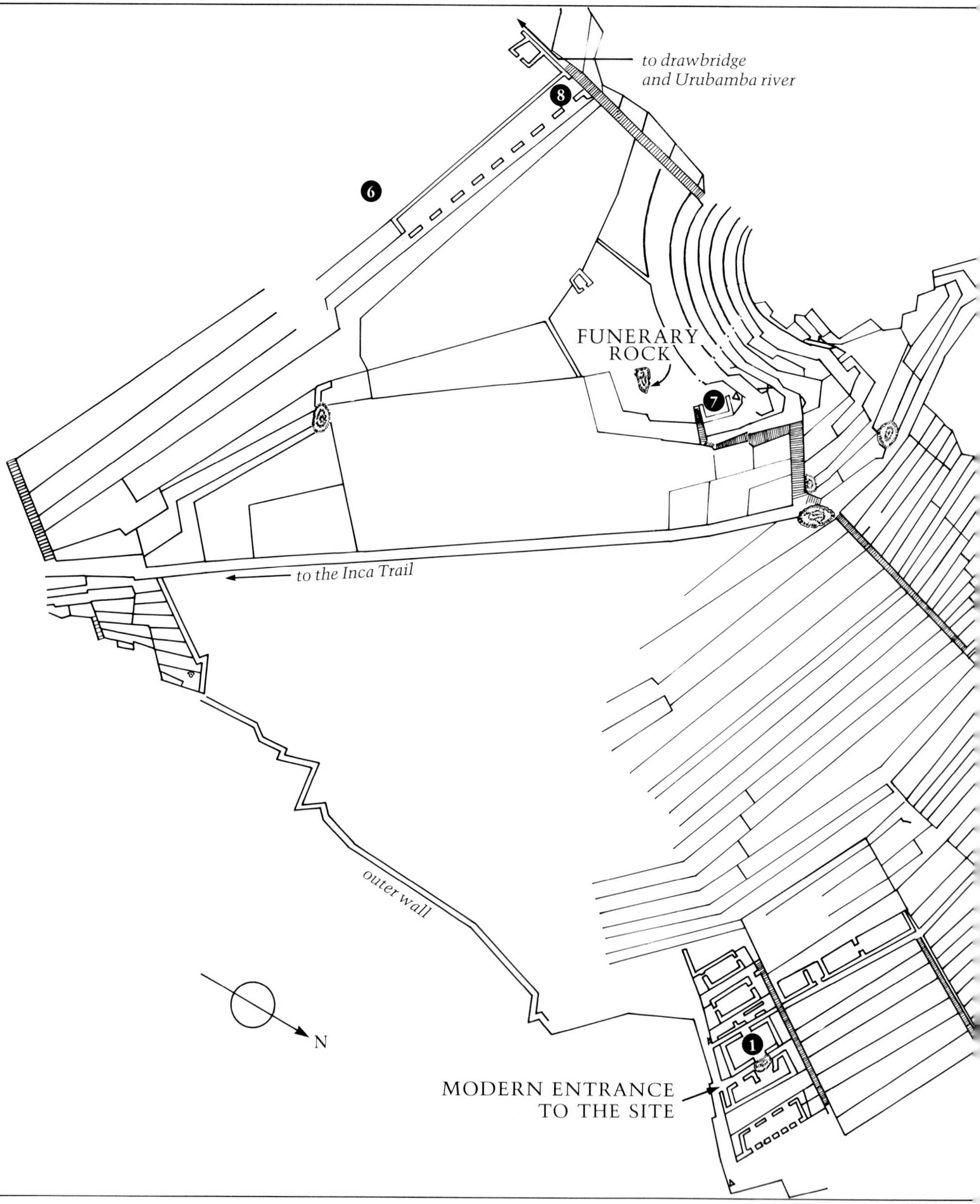

to drawbridge and Urubamba river

FUNERARY ROCK

to the Inca Trail

outer wall

N

MODERN ENTRANCE TO THE SITE

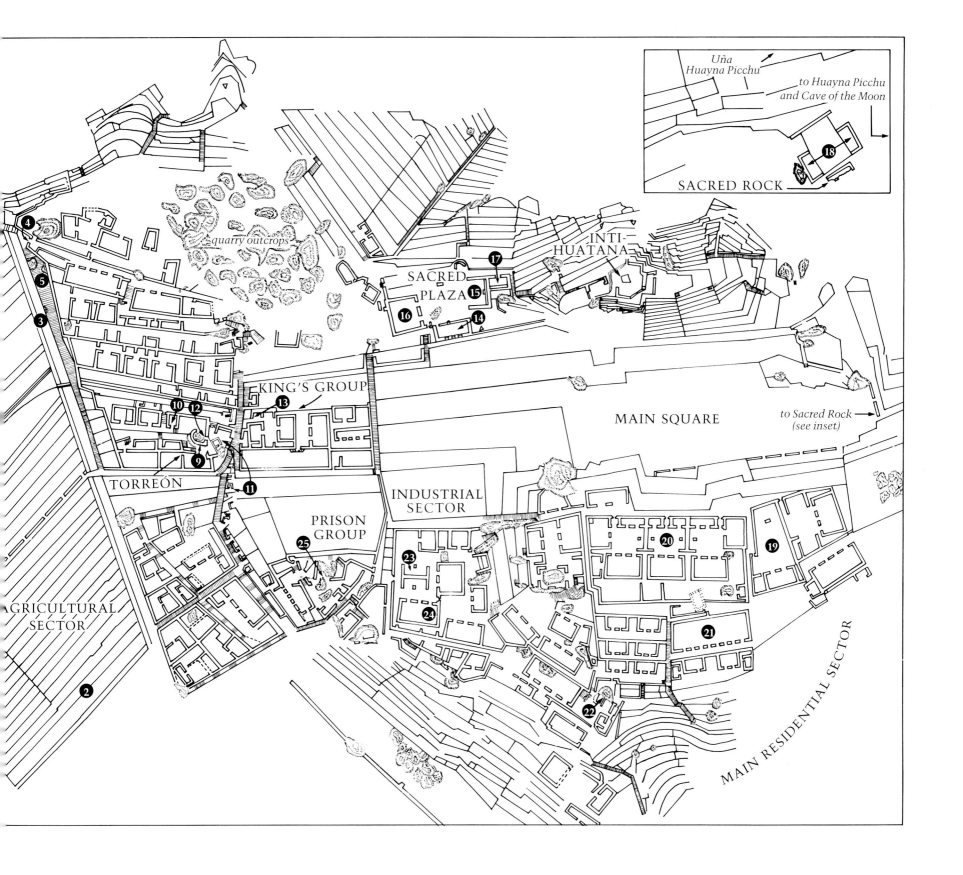

Uña Huayna Picchu

to Huayna Picchu and Cave of the Moon

⓲

SACRED ROCK

quarry outcrops

④

⑤

③

INTI-HUATANA

⑰

SACRED PLAZA

⑮

⑯

⑭

KING'S GROUP

⑬

MAIN SQUARE

to Sacred Rock (see inset)

⑩ ⑫

⑨

TORREÓN

⑪

INDUSTRIAL SECTOR

PRISON GROUP

⑳

⑲

㉕

㉓

㉔

㉑

AGRICULTURAL SECTOR

②

㉒

MAIN RESIDENTIAL SECTOR

When Hiram Bingham discovered Machu Picchu it was choked by vegetation. In his photograph of 1915, both the torreón (lower foreground) and the principal temple (center left) are visible

Machu Picchu, 1971

He set out on the misty morning of 24 July 1911 with Arteaga and a Peruvian sergeant. They crept across the plunging rapids of the Urubamba on a spindly bridge of logs fastened to boulders, and then clambered up a rough path through the jungle on the far side. They paused for lunch with two Indians who had made themselves a farm on ancient agricultural terraces two thousand feet above the river. After lunch, Bingham left their hut, unenthusiastic at the prospect of more climbing in the humid afternoon heat. But just around a promontory he came upon his first thrilling sight: a magnificent flight of stone terraces, a hundred of them, climbing for almost a thousand feet up the hillside. These terraces had been roughly cleared by the Indians. But it was in the deep jungle above that Bingham made his breathtaking discovery. There, amid dark trees and undergrowth, he saw building after building, a sacred cave, and a three-sided temple whose granite ashlars were cut with all the beauty and precision of the finest buildings of Cuzco. Bingham left an unforgettable account of his excitement that afternoon, of the dreamlike experience of entering the untouched forest and seeing archaeological wonders, of finding each successive treasure of the lost city on that sharp forested ridge: "I suddenly found myself in a maze of beautiful granite houses! They were covered with trees and mosses and the growth of centuries, but in the dense shadow, hiding in bamboo thickets and tangled vines, could be seen, here and there, walls of white granite ashlars most carefully cut and exquisitely fitted together." On his first attempt, he had discovered the most famous ruin in South America.

In that first year, Bingham's team merely mapped their spectacular discovery. They returned the following year, 1912, to clear and excavate the site. Bingham described this as a discouraging task. The ruins were deeply overgrown. His reluctant Quechua workers had to cut down a hardwood forest and thick undergrowth. In places he found "massive trees, two feet thick, perched on the gable ends of small, beautifully constructed houses." Machu Picchu is now well trodden by the daily influx of visitors, and the site is continually being restored and maintained. It is only by looking at Bingham's early photographs that we can visualize how choked it had been by centuries of invading vegetation.

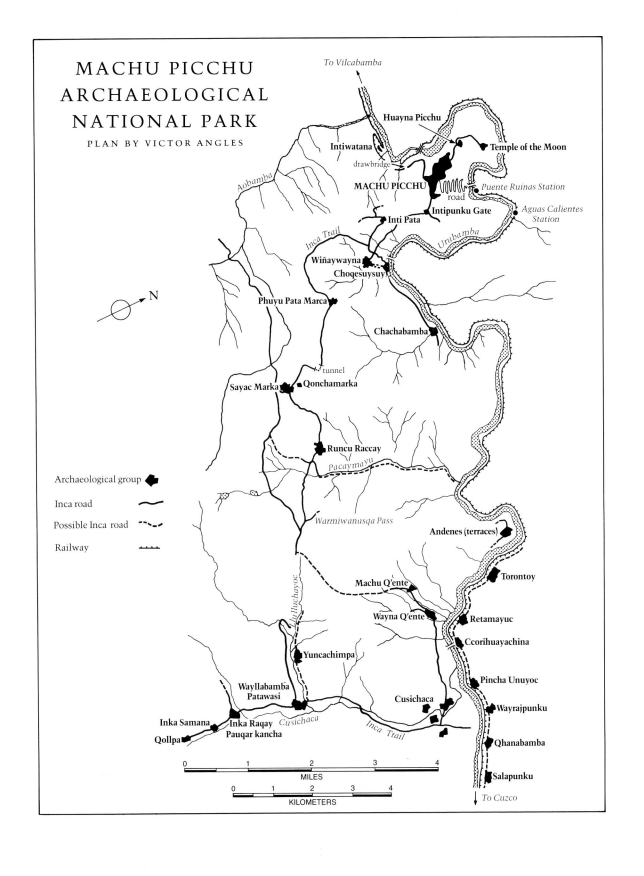

MACHU PICCHU ARCHAEOLOGICAL NATIONAL PARK

PLAN BY VICTOR ANGLES

To Vilcabamba

Huayna Picchu

Intiwatana

Aobamba

drawbridge

Temple of the Moon

MACHU PICCHU

road

Puente Ruinas Station

Aguas Calientes Station

Intipunku Gate

Inti Pata

Inca Trail

Urubamba

Wiñaywayna
Choqesuysuy

Phuyu Pata Marca

Chachabamba

tunnel

Sayac Marka   Qonchamarka

Runcu Raccay

Pacaymayu

N

Archaeological group

Inca road

Possible Inca road

Railway

Warmiwanusqa Pass

Andenes (terraces)

Torontoy

Machu Q'ente

Wayna Q'ente   Retamayuc

Ccorihuayachina

Mulluchayoc

Yuncachimpa

Pincha Unuyoc

Wayllabamba
Patawasi

Wayrajpunku

Cusichaca

Inka Samana   Inka Raqay
Qollpa   Pauqar kancha   *Cusichaca*   *Inca Trail*

Qhanabamba

Salapunku

| 0 | 1 | 2 | 3 | 4 |

MILES

| 0 | 1 | 2 | 3 | 4 |

KILOMETERS

To Cuzco

Bingham led a third expedition to this part of Peru in 1915. In addition to work at Machu Picchu, it explored the Inca approach roads high in the hills and forests above the Urubamba and located a number of other Inca sites along what is now known as the Inca Trail. He invented Inca names for those that had no local name: Ccorihuayrachina (the place where gold is washed), now called Phuyu Pata Marca; Cedrobamba, now called Sayac Marka; and Runcu Raccay—and Llactapata (high town) farther down the Urubamba. These sites were cleared and investigated again by the Peruvian archaeologist Luis E. Valcárcel in 1934, and were carefully mapped by another large American expedition under Paul Fejos in 1940–1941. The latter expedition discovered two more sites, Wiñaywayna and Inti Pata (sun terrace), both with massive hillsides of terracing. Bingham's expeditions had also noted Inca ruins down along the Urubamba river, at Choquesuysuy near Machu Picchu railway station and at Torontoy and Cusichaca between there and Ollantaytambo. Cusichaca and its associated ruins were thoroughly explored between 1977 and 1982 in a project led by Ann Kendall: the urban complex Llactapata and the fort of Willkaraqay facing it were excavated and restored, and Inca irrigation channels were rebuilt to help local farmers. It thus became clear that Machu Picchu lay at the end of a chain of Inca towns and agricultural stations. The left bank of the Urubamba was evidently well peopled in Inca times. But none of the later discoveries rivaled Bingham's first find, Machu Picchu, in size, excellence or beauty.

Machu Picchu is full of enigmas, mysteries that cannot be fully resolved. Like most Inca sites, it was built on previously unoccupied land, so that excavation would reveal little that cannot be seen now; and there seems no chance of any new documents being found to shed light on a place never visited during the Spanish occupation.

One of the many unanswered questions is the extent to which Machu Picchu was fortified. Was it a bastion to defend the Inca homelands from the peoples of the Antisuyo, the forest tribes to the north? Was it part of a defensive network

to protect Vilcabamba from the Chancas living to the west across the Apurímac? The place does have some defenses. The approach trail from the south passes through tunnels that could easily be closed and, as it comes in sight of the city, it is blocked by an outer gate. Another road that comes up the Urubamba from the southwest runs along the face of a sheer cliff and is broken by a deliberate void once spanned by a log drawbridge. The inner city of Machu Picchu is on a mountain saddle that drops precipitously to river gorges to the east and west. To the north the spur of land ends in the granite sugarloaf of Huayna Picchu, which rises like the horn of a rhinoceros, with the Urubama roaring in a hairpin bend below its sheer walls. The only vulnerable flank was thus the south. On this there were two defensive walls. One crosses the ridge south of the agricultural terraces. The inner city is further protected by a dry moat between it and these terraces. Inside the moat the houses of the town form an unbroken line and stand on terraces to form the second defensive wall. The old Inca road enters the city at the top of this steeply sloping bulwark. It passes through a massive trapezoidal gate whose outer face is flanked by a defensive platform. Inside this powerful stone gate are the reminders of its vanished door: a stone ring (eye-bonder) in the stone immediately above the lintel, from which the wooden door was doubtless suspended, and vertical stone cylinders, "barholds" sunk into the jambs to hold some form of horizontal locking beam. It is extraordinary that no chronicler described the mechanism of an Inca gate, and none has survived the centuries since the empire's overthrow. A final defensive feature of Machu Picchu is a web of lookouts to warn of any approaching enemy. The pinnacle of Huayna Picchu has the remains of Inca structures that clearly served as such an observatory, a signal station visible from hilltop eyries up and down the valley.

Bingham had a high regard for these defenses. He felt that they could have held off attackers who penetrated this far; and they also isolated the holy parts of the city from unauthorized intruders. Paul Fejos was less impressed by their military value. He noted that most of the chain of sites farther

Wiñaywayna was photographed by Martín Chambi shortly after it was cleared by the Fejos expedition in 1941

up the valley were undefended and concluded that none of them had been built primarily for defense. Machu Picchu's gates and wall were therefore more probably for religious seclusion. They are reminiscent of the enclosure walls around the temple of Viracocha at Raqchi, at the sacred end of the Island of the Sun in Lake Titicaca, and around the temple areas of Pisac, Coricancha and Ollantaytambo.

If Machu Picchu's purpose was not primarily military, was its function agricultural or was it religious? There is good evidence for either theory. All the Inca towns along this flank of the Urubamba have a very high ratio of agricultural terracing to dwellings. Inti Pata in particular has only about a dozen houses tending a wide hillside of terraces. The builders of Machu Picchu made the greatest possible use of its awkward site, terracing the slope between the defensive walls to the south and terracing the mountainside below the city on the east. Even the flat plazas that divide the inner city could have been used for agriculture. This chain of sites may therefore have served a special agricultural purpose, growing coca or other tropical luxuries for the imperial court in Cuzco. It is not immediately obvious what those luxuries can have been. Coca grows better in hot, still valleys than on the turbulent hills above the Urubamba, where between October and April rains, mists and electric storms are so frequent. At present the mighty terraces of Machu Picchu support only a few alpacas, who are there for decorative purposes, and in July and August a mass of wild strawberries.

A modern visitor to Machu Picchu generally descends the Urubamba on a narrow-gauge railway built along the path blasted in 1909, and climbs to the site on a zigzag road built during Valcárcel's cleaning operation of 1934. The ruins are entered near the modern tourist hotel. This entrance leads to a group of houses at the outer edge and near the foot of the main flight of terraces. Bingham called them the houses of the agricultural guardians. These five rectangular houses are built on different levels, but are larger and higher as they descend. The lowest and tallest has three doors on its upper side and a series of six openings from which to admire the

canyon below. One house has been restored with a thatch hip roof resting on four level-topped walls.

From this group, visitors walk along a terrace to reach the dry moat, the inner city wall, and one of the longest of Machu Picchu's hundreds of staircases. The hillside above and below is contoured in a magnificent flight of over forty terraces. Quite apart from their agricultural value, these terraces were the Incas' way of taming the unstable mountain against erosion. Such is the steepness of the slope that most of the terraces require retaining walls 3.5 meters (11½ feet) high to provide only 3.0 meters (10 feet) of horizontal platform. This main group of terraces faces north to enjoy the longest possible exposure to the subequatorial sun. Other terraces to the west of the inner city, below the inti-huatana group, are far steeper and served largely as buttresses.

Before entering the inner city, it is worth climbing to the top of the agricultural sector between the two defensive walls. The staircase between the moat and the inner wall ascends to the city's main gate. From here the visitor walks back along the old Inca road, on a terrace, and then climbs other staircases to an area that is known as the Upper Cemetery. Bingham gave it this name because his men excavated a number of skeletons in a cave here and from the narrow plateau above the great flight of terraces. The cave was only one of some fifty burial caves found near Machu Picchu, most of them on the slopes below the city. Bingham offered rewards to any of his men who could find a cave. By the end of his explorations he was sure that his men had scoured "every accessible—and many seemingly inaccessible—parts of Huayna Picchu and Machu Picchu Mountains and the ridge between. . . . Practically every square rod of the ridge was explored."

The Upper Cemetery was guarded by the "watchman's hut," a masma whose steeply pitched roof has been restored (see plate, page 31). The hut now provides welcome shelter for visitors on the many days of heavy rain at Machu Picchu. The trapezoidal windows in its end walls give a famous view over the legendary city.

The canyon of the Urubamba river, seen from the Inca Trail en route to Wiñaywayna. The railroad runs close to the river, along the trail that had been opened shortly before Bingham's expedition in 1911

*The southern end of Machu Picchu. Agricultural terraces beyond the Sacred Plaza
lead up to the gabled watchman's hut and the start of the Inca Trail*

*The modern road zigzags up the slope climbed by Bingham in 1911 and ends
well below the watchman's hut, which overlooks the city from the south*

The sculpted Funerary Rock beside the watchman's hut

The watchman's hut faces an open space containing one of the many worked rock outcrops that abound here or in any Inca site (see page 2). This sculpted rock, with its flattened surface, molded protuberances and tiny access steps, was obviously a huaca (shrine). It may have served as a funerary altar, a place for mummifying the bodies of important dead persons or for animal sacrifices, and Bingham therefore called it the Funerary Rock. It was in a prominent, public place, overlooked by another terrace and plaza that might have held the spectators of such rites.

On the far side of this upper plaza is the so-called tambo (posthouse barracks): a long rectangular building with eight large doorways in its façade and one in either end. This is a familiar Inca plan, not large enough to be called a kallanka, but perhaps similar to the buildings around the square of Cajamarca, from which Pizarro's cavalry launched their murderous charge against Atahualpa's entourage. There are similar long buildings at Pisac, at Caquia Xaquixahuana above the Yucay valley, and at Vitcos thirty-five kilometers (twenty-two miles) west of Machu Picchu. The tambo stood at the junction of the two Inca roads to the city: the Cuzco road, the "Inca Trail," which came down the slopes of Machu Picchu mountain from the southeast; and the other, which climbed to the western end of the "barracks" from the Urubamba river and the cliff-hanging drawbridge two kilometers (one and a quarter miles) from the city.

Looking down from the vantage point of the cemetery lookout, the dual nature of Machu Picchu becomes evident. The inner town is very obviously divided by the line of grassy central squares. In this it was the mirror of Cuzco, which was split into Hanan-Cuzco and Hurin-Cuzco. As Bernabé Cobo explained, the Incas "divided every town or chiefdom into two sections or groups known as hanansaya and hurinsaya, which mean the upper ward and the lower ward." Cobo stressed that the two ranked equally. The Inca rulers made the distinction so that their subjects' loyalties would be divided—an obvious insurance against sedition—and to facilitate tribute and labor levies. It was also done to "give their subjects an incentive for competition and emulation in any craft or task they undertook on royal orders. . . . The two divisions always performed on their own; the men of one never interfered with those of the other. At festivals and public celebrations each group did its utmost to excel, to gain an edge over its competitor in the innovations or entertainment they devised."

Manuel Chávez Ballón, creator of the Machu Picchu museum and for many years custodian of the ruins, propounded this dual interpretation. He was able to show that Machu Picchu had two moieties (sayas) to east and west of the central plazas. Each contained the essential elements of an Inca ceremonial center: royal lodging, acclahuasi for the chosen women, temples to the sun and to Viracocha, yachahuasi college for sons of the nobility, storage area and accommodation for court officials and soldiery. It is also possible to argue that Machu Picchu, like Cuzco, had ceques—lines of shrines radiating down from a central point, like stations along a Christian pilgrimage route. Sacred rocks, caves and other huacas were arranged along ceque paths around the holy city.

Not everyone agrees with this theory of duality. Bingham, George Kubler, Víctor Angles and others note a different character in each compound or cluster of buildings in Machu Picchu. They assign a different function to each part of the city. They see the central squares as fortuitous: the buildings that rise on either side of these squares are grouped around them only for convenience and to exploit the topography. They do not mirror one another in hanan and hurin wards. Kubler described the city's design as "a patterned blanket thrown over a great rock: the pattern falls in many folds." The attraction of Machu Picchu is that it is sufficiently enigmatic to support both these interpretations. Its ruined buildings are wonderfully preserved and untouched by later occupation; but it is impossible to say for certain what happened in any individual structure.

Some things can be said with certainty about Machu Picchu. The quality and quantity of its stonework are impressive. So much stone would indicate an important or holy place. (It does, however, rest on a mountain of granite, with plenty of stone but little mud available for adobes; stone was also the best building material for any permanent structures in this humid region.) The town has a remarkable number of shrines—caves or rock outcrops of obvious spiritual importance. Its spectacular location on a spur with a commanding view—reminiscent of Pisac or Choquequirau and to a lesser extent of Ollantaytambo, Vilcashuamán or Vitcos—seems to mark it as a sanctuary. With only two hundred habitable structures and relatively little level agricultural land, Machu

In Martín Chambi's photograph of 1934, most of Machu Picchu had been cleared, but the Prison Group of buildings (on the slope to the right of the circular torreón) was still overgrown

The inner city was entered by a single gateway, which is seen at the lower left of the facing photograph

tained more than about a thousand people. The architecture is very uniform and hardly any building shows signs of alteration. The style is late imperial Inca, and Cobo confirmed that Pachacuti occupied this region immediately after the defeat of the Chancas: "He started his conquests with the provinces of Vitcos and Vilcabamba, a difficult country to subdue because of its wildness and extensive undergrowth and dense jungles."

Machu Picchu's inner city or urban sector was apparently its sacred sector—an area full of holy buildings, masked by a wall that served as much to exclude the uninitiated as to protect it from enemies. Entering through the main gate, at the southernmost point of the inner city and at the top of the dry moat and broad staircase, a visitor passes above a sector of buildings arranged on seven terraces. These houses are of pirca, fieldstones roughly shaped and set in clay mortar. The doors of each row of buildings face inwards toward the terrace wall of the tier above. It is an apparent labyrinth of enclosures and courtyards, but there is a pattern, a plan adapted to the slope of the hill. Some of these structures were habitations— notably a fine house with four doors onto the street just inside the main gate—but others may have been for storage.

Staircases at the northern end of this upper group lead down to the famous torreón, the "bastion," so called because its curved wall recalls the towers of medieval fortifications. There was, of course, nothing military about the torreón: its purpose was entirely religious. The beautiful curving wall is built of regular courses of tightly fitting ashlars, leaning slightly inward toward the top. The inner walls of the curve and its attendant rectangular temple are equally perfect, with splendid niches and stone bosses of impeccable precision. The curved wall surrounds a sacred outcrop of rock, and beneath is the mysterious grotto known as the royal mausoleum. Such a curving wall is rare in Inca architecture. Similar curved walls contain huacas (shrines) in the sun temples of Coricancha in Cuzco and at Pisac. Hiram Bingham was therefore justified in calling the torreón the sun temple of Machu Picchu.

Picchu hardly qualifies as a city. If there was a large population in this region it lived in huts of perishable materials, perhaps in the Urubamba valley reached by the Inca road that crosses the drawbridge. The sanctuary itself cannot have con-

The rock altar inside the torreón

The curved wall of the torreón encloses a sacred outcrop. The house of the ñusta is on the right (Martín Chambi, 1934)

The southern part of the temple complex is a lovely two-storied building of the finest masonry. As usual in Inca building, there is no internal staircase: the upper story opens toward the temple courtyard while the lower faces west onto the terrace below. This two-story building is known, for no good reason, as the house of the ñusta (princess). It was more probably the residence of a high priest, or chapels dedicated to lesser celestial deities such as the thunder, moon or rainbow. Whatever its purpose, the building demonstrates some of the triumphs of Inca masonry: coursed ashlars fixed with stunning virtuosity; courses diminishing in size as they rise; tapering and inward lean of the walls; blocks cut to turn at the corners and bonded for exceptional strength; perfect trapezoidal doors and window looking out over the Urubamba valley. The sacred nature of this temple group is confirmed by the remains of a defensive gate—with lintel ring and horse-shoe-shaped grooves and barholds for securing cords in either jamb—in an unroofed entry passage alongside the house of the ñusta (see plate, page 29).

The grotto beneath the torreón outcrop (Martín Chambi, 1934)

The core of this temple area is a mighty granite boulder that thrusts upwards from the slope of the hillside. Its top is the rounded "altar" surrounded by the curving wall. Below this, Inca masons have skillfully converted the rock's overhang into a grotto, sealing part of its entrance with a coursed wall rising out of a stepped outcrop. The bedrock within the "tomb" blends smoothly with Inca walls that contain niches

The sculpted grotto, known as the royal mausoleum, below the torreón

large enough to hold royal mummy bundles. The angles of this chamber are cut sharply but they are asymmetrical. Such stoneworking is sufficiently surprising to constitute a hollow sculpture of great beauty, three-dimensional and plastic, with strange shadows and a deep sense of religious mystery.

The curving wall of the torreón has fine trapezoidal windows facing east and south. Stone bosses that project at the corners of these openings defy precise analysis. Were they purely decorative or did they have a religious significance now unknown? Or are they weathered corbels that once supported some form of shutter or monstrance for holy symbols? The opening to the north of the temple is even more curious.

Steps cut into the bedrock lead to the house of the ñusta and the torreón

Trapezoidal niches and stone pegs inside the grotto

Coursed masonry and stepped rock at the grotto entrance

The carved steps leading to the house of the ñusta

A gnomon carved within the grotto

The trapezoidal "serpent gate" in the north wall of the torreón overlooks the principal liturgical bath

It is a full-length trapezoidal doorway that opens onto the void; and its base is carefully stepped, with a narrower opening at the center, and surrounded by strange holes that pierce the surrounding stones. One theory was that sacrificial efflu-

ents might have poured from these holes, or that snakes were made to glide through them. Bingham later surmised that the holes were used to attach the punchao, the golden image of the sun at daybreak. The opening does not face the dawn, but it does face north toward the equator, and, with its surrounding holes, is reminiscent of the niche in Coricancha that probably held *its* sun image.

This strange gateway looks down onto another of Machu Picchu's enigmatic features: the cascade of stone baths. There are sixteen of these cisterns, with the water tumbling from one to another from the upper part of the city to the start of the terraces below. The bath beneath the torreón is the fourth from the top, the finest in the quality of its stonework and evidently the most important of the series. Each bath has stone sides up to 1.5 meters (5 feet) high, with narrow door openings and some with small internal niches. The channels that fill and drain each tank are obvious but perplexing, for they are too low to permit much water to stand in each bath unless the drain holes were plugged. It is difficult to imagine these tanks being used as human baths. They seem equally impractical as cisterns to supply the city's inhabitants with their daily water supply. Bingham imagined Inca women coming to fill their narrow-necked jars at these basins, using the niches to hold cups or fiber stoppers for their bottles. But the elaborately cut basins do not seem right for this purpose. Such communal cisterns are not a feature of Inca towns, for the Incas had no difficulty in piping or channeling water to all residential areas, as can be seen at Pisac, Cusichaca, Tipón near Cuzco, Huánuco, Chinchero and other sites. The baths of Machu Picchu must therefore have been liturgical fonts or some form of ceremonial water garden. There are many sacred springs or baths in other Inca ruins, in such places as Tambo Machay (see plate, page 47), Choquequirau, or the inti-huatana group at Pisac; and there are cascades of water on the Island of the Sun in Lake Titicaca, at Wiñaywayna, 3.5 kilometers (2.2 miles) from Machu Picchu along the Inca Trail, at Ollantaytambo and at Choquesuysuy. But none of these can compare with the flight of cisterns at Machu Picchu. The water that

The principal liturgical bath, below the "serpent gate" of the torreón sun temple

once flowed into them from some vanished spring must have given the town a delightful splashing counterpoint to the thundering of the Urubamba in its canyon far below.

Just above the central flight of basins is a lovely three-sided shelter, with a stone bench looking down on this cere-monial center. The shelter must surely have been the scene of rituals connected with the sacred sites nearby. As one looks out from it, to the right is the torreón sun temple with its

Water flows into the principal liturgical bath through a channel six feet long

strange "serpent gate" and the royal mausoleum below; look-ing down are the basins and a stupendous view across the Urubamba valley; and to the left, the city's finest residential group of buildings.

The "serpent gate" of the torreón, with the Urubamba gorge beyond

Looking out over the King's Group toward the Prison Group

Hiram Bingham called the residence beyond the baths the King's Group because of the great strength and beauty of its masonry and the steep pitch of its roofs. He reasoned that "no one but a king could have insisted on having the lintels of his doorways made of solid blocks of granite each weighing three tons. . . . Even had he possessed cranes, pulleys, and steam winches, he would have found it no easy task. Since he had none of these things, he must have built up a solid inclined plane side by side with the wall as it rose so that the workmen could raise the heavy lintels with levers. What a prodigious amount of patient effort had to be employed!" This mighty door has a lintel whose "artistic workmanship" defies descrip-

Two chambers of the King's Group open onto a small courtyard

The long staircase from the Sacred Plaza to the lower city

tion or even photography to be properly appreciated. Once through it, a visitor passes below a ring, 2 meters (6½ feet) from the ground, cut into a boss projecting from the rock above. This doubtless held some lamp or image; but to the popular imagination it is the Hanged Man's Rock. Beyond is a central, service courtyard with two fine, niched buildings facing onto it. These are traditionally thought to have been the ruler's dormitory—a building with an audience chamber and a water channel that runs into a narrow internal passage. Beyond lie "servants' quarters" in more rustic masonry; and below the King's Group is what may once have been a delightful walled garden.

The surviving ruins of this small palace remind us of the Spaniards' descriptions of their first meeting with the Inca Atahualpa, on the day before they kidnapped him in the square of Cajamarca. He was in a small palace at some natural hot baths a few miles from the city. Juan Ruiz de Arce, Francisco de Jerez and Hernanado Pizarro described his lodging as consisting of four chambers around a patio. There was a stone bath into which hot and cold water were piped. The Inca slept in a room with a corridor overlooking a walled garden. Its walls and roof beams were painted with a red bitumen. The chamber opposite was plastered white as snow and was roofed by four false domes incorporated into a larger thatch dome. Two other chambers were for servants. All those early eyewitnesses stressed the fine textiles that surrounded the Inca—carpets covering his stool and draperies held over him by a flock of women constantly in attendance.

The holy character of Machu Picchu emerges most strongly on the ridge that rises northwest of the King's Group. This

The Sacred Plaza from the south. The winding staircase leading to the inti-huatana begins behind the U-shaped wall of the principal temple. To the right is the gabled end of the temple of three windows, with the Main Square beyond

is the dominant feature of the inner city. To the east of it are the tiers of central plazas with the lower wards of Machu Picchu beyond. To the west, the mountain drops almost sheer to the raging river. Every building on this ridge has obvious religious significance.

The long staircase behind the King's Group leads toward

A monolithic pier once supported the roof on the open side of the temple of the three windows

the "Sacred Plaza" at the heart of this religious complex. On one side of the plaza is the famous temple of the three windows, looking down over the city's central squares. The three windows and their attendant niches are roughly trapezoidal, but with rounded lower corners and subtle, highly satisfying curves on their sides to widen the frames of the view. Bingham argued very plausibly that these great windows might have symbolized the three caves of Tambo-toqo, the mouths

The snowcapped Vilcambamba mountains on the western skyline beyond
the Sacred Plaza seen from within the temple of the three windows

of the tunnels from which the legendary Ayar brothers emerged on their migration from Titicaca toward Cuzco. This temple is a masma: three-sided, with the open side toward the plaza. A magnificent monolithic pier once supported the roof beams in the center of the open side; and the end walls have large sockets for the missing horizontal beams. A rock in front of this pier is sculpted with steps and polished planes, and carries the stepped symbol found in Pisac, Ollantaytambo and the cave passages of Laqo near Kenko: a motif so familiar from the Tiahuanaco civilization of Lake Titicaca. On the side with the three windows, the building drops down far below its inner floor, which is level with the plaza. The outer face is thus 5.2 meters (17 feet) high, an imposing sight from below, with the three great windows apparently in an upper story (see plate, page 160).

The buildings around the Sacred Plaza are built in monolithic style, with vast boulders sunk into their walls. These huge stones are so audaciously cut and fitted that they could only be the work of the most skilled and flamboyant Inca masons. The principal temple, presumably to Viracocha, occupies the northern side of the Sacred Plaza. Huge blocks at the bases of its walls are foundations for neat coursed ashlars and symmetrical niches above. The side walls show vestiges of a sloping gable and notches for roof beams. Like the temple of the three windows, the principal temple was evidently a masma, open on the side facing the square. The building measures 8 by 11 meters (26 by 36 feet). It is not clear whether a gigantic forest tree was found to span the open long wall, or whether this side once had a central pier, as did the adjacent temple. At the center of the back wall is an enormous stone altar 4.2 meters long by 1.4 high and 0.9 wide (almost 14 by 4½ by 3 feet) flanked by smaller stone benches or altars. Across the plaza there is a building of slightly less brilliant masonry, traditionally thought to have been the house of the high priest; and to the west, semicircular foundations of a vanished enclosure. Perhaps the curved wall of this lost building was once another sun temple, directed toward the rays of the setting sun.

The western wall of the principal temple was extended to the rear and enclosed one of the most perfect of Machu Picchu's many beautiful buildings. Bingham first identified it as the high priest's house; but he later decided that it was a royal mausoleum, with a bench for displaying the mummies of Inca rulers. Others have called it the ornament chamber. It is quite small, only 7 by 4 meters (23 by 13 feet), but built of white granite cut and fitted with breathtaking brilliance. A great block forms the base of the wall to the left of this chamber's only door. Visitors are shown how this one stone has no less than thirty-two corners, in three dimensions, each fitting tightly with its neighbors; and the rock at the base of the opposite wall, to the right on entry, also has the same number of angles. The masons' virtuosity is manifested just as strikingly in the niches—startlingly crisp and regular—in the turning of stones at the chamber corners, and in the precision and polish of every ashlar. Bingham boasted, justifiably, that this building in his discovery equaled in proportions, beauty and the artistic care with which it was built any ancient building anywhere.

The ornament chamber is at the edge of the most spiritual of all sectors of this holy city. A corridor leads around its northern end and then climbs some sixty steps, in four small flights, toward the summit of the inti-huatana. The Incas converted a natural outcrop of granite into a stepped pyramid, a form of usnu. The temple that surrounds the crowning gnomon seems elevated by tiers of terraces or walls of natural rock. The mystery and expectancy of the approach is heightened by changes of direction, successive flights of steps, small walled courtyards, and clusters of buildings.

The inti-huatana itself is a simple pillar of stone rising from a roughly rectangular platform. It is the pinnacle of the ridge's natural bedrock. The gnomon rises 1.8 meters (almost 6 feet) above its base, the highest such rock projection to survive among the Inca ruins of Peru. It is also the most powerfully elegant, a masterpiece of sculpture, rising in tapering planes from its curving base in a single strong upward thrust.

*The approach to the inti-huatana from the south. The trapezoidal openings
on either side have been partially filled by Inca masonry*

No one knows the precise ceremonial that took place at the inti-huatana of Machu Picchu, Pisac or other shrines. The assumption is that these gnomons were used to record movements of the sun, inti. Garcilaso de la Vega explained that "for all their simplicity, the Incas realized that the sun completed its course in a year, which they called *huata*. The noun means 'a year,' but used as a verb, similarly pronounced and accented, it means 'to tie.'" Hence, inti-huatana is translated as "hitching post of the sun"—like the great masts once used to moor airships.

The Incas clearly had an accurate awareness of the seasons and equinoxes. Felipe Guaman Poma noted that the Incas knew that the sun was farther away than the moon and paid particular attention to eclipses. "They calculated the month, day, hour and precise moment for sowing their crops, observing the movements of the sun. They observed the way in which its rays illuminated the highest peaks in the mornings and how they penetrated the windows of their houses. Variations in its direction and intensity acted as a precise clock to regulate the sowing and harvesting of their foods." Pedro Sarmiento de Gamboa described special solar observatories called *sucanas* on hills near Cuzco: "In order to know the precise time of sowing and harvesting, . . . the Inca caused four poles to be set up on a high mountain to the east of Cuzco, about four varas [3.3 meters or 11 feet] apart, on the heads of which there were holes by which the sun entered, in the manner of a watch or astrolabe. Observing where the sun struck the ground through these holes at the time of sowing and harvest, marks were made on the ground. . . . Thus the whole became an instrument serving as an annual timepiece."

If the inti-huatana of Machu Picchu was a solar observatory, we have an indication in the chronicles of the ceremonial that once surrounded it. Garcilaso wrote that there were solar columns throughout the empire. "To ascertain the time of the equinoxes they had splendidly carved stone columns erected in the squares or courtyards before the temples of the sun. . . . The columns stood in the middle of great rings filling the whole extent of the squares or open spaces. Across the middle of the ring a line was drawn from east to west by a cord. . . . When the shadow fell exactly along the line from sunrise, and at midday the sun bathed all sides of the column and cast no shadow at all, they knew that that day was the equinox. They then decked the columns with all the flowers and aromatic herbs they could find, and placed the throne of the sun on it, saying that on that day the sun was seated on the column in all his full light."

Worship of the sun culminated during the months corresponding to June and December, in each of which there was a great Inti Raymi (sun festival). The young priest Cristóbal de Molina was privileged to observe such a festival during the first few months after the Spanish occupation of Cuzco. He wrote that "the Inca opened the sacrifices and they lasted for eight days. Thanks were given to the sun for the past harvest and prayers were made for the crops to come. . . . They brought all the effigies of the shrines of Cuzco onto a plain at the edge of the city in the direction of the sun's rise at daybreak." The effigies were housed under magnificent featherwork awnings, arranged in an avenue, and attended by the lords of Cuzco, "all magnificently robed [in] rich silver cloaks and tunics, with brightly shining circlets and medallions of fine gold on their heads. . . .

"As soon as the sunrise began they started to chant in splendid harmony and unison. While chanting each of them shook his foot, . . . and as the sun continued to rise they chanted higher." The Inca presided from a rich throne, and it was he who opened the chanting. "They all stayed there, chanting, from the time the sun rose until it had completely set. As the sun was rising toward noon they continued to raise their voices, and from noon onward they lowered them, keeping careful track of the sun's course.

"Throughout this time, great offerings were being made. On a platform on which there was a tree, there were Indians doing nothing but throwing meats into a great fire and burning them up in it. At another place the Inca ordered [llama] ewes to be thrown for the poorer common Indians to grab, and this caused great sport. At eight o'clock over two hundred

Northernmost Machu Picchu. Uña (small) Huayna Picchu is to the left; Huayna Picchu, to the right, rises above the gabled buildings (masmas) attending the Sacred Rock

girls came out of Cuzco, each with a large new pot of . . . chicha that was plastered and covered. The girls came in groups of five, full of precision and order, and pausing at intervals. They also offered to the sun many bales of a herb that the Indians chew and call coca, whose leaf is like myrtle.

"There were many other ceremonies and sacrifices. Suffice it to say that when the sun was about to set in the evening the Indians showed great sadness at its departure, in their chants and expressions. They allowed their voices to die away on purpose. And as the sun was sinking completely and disappearing from sight they made a great act of reverence, raising their hands and worshipping it in the deepest humility." Similar ceremonies may have been performed in the sun temples of Machu Picchu. It is no accident that to the west the hill of the inti-huatana drops dramatically, sheer to the river, and the setting sun strikes the snows of the Vilcabamba mountains in the distance.

Modern visitors follow a route doubtless once used by Inca priests, off the inti-huatana to the north, away from the Sacred Plaza. Ahead is a small hill called Uña Wayna Picchu (small Huayna Picchu—small young peak). Facing it, at the northernmost part of the town, along the path to Huayna Picchu and the temple of the moon, is a great thin slab of rock set in a platform of Inca masonry—the Sacred Rock (see plate, page 52). There is a sunken plaza in front of this shrine, and on either side of it fine examples of masmas. These doubtless sheltered participants in the ceremonies from sun or rain (see plates, pages 31–32). One has had its roof restored, with the roof beams slotted into the gables, the thatch tied down to bosses and eye-bonders, and a trace of original clay plaster on the walls.

From the Sacred Rock the lower city, Hurin Machu Picchu, stretches along the northeastern side of the central squares. This is the largest concentration of dwellings, with a series of wards arranged along a low ridge. These wards contain the greatest variety of housing. Closest to the Sacred Rock is the so-called Upper Group, which overlooks the main square. It is enclosed by a wall with only two gates, the main one a double-jambed door toward the square. Within this perimeter is an irregular group of houses and courts, of relatively rustic workmanship. To the south is the Three Doors Group or Group of Identical Houses, named because three identical buildings overlook the square. Each of these has one double-jambed door toward the square, with other gates leading onto courtyards within the compound. The doors over the square stand above three handsome tiers of terraces. It is possible to imagine participants emerging from them for some ceremony. As with other important compounds, these gates are protected within by vertical cylinders in the jambs to secure vanished doors. On the inner side of each of the three courtyards is a fine three-doored building, and on the flanking sides are back-to-back, open-fronted masmas. The entire group is well isolated by its enclosure wall.

Behind the Three Doors Group, to the north, is the largest building in Machu Picchu, almost a kallanka, possibly a dor-

The inti-huatana

The Three-Doors Group in lower Machu Picchu, seen from the inti-huatana pinnacle

mitory for agricultural workers since a long staircase nearby leads down to the terraces. With eight doors on one long wall, it is similar to the barracks-like tambo at the junction of the two roads entering Machu Picchu from the south. Near here, Bingham's men excavated a rubbish midden that showed signs of long occupation, with sherds from well over a hundred pots. The side of the hill facing northeast has the feel of a residential district, with terraces of identical simple houses, courtyards, internal streets, rock-outcrop shrines, caves, tombs and short terraces overlooking the steep mountainside.

*The lower, eastern side of Machu Picchu. In the Industrial Sector
(to the right) is the double masma with its high gables*

The stone projections identified by Bingham as "household mortars" may have had a ceremonial rather than a practical function

A carved rock shrine on the easternmost edge of Machu Picchu, near terraces above the Urubamba river

The finest of these clan compounds is across the square from the temple of the three windows and the Sacred Plaza. A splendid tall gabled building dominates the center of this ward. It is a double masma, with a high central wall supporting the roof apex, and piers in the center of each open side. The buildings around it have flat stone walls and were once hip-roofed, with the thatch rising from each of the four walls in a near pyramid. But the building that gives this group its name (Mortar Group) faces the double masma to the east. In its floor are two round stone projections whose tops are carved to form shallow flat cups. Bingham took these to be "permanent and unbreakable mortars or grinding stones, where maize could be ground and frozen potatoes crushed under the smooth-faced mullers, or rocking stones, which have been used throughout the central Andes since time immemorial. Near the mortars we actually found one of the ancient mullers which had been rocked here centuries ago." The only trouble is that these bosses in Machu Picchu do not resemble either the mortars or

the rocking grinding stones that have always been used by Andean Indians. Stones with hollowed tops similar to the ones in Machu Picchu have been found elsewhere, but in Inca shrines rather than dwellings. Víctor Angles mentions seeing them in Sacsahuaman, at Tarapata in Quente and in other outcrops near Cuzco. He confesses that Bingham's stones "up to now have not been explained; but it is clear that they were not mortars."

The Incas, like all Andean Indians, were orderly, docile, honest and law-abiding by European standards. Their communal spirit and unquestioning obedience to authority greatly facilitated the Spanish Conquest. However, despite their natural good behavior, their society demanded absolute conformity to established laws and customs. Any transgression or deviation was punished implacably. The chroniclers describe a scale of harsh punishments for crimes ranging from treason and murder to adultery, abuse of royal possessions, sorcery and common theft. Different chroniclers give slightly differ-

A vault, or passageway, within the Prison Group

The offertory stone and the central outcrop of the Prison Group

ent lists of punishments for different crimes, but most agree that there were two main prisons in Cuzco and equivalent prisons in provincial cities. Guaman Poma described one prison as "constructed below ground in a form of crypt, very dark, where they raised snakes, poisonous serpents, pumas, jaguars, bears, foxes, dogs, wildcats, vultures, eagles . . .— creatures that could be used to punish criminals and delinquents. . . . Those who committed serious crimes were placed

in those vaults in order that the beasts would devour them alive." Lesser crimes might be punished by "tying the hands and feet with a cord and twisting it to obtain confession," but for other serious crimes there was stoning or clubbing to death or, as we have seen at Ollantaytambo, execution by being hurled from high precipices. Cobo spoke of habitual criminals being "executed by hanging with their heads downward and being left hanging in this way until they died."

The compact enclosed area of the Prison Group from the north. Within it is the flat rock known as the condor stone

It is possible to identify one group of buildings in Machu Picchu as the prisons: the ward to the southeast of the Main Residential Sector and the Industrial Sector of the city. This group is overlooked by a handsome three-story building, which could conceivably have housed the prison governor or legal authority. It is an admirable structure that makes good use of the steep slope to give access to each floor. Its gables, walls, windows and niches are intact and the stepped cornice that once held the upper floor is clearly visible. The view from the top story is superb. But the basement and the rocky vaults and caverns alongside could well have been the subterranean prisons that once held dangerous beasts. A large, flat rock in the small courtyard outside has been carved to resemble a reclining condor. The head, knobbed beak and white collar of the largest of all birds of prey are clearly visible. Above this rock are niches large enough to take prisoners; they even have holes in their stone walls through which the cords described by Guaman Poma could have passed. There is another row of nine full-length niches along the wall that faces westward toward upper Machu Picchu. These might also have been used for some form of incarceration.

As so often in Machu Picchu, nothing is certain. The "Prison Group" seems to have the vaults, punishment cells and suitably symbolic condor that would be required in an Inca prison. But the place could equally well have been used for some religious purpose. The condor stone might have been a sacrificial altar—it does seem to have grooves to carry off sacrificial fluids. The tunnels and caverns under the rock outcrops—which remind a visitor of Kenko above Cuzco—may have had religious rather than judicial purposes. To Bingham, the niches with holes in their sides were just the right size and shape to hold royal mummy bundles. Bodies were mummified with their knees drawn up under their chins and were then swathed in successive layers of cloth. "Each of these three niches was large enough to receive such a bundle and was provided with a stone barhold so that the mummy could be tied in, or taboo sticks could have been fastened in front of each niche to ward off any interference with the mummy. Each niche in turn had three little niches, one on the back wall and one on each of the side walls. The little niches were probably for the reception of offerings, articles presumed to be of value and interest to the departed." The stone platform below could have been used to dry the mummies in the sun, to maintain their preservation. The problem is one of identification. The structures are well preserved and their baffling details are intact. But none can say for sure what was their function: prison, mummy store, or temple.

One of the holiest of Machu Picchu's many shrines was discovered only in 1936. This is the Cave of the Moon, on a densely forested mountainside below the pinnacle of Huayna Picchu. It is reached by a forty-minute walk down a fine Inca road that plunges around the western flank of Huayna Picchu. It is a dramatic journey, vertiginous where the slippery trail clings to granite cliffs. The cave is in deep rain forest. When it finally comes into view in a break in the tropical vegetation, it is as unexpected as the first view of Petra's temples at the end of their ravine. It is almost as theatrical as the famous Jordanian ruin.

Masonry walls rise above the central rock spur of the Prison Group.
The niches may have held mummies or been used to incarcerate prisoners

The condor stone

The upper cavern, the Cave of the Moon

There are two caverns in the Cave of the Moon, with the upper and lower chambers linked by an ornamental façade. The upper cavern has various small niches and five of full height. The interior is completely filled with the most brilliant masonry, remarkable even among Inca ruins for the skill of its cutting. The niches are particularly impressive. The five large niches have double jambs, with their recessed edges carved from single blocks—not, as is usual, from different blocks interlocking at the inner angle. A lateral chamber of this upper group has a long outer wall, with the receding rock outcrop as its back wall. The screening wall has three fine trapezoidal doorways, 1.6 meters (5¼ feet) tall, with a similar door at the south end. One doorway leads to a passage and stair down the rock face to the lower cave group. Here again, the cavern is associated with an ornamental façade that faces south, above the cave's entrance, with niched wings projecting on either side. Opposite, a rock outcrop has been sculpted into a huge throne, with a view of the tall forest and the entrance to the sacred cave. There are other carved and ma-

The cave of Choquequilla, above the Huarocondo river

sonry-lined caves, notably at Choquequilla (see plate, page 174) above the valley of the Anta river fifty-two kilometers (thirty-two miles) along the railway from Cuzco to Machu Picchu. These were evidently more than burial mausoleums: they were temples connected with the Incas' worship of the earth and all its unusual features.

Two final questions about Machu Picchu are these: When was South America's most famous ruin built, and when was it abandoned? The date of construction is fairly sure. The few

The temple of the three windows, from the east

chronicle mentions of Vilcabamba say that Pachacuti invaded this region immediately after his defeat of the Chancas in about 1438. A glance at the map of the Inca empire (page 14) shows why the Inca wanted to secure the north bank of the Apurímac: to protect the forest flank of Cuzco and to prevent remnants of the defeated Chancas from breaking out in this direction. The architecture of Machu Picchu confirms this "late imperial" Inca attribution. Although Bingham's excavators found large rubbish middens, the contents were all Inca; and there are no signs of prior occupation of the site, or of much alteration or rebuilding of its structures.

Bingham argued with characteristic gusto that Machu Picchu was far older. He claimed that it was no less than Tambo-toqo of the Incas' origin legend. This was the cave with three openings from which the Ayar brothers emerged on their migration toward Cuzco. The native chronicler Santacruz Pachacuti Yamqui wrote that the first Inca, Manco Capac, ordered that in his birthplace his Indians "should build masonry with a form of opening, consisting of three

windows, that signified the home of his fathers from whom he was descended. The first of these was called Tampottoco, the second Marasttoco, and the third Suticttoco." The building with three windows sounds very much like Machu Picchu's famous temple of three windows. And the "Tampu" of Tambo- or Tampu-toqo might have referred to the Tampu tribe that lived near Ollantaytambo and may have given that town its name. The cave of Tambo-toqo was located by all chroniclers at Paccaritambo, south of Cuzco. But there are virtually no remains there, which is surprising for a place that was so important in the Inca religion. Bingham's conviction that this legendary cave and the birthplace of the first Inca, Manco Capac, were in fact northwest of Cuzco is not entirely impossible. If only Machu Picchu's forested location and the antiquity of its buildings coincided with other elements of the legend, his bold claim could be correct. Machu Picchu has enough sacred architecture to mark it as a very holy place. But the weight of other evidence seems to rule out Bingham's attractive theory. Machu Picchu is on the wrong side of Cuzco to have been on the Ayar brothers' migration route.

Bingham went on to argue that Machu Picchu was Vilcabamba, the last refuge of the Incas after the Spanish invasion. When Manco Inca's rebellion of 1536–1537 failed, he retreated to the valley of the Vilcabamba river northwest of Cuzco. He hoped that the barrier of the high Vilcabamba mountains, the gorges of the Urubamba, and the forests of the area around Machu Picchu would prevent pursuit by the dreaded Europeans. His first refuge was a place called Vitcos, high up the Vilcabamba river. He reached it by taking the road that started near Ollantaytambo and ran northeast of Mount Verónica, to rejoin the Urubamba downstream of Machu Picchu at the bridge of Chuquichaca. Manco was wrong to think that he was beyond the reach of the Spaniards. As early as July 1537, a dashing conquistador called Rodrigo Orgóñez pursued the fugitive Inca along this road and came within a few minutes of capturing him at Vitcos. Manco himself escaped in the arms of his swiftest runners. Orgóñez returned to Cuzco with important spoils: twenty thousand of the Inca's followers, in-

The Urubamba river, at the eastern edge of Huayna Picchu

lated isolated groups of Spanish soldiers; and in 1539 he attempted to raise all Peru in a second valiant rebellion. The Spaniards were now more numerous and more firmly in control of the country. The second rebellion failed, and Francisco Pizarro sent his youngest brother, Gonzalo, to try to capture the fugitive Inca. Gonzalo marched to Vitcos, then on to a place called Pampaconas, and thence on foot down into the forests toward Vilcabamba. The Incas' attempts to defend their new refuge were defeated. Gonzalo Pizarro actually reached Vilcabamba but, like Orgóñez before him, he just failed to capture Manco. The Inca slipped off into hiding with friendly forest Indian tribes. The Spaniards again left the Vilcabamba region, convinced that it was too wild and remote to be worth occupying.

Manco established a neo-Inca state in this small corner of his father's former empire. The Spaniards were soon preoccupied with internecine quarrels over the rich empire they had seized. Their occupation of Peru degenerated into civil war between two factions of conquistadores. After the defeat, in 1542, of the faction opposed to the Pizarros, Manco—who regarded the Pizarros as his personal enemies—made the fatal mistake of giving sanctuary to six Spanish fugitives from the defeated side. He lodged these men at Vitcos and entertained them for some three years. But in 1545 they repaid the young Inca's hospitality with Spanish perfidy: they murdered him during a game of bowls or quoits, and tried unsuccessfully to escape to Spanish-occupied Peru.

Manco was succeeded in Vilcabamba by three sons, each of whom ruled the remote kingdom during the twenty-eight years after his death. The first, Sayri Tupac, eventually agreed to leave Vilcabamba and live as a puppet Inca in Spanish-occupied Peru. He built a palace of adobe and stone, part of which still stands at Yucay, between Pisac and Ollantaytambo (see plate, page 22). He was succeeded in 1560 by a less legitimate younger brother called Titu Cusi Yupanqui, an endearing extrovert who succeeded in spinning out fruitless negotiations with the Spaniards for a full decade. Titu Cusi also dictated a memoir that is the most powerful record of the

cluding some of his wives and children, vast herds of llamas and alpacas, and holy relics, including mummies of Inca rulers and one of the stone effigies from the shrine of Huanacauri. After such a defeat, Manco decided that Vitcos was too exposed. He started to build another capital called Vilcabamba deeper in the security of the Amazon forests.

During the ensuing years, Manco acted as a true guerrilla leader. His men raided convoys and travelers on the long road between Cuzco and the Pacific coast; he trapped and annihi-

The Urubamba river from the watchman's hut. The Prison Group, on the southeastern edge of the city, is on the left

Conquest from native eyes. Titu Cusi died suddenly, of disease or a stroke, in 1571. His brother Tupac Amaru succeeded, and sought to break off relations with Spanish Peru and revert to a traditional Inca way of life. Within a year of his accession, powerful Spanish forces invaded Vilcabamba and occupied Vitcos and the city of Vilcabamba. Tupac Amaru tried to imitate his father by fleeing to jungle tribes down the Urubamba; but he was pursued, captured, and led back to Cuzco for a hasty trial and execution on 24 September 1572.

After Hiram Bingham discovered the ruins of Machu Picchu in July 1911, he went on to the Vilcabamba region, downstream to the northwest. With characteristic energy and good luck, he rapidly discovered a ruin above a place called Rosaspata that is generally accepted to be Manco's first refuge, Vitcos. Still seeking Inca ruins, Bingham then moved off to the northwest, over a pass and down into the lowland forests. His reward was to discover more remains, heavily overgrown with jungle, at a place called Espíritu Pampa.

The problem now was to establish which of these ruins was Vilcabamba, the last Inca capital. Various Spanish envoys and missionaries had been admitted to the neo-Inca state, and their reports together with those of the Spaniards who finally invaded Vilcabamba provide clues about locations in this remote region. The evidence supporting Bingham's identification of Rosaspata as Vitcos seems conclusive. It was known that the city of Vilcabamba lay two long days' march from Vitcos. Bingham argued that Machu Picchu, which is this far to the east of Vitcos (Rosaspata), was in fact the lost capital city. He put forward various arguments to support his claim. But a careful study of the documentary evidence—including some manuscripts unknown to Bingham—demonstrates that the last refuge was the ruin, also discovered by Bingham, at Espíritu Pampa, two days' march to the northwest of Vitcos. The chronicles described Vilcabamba as being in a broad valley with semitropical vegetation at low altitude. This, together with the names of places on the road toward the missing Vilcabamba, made it clear that Espíritu Pampa was that lost city. None could describe Machu Picchu, on its knife-edge ridge, as being in a broad, low valley. But the conclusive evidence was a report of 1572 that Manco Inca's palace in Vilcabamba had been roofed in imitation curved Spanish roofing tiles instead of the traditional thatch. Bingham himself and later explorers found precisely such native-made roofing tiles embedded in the forest floor at Espíritu Pampa. It is therefore now accepted that Manco's Vilcabamba was at this site, far down in the Amazonian jungles.

How, then, did Machu Picchu fit into the post-Conquest Inca state? Bingham's excavations of burial caves and graves near Machu Picchu revealed over a hundred skeletal remains, the majority of which were of women. On the strength of this, he imagined Machu Picchu as a city of mamaconas, the hiding place of the holy women of Cuzco. He also imagined Manco's sons Titu Cusi and Tupac Amaru living in the King's Group of buildings and pampered by the temple women. The identification of Vilcabamba far away to the northwest at Espíritu Pampa has ruined this romantic vision. There is no evidence of any post-Conquest occupation of Machu Picchu and no reference to it in any contemporary literature of the state of Vilcabamba. We must therefore accept the sadly unromantic truth that Machu Picchu was already abandoned by the time that Manco retreated to Vilcabamba. The beautiful mountaintop city was unoccupied and forgotten, shrouded in mists and overgrown with tropical vegetation, until its thrilling rediscovery in the twentieth century.

The deep gorge of the Apurímac river, which defended the western approach to Cuzco, was crossed by a famous suspension bridge

SAIHUITE

O NE OF THE MOST IMPORTANT FUNCTIONS OF THE Inca priesthood was prediction and divination. A few shrines in different parts of the empire were venerated as places where priests could converse with the spirit world. Spanish missionaries were naturally determined to crush such manifestations of a rival religion—but they were slightly in awe of native sorcerers who might be in communication with the true devil. Cristóbal de Molina admitted the possibility that some of the predictions might be correct: "There were other shamans who had charge of the huacas [shrines], and among these were some who at certain shrines spoke with the devil and received his answers. They would tell the people whatever they wanted to learn ... and on a few occasions they gave true answers." Another priest, Pablo José de Arriaga, agreed: "Huaca-villac means 'he who speaks with the shrine': this is the chief priest, he who is responsible for guarding the huaca and speaking to it. He tells the people what he pretends it has told him—although sometimes the Devil really does speak through the stone."

One of the most holy oracle-shrines was located above the canyon of the Apurímac. This mighty river, whose name means great speaker or great oracle, was probably named after this famous oracle-shrine. According to Hernando de Santillán, a Spanish administrator who was particularly knowledgeable about the Incas, the coastal oracle of Pachacamac, the holiest of all pre-Inca shrines, told Topa Inca Yupanqui that it had four "sons," oracle-shrines that would tell the Inca whatever he wanted to know. One of these overlooked the Apurímac near Andahuaylas. Francisco Pizarro's secretary Pedro Sancho reported that when the invading Spaniards passed this place on their march to Cuzco, they found a temple full of silver slabs "twenty feet long by a foot wide and an inch or two thick" (6.10 meters by 31 centimeters by 2–5 centimeters).

By far the most detailed description of the Apurímac shrine came from the conqueror's cousin Pedro Pizarro. He learned about it from a soldier called Francisco Martín who had been captured by Manco Inca's men. This man had actually seen Manco Inca consult the oracle: "Manco Inca made the devil speak to him in front of this Francisco Martín, who says that he heard the voice of the devil answering what Manco Inca had asked him. [The Inca] said to [Martín]: "Look how my god speaks to me!" For here at Apurímac there was a highly painted hall inside which a thick pole was erected— thicker than a very fat man. This pole had many pieces broken off it, and it was covered in the blood of sacrifices offered to it. It was completely encircled by a band of gold, the width of a hand, which was welded to it in a form of inlay. In front it had two golden breasts the size of a woman's, fixed to the same band. They had this pole clothed in very delicate women's clothing, with many gold *copos*, which are a form of pin that the women of this land used. . . . Beside this thick pole there were other smaller ones in a line on either side, occupying the entire chamber from end to end. These poles were also bathed in blood and dressed in mantles like the large one, so that, with their copos, they resembled statues of women. The [Indians] said that the devil spoke to them from the large idol, and they called it Apu-rímac. The guardian of this was a lady called Asarpay, a sister of these Incas. She later jumped to her death from a very high pass on the descent toward the bridge over the river Apurímac. She covered her head and threw herself into the river where it runs near this cliff, from a height of over two hundred estados [315 meters or over a thousand feet], calling on Apurímac, the idol whom she had served." The priestess' suicide was a protest against Spanish desecration of her shrine.

The remains of this important shrine are still visible, on

The complex carvings on the principal, or upper, stone of Saihuite may have been a topographical model

rolling hills high above the Apurímac canyon. They are on the land of a hacienda called Sahuite, not far from the main road between Cuzco and the coast. The stones and shrines that survive are called either Saihuite or Concacha. They are near the town of Curahuasi, 190 kilometers (118 miles) along the road from Cuzco, and 45 kilometers (28 miles) from Abancay. This is high country, with rolling hills surrounded by mountains, but it is fertile. Tough Andean horses graze here, on highland meadows often broken by outcrops of lichen-covered rocks (see plates, pages 11–12).

The most striking of the Saihuite stones—known as the principal, or upper stone—looks from a distance like a broken flint: half a petrified orange resting on its hemisphere in the midst of a treeless meadow. As one approaches closer, the jagged top is seen to be covered in an intricate mass of carving: numerous figures, some in high relief, others almost freestanding. There are human beings armed with arrows, pumas, llamas, vicuñas, snakes, frogs, monkeys, lizards and even a crab. The faces of all but one of these figures have been smashed, presumably by some Spanish zealot charged with the extirpation of native "idolatry." The sole survivor is a puma who crouches severely at one side of the rock, almost as its guardian spirit. Between the figures is a labyrinth of tiny altars, stairways, gates and platforms. A most important feature is the network of grooves and channels that doubtless once carried liquids past the various figures, in some complicated ceremony of divination. All the grooves run down from the stone's highest point. The stone itself has been tilted by erosion or treasure seekers, so that the channels do not now run freely; but it is easy to imagine the mysterious rites that once took place at this oracle. The stone stands 2.6 meters (8½ feet) high, and its oval surface varies from 3.0 to 4.1 meters (10 to 13½ feet) in diameter. Its curving rim has notches that may once have held a golden cladding. Other places, such as the rocky shrine of Kenko above Cuzco, have similar carving and divination channels; but nothing is as elaborate as the upper stone of Saihuite, and no other stone stands so dramatically isolated. It has even been suggested

Terraces, channels, and small creatures cover the upper Saihuite stone. Notches along its rim may have held a golden cladding

that the rock's surface is a map. To the nineteenth-century French traveler Charles Wiener it was "a faithful reproduction of the region of the Andes and the works of the Peruvian architects and engineers: a form of topographical synthesis."

Over the brow of the hill, the land slopes down toward the distant Apurímac. There are more Saihuite stones here, notably a mighty carved boulder that the natives know as Rumihuasi (stone house). This rock, 6.1 meters (20 feet) wide, has been split, perhaps by lightning. The Incas had previously smoothed and shaped it into a gigantic sculpture. It is geometrical and abstract, with altar tables and small flights of steps. But its purpose was clearly prediction or divination. Eight shallow dishes are carved into its upper surface, and from one of these runs a groove intended for ritual effluents. The groove divides at the edge of the stone into two channels that end in rectangular basins.

Other rock outcrops in this area are similarly carved with channels and rectangular planes. Wiener reported a cyclopean

In the terraced valley north of Chinchero, there are three unusual rock shrines. The largest (center), known locally as Titicaca Rock, is carved with two stairways: one on its upper surface, visible here; the other in the dark cleft to the right (see plate, page 16). Another, the Chingana stone (see facing page), appears farther down the valley to the right. A third is pictured on page 176 (lower right plate)

A ceremonial stairway is carved on the face of the Chingana stone at Chinchero. A small stream runs below

wall almost sunk into swampy ground. He also described and sketched a large Inca hall half a day's ride across the hills to the north. This building, known as Incahuasi (Inca's house), looks across the great cleft of the Apurímac toward Vilcabamba and the Inca ruin of Choquequirau. It is a tall structure with three levels of niches one above the other. It corresponds best to Pedro Pizarro's description of the temple containing the Apurímac oracle. But the extraordinary rocks of Saihuite have a more powerful religious presence; and their location is closer to the foundations of the famous suspension bridge that once carried the royal Inca highway across the Apurímac.

In addition to shrines devoted to prediction and divination the Incas worshipped at many isolated landscape shrines and carved rock outcrops, the symbolism and meaning of which are only partially understood. In the immediate vicinity of

Cuzco there were over three hundred of these huacas, located on ceques that radiated from the temple of the sun and created a pattern possibly symbolic of the Inca calendar. Huacas were specific places or objects, distinguished by some special peculiarity, in which supernatural forces and spirits resided. To the Quechua Indian, even a small stone or stick from the vicinity of his home huaca could serve as a talisman, enabling him to carry the protective power of his huaca with him. Most huacas possessed the power of speech, or oracle. Some possessed demonic power, were feared, and destroyed if possible.

Caves and rocks, particularly those near rivers, streams or springs where the sound of rushing water spoke as the oracle, were the most prevalent huacas. These were often carved with shapes that embodied the power of the sun, the mountains, or the earth's forces, or were related to them. Virtually all carving of the huacas was nonrepresentational, made to mark the presence of man without depicting him, and was often in the form of ceremonial seats or niches. Some of the most precise work, such as that at Quillarumi, or the intihuatana at Machu Picchu, appears to have been dedicated to the worship of the sun, to mark specific points of the solar year. Some carving was more symbolic, such as the recurrent stepped design, the puma, and the incised channels used for offertory rites and divination ceremonies. Rarely, as far as we know, was representational carving employed, as on the principal, or upper, stone of Saihuite.

It was the Incas' acts of worship and ritual which endowed these shrines with meaning. Many of the small huacas outside Cuzco were cared for by the clan groups living near them, thus enabling much of the population to serve as their own priesthood. In addition, participation in public ceremonies relating to the Inca calendar and ancestor worship, annual initiation rites of noble youths at Huanacauri hill, and pilgrimages to religious sites like the Island of the Sun provided involvement in rituals and assured cultural continuity.

Offertory, or divination, channels on Rumi-huasi, one of the stones of Saihuite

The zigzag offertory channel at Kenko flows down to a cave shrine associated with the underworld and was probably related to rites venerating the dead as well as to divination ceremonies

The massive outcrop at Kenko, above Cuzco, is covered with carving as well as with natural faults and cavities. A cavelike passageway beyond the wooden rail was apparently associated with the forces of the underworld and worship of the dead. To the left of the outcrop is a large stone shaped like a puma (see facing page)

The puma on the summit of Puma Orco, thirty miles south of Cuzco

The seated puma at Kenko

The offertory channel at Urco, near Calca, ends in the head of a snake

The altar stone at the mouth of the cave shrine of Choquequilla, near Pachar. The top of the stone was destroyed by vandals. The stepped design is repeated at the base and sides of the altar

A semicircular cut, eight feet across, at Quillarumi, near Anta

A ceremonial seat below the cave openings at Puma Orco (see page 62)

The stepped design at Quispihuara shrine, north of Sacsahuaman

The Tired Stone, at Sacsahuaman north of Rodadero hill

A pumalike stone at Saihuite

A post-Conquest shrine near Vitcos and the Vilcabamba valley

The gnomon at Intiwatana, downstream from Machu Picchu

The third rock shrine in the valley near Chinchero

The "white rock" Yurac Rumi, near Vitcos, an important shrine of the post-Conquest state of Vilcabamba. It was discovered by Hiram Bingham a month after finding Machu Picchu

TARAHUASI

THE ROAD FROM CUZCO WEST TOWARD THE COAST drops dramatically into the mighty canyon of the Apurímac. As we have seen, Apu-rímac means great oracle; and on the Cuzco side of the canyon was a royal lodging called Rimac-tampu (oracle's inn), a name that Spaniards have contracted to Limatambo. Two kilometers south of the modern town of Limatambo—seventy-six kilometers (forty-seven miles) from Cuzco—is the magnificent but isolated ruin of the tambo, just off the main road on a farm called Tarahuasi. The ruin does not look like the remains of an inn or a lodging. There is a long terrace wall of strongly rusticated polygonal masonry. In its center a monumental stairway leads up to the terrace, and above the stair is an earth-filled platform projecting from the hillside. The Incas clad three sides of this rectangular platform with masonry of the very highest quality. A solemn line of tall, trapezoidal, sentry-box niches adorns its three faces: twelve along the front looking down over the valley, and eight in each side wall. The two walls are imposing, almost theatrical. It is a place for ritual, with mummies or liveried attendants in the tall niches. At the time of the Conquest, this hill was called Vilcaconga, and the chronicler Miguel de Estete mentioned that on this hillside the natives had an idol also called Vilcaconga. Such an idol would have corresponded to the famous Apurímac oracle at Saihuite. The ruins of Tarahuasi look more like a shrine to this idol than part of an inn, and no further building remains were found here when the site was excavated and restored by Luis Valcárcel and J. M. Franco Inojosa in the 1930s.

The slope of Vilcaconga played an important role during Pizarro's march toward Cuzco at the start of the Conquest. The dashing Hernando de Soto had pushed ahead of Pizarro, Almagro and the slower part of the small invading army. He decided to hurry forward with his force of forty mounted men in order to be the first to reach Cuzco. His men successfully forded the Apurímac and climbed the eastern wall of its canyon, on the last lap. They rested for two days at the lodgings of Rimac-tampu.

On Saturday, 8 November 1533, they set off up the hill of Vilcaconga. As Juan Ruiz de Arce recalled: "We were marching along with no thought of a line of battle. We had been inflicting very long day's marches on the horses. Because of this we were leading them up the pass by their halters, marching in this way in groups of four." The Spaniards paused in the midday heat to feed the horses some maize. At this moment three or four thousand Inca warriors appeared along the crest of the hill. They charged down, completely covering the hillside. Soto shouted to his men to form line of battle, but it was too late. The Indians hurled a barrage of slingstones and missiles, which caused some Spaniards to scatter. Others ran to their horses, mounted, and tried to spur them up to the crest of the hill. "The horses were so exhausted that they could not catch breath sufficiently to attack such a multitude of enemy with any dash. [The natives] never stopped harassing and worrying them with the javelins, stones and arrows they were firing. They exhausted them to such a degree that the riders could hardly raise their horses to a trot, and some not even to a walk. As the Indians perceived the horses' exhaustion, they began to attack with greater fury." For once the natives had caught the Spaniards in hand-to-hand combat, at a time and place where the dreaded horses could not function. They killed five Spaniards—two on their horses, and three before they could mount—and wounded seventeen. The dead Spaniards all had their heads split open by stone battle-axes. It was the conquerors' worst defeat.

*The shrine of Tarahuasi near the town of Limatambo above the Apurímac river
has one of the finest stretches of polygonal retaining wall in Peru*

Polygonal masonry in the lower retaining wall

As night fell, the remainder of Soto's force huddled on a hillock and tried to tend their wounded. Diego de Trujillo wrote, "We were in great hardship that night, for it snowed and the wounded men complained greatly of the cold. The Indians, who kept us encircled with many fires all round us, shouted at us: 'We do not want to kill you by night, but rather by day, so that we can have sport with you!'" The Spaniards spent the night on guard, armed and fearful. Then, in the middle of the night, they heard the distant sound of a Spanish trumpet. No noise could have been more welcome. Francisco Pizarro had, with amazing foresight, sent a further force of cavalry ahead to reinforce Soto. These men had hurried forward and at Limatambo they were told about the battle of Vilcaconga. Their trumpeter Alconchel sounded his bugle like a foghorn in the night, and the two forces managed to link up in the darkness. So, when the mists cleared next day, Soto's battered force was miraculously doubled. It charged

into action with characteristic courage and the Inca army was soon dispersed.

A chastened Hernando de Soto rested his men near the top of the ascent and awaited the arrival of his leader. Pizarro came the following day and the combined force marched forward toward Cuzco. It was at this moment that the young Manco Inca first made contact with the invading Spaniards. He was a prince of the royal faction that had been defeated by Atahualpa's generals. He was therefore a fugitive, "fleeing from Atahualpa's men to prevent their killing him. He came all alone and abandoned, looking like a common Indian." He seemed younger than his twenty years and was wearing a yellow cotton tunic. The Spaniards were delighted to have in their midst so important a pretender to the Inca throne, particularly as he regarded them as his saviors in the native civil war. The Spaniards had with them Atahualpa's most senior general, the formidable old warrior Chalcuchima. They had him in chains and under guard, for they suspected that he wanted to avenge the murder of his Inca, Atahualpa. Manco Inca now told them that Chalcuchima had passed a message to his fellow general Quisquis in Cuzco. Chalcuchima was thus responsible for the ambush by Quisquis' men on the slope of Vilcaconga.

Pizarro delivered a chilling announcement to his prisoner Chalcuchima: "'You have seen how, with the help of God, we have always defeated you Indians. It will be the same in the future. . . . You can rest assured that you yourself will never see Cuzco again. For . . . I shall have you burned alive!'" Chalcuchima was brought out into the square of a town called Jaquijahuana, at the top of the ascent of Vilcaconga. The Dominican friar Vicente de Valverde tried to make him accept a deathbed conversion to Christianity. But the warrior would have none of it. He declared that he had no wish to become a Christian, and found Christian law incomprehensible. So he was set alight. As he burned to death he called on the god Viracocha, and on his friend Quisquis, to avenge him.

VILCASHUAMAN

THE INCAS CONSIDERED VILCAS OR VILCAS-HUAMÁN as the central point of their empire. It lay halfway between Cuzco and the Pacific coast, and "they say that it is exactly as far from Quito to Vilcas as it is from Vilcas to the farthest limit of the Incas' conquests on the Maule river in Chile." This measurement was not strictly accurate. From Vilcashuamán to the northern limit of Inca rule, at Pasto in what is now Colombia, is under two thousand kilometers (about twelve hundred miles), whereas from Vilcashuamán to the Maule river in Chilean Araucania is over three thousand kilometers (about nineteen hundred miles). It was, however, the main crossroads, the place where the road from Cuzco to the coast crossed the highway running along the length of the Andes. The name Vilcas means sacred and Huaman is a falcon.

Vilcashuamán was once in the lands of the Chanca tribe, the people who tried to capture Cuzco in about 1440 and were then overwhelmed in the first rush of Inca expansion. The chroniclers agree that Pachacuti and his son Topa Inca Yupanqui conquered this region and founded Vilcashuamán. A Spanish corregidor called Pedro de Carvajal described the place in 1586. He said that the rulers "founded in this location of Vilcas Huamán a city and frontier post with thirty thousand Indians as garrison. [They] began to construct forts and buildings in it. Parts of these and their foundations are visible at present, for they were all of cut stone." Pedro de Cieza de León also wrote that local people made these buildings, but under the direction of "masters from Cuzco to measure out the plans and show the way in which they must lay the stones and bricks in the building."

The most important structure in Vilcashuamán was the temple of the sun. It rose on one side of a vast square, with the temple to the sun itself and an adjacent temple to the moon all built of characteristically excellent masonry. Cieza de León visited it and wrote: "The temple of the sun, which was made of stones laid upon one another with great skill, had two main doorways. To enter them, there were two stone stairways which, by my count, had thirty steps each. Inside this temple there were rooms for the priests and for those who watched over the vestals, the mamaconas, who observed their vows faithfully." Inside the temple was a golden effigy of the sun. "The Indians tell that the image of the sun was of enormous value, and that there was great treasure both in the temple and buried." Such grandeur was an element of Inca policy: "The Incas worshipped [the sun and moon] and ordered all the Indians they were conquering to worship these gods and to destroy the stone idols that they already had."

Fifty years after the Conquest, Pedro de Carvajal wrote, "This temple or house that contained the sun effigy is still standing. It serves as a church, where Mass is . . . said for people at the royal market that is founded here." Four centuries later the ruins of Vilcashuamán are pathetically overgrown, fallen and buried under the houses of a Peruvian village. It is just possible to imagine the disposition of the original temple. The parish church of Saint John the Baptist used to occupy most of the temple building along the south side of the large square. The French artist Léonce Angrand sketched the church in 1849 and showed clearly how its adobes rose above a wall of Inca masonry that contained five trapezoidal doors or niches. The Inca wall is still there, built of dark granite in beautiful courses of rectangular ashlars, but the church has been rebuilt on a north-south axis with its end wall against the Inca façade. A Spanish colonial arch, fluted pilasters and a cornice have been added, superfluously, to the austere Inca door.

A terrace wall with tall niches is one of the few remains of the sumptuous sun temple at Vilcashuamán

The original temple occupied the crown of the hill on which Vilcashuamán is built. The temple itself was raised on three tiers of terraces, and enough is visible above ground and in Angrand's sketch to reconstruct part of these terraces. The upper level had a smooth polygonal wall, broken only by the two flights of stairs. The middle level had a satisfying pattern of niches: some the height of a man alternating with smaller ones at shoulder level. The lowest tier had a curious

arrangement of alternating salient and entrant stretches of wall. It is a plan peculiar to Vilcashuamán. Such regular buttressing may have given added strength to the terrace walls. The lines of terraces project northward at one side of the church to form another platform, and it is here that we can see them best. A fine stretch of the middle and lower levels rears above the detritus of centuries. As Cieza de León observed in the 1540s, "What can be seen are only the foundations of the buildings and the walls and enclosures of the shrines . . . and of the temple with its stairways. For it has fallen into ruins and is overgrown with grass, and the storehouses have fallen down. In a word, it was once what it no longer is; and by what it is, we can judge what it was." It is surprising that so famous a ruin was never excavated or restored until the 1980s.

The most spectacular surviving structure in Vilcashuamán once faced the sun temple, in the middle of the great square, but is now separated from it by streets of the modern village. This ruin is a stepped usnu. It rises in four terraces of superb masonry, a building unique among Inca ruins, more like a small version of the mighty stepped pyramids of Mexico. It was a monument worthy of South America's most powerful ruler. Carvajal said of the square that it was "very large, capable of holding twenty thousand men. The Inca ordered it built by hand, and he drained a very large lake that used to be there for this purpose." And Cieza de León wrote that "to one side of this plaza, toward the rising sun, there was a shrine of the [Inca] lords, made of stone and surrounded by a low wall from which a smallish terrace emerged, some six feet wide, with other terraces successively mounted upon it, until on the summit there was the throne to which the lord went to make his oration. This throne was made of a single rock, so large that it measures eleven feet long by seven wide, and on which two seats had been cut for this purpose. They say that this stone used to be covered in ornaments of gold and precious stones to adorn the place that they venerated and esteemed so greatly. [There was similar decoration] on another stone, not small, which is still in the middle of this

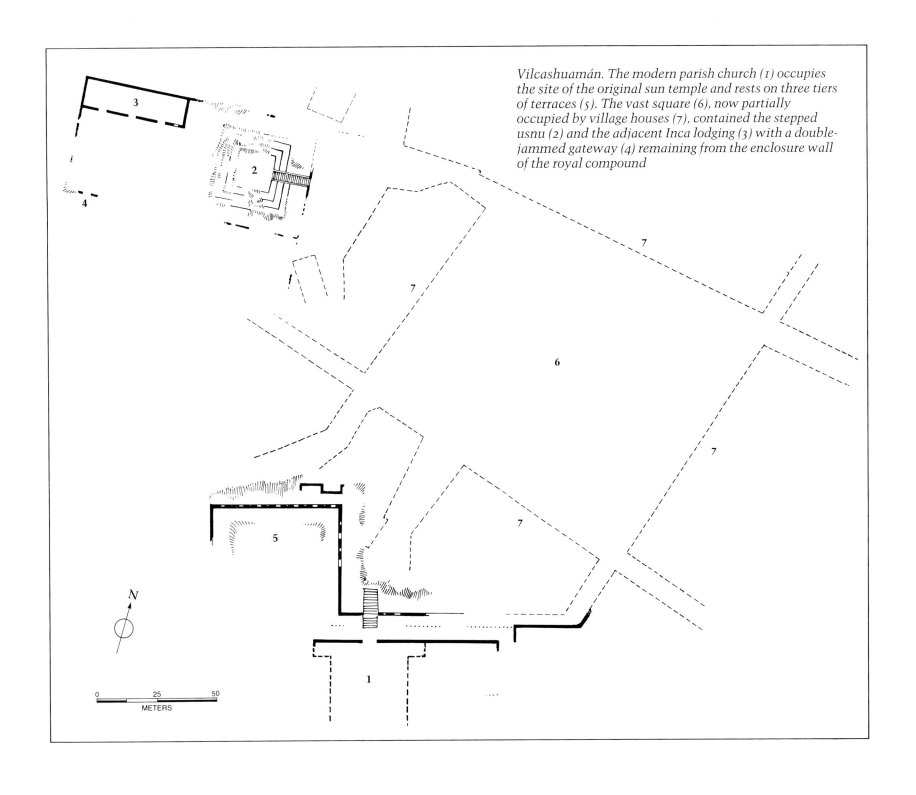

Vilcashuamán. The modern parish church (1) occupies the site of the original sun temple and rests on three tiers of terraces (5). The vast square (6), now partially occupied by village houses (7), contained the stepped usnu (2) and the adjacent Inca lodging (3) with a double-jammed gateway (4) remaining from the enclosure wall of the royal compound

N

0   25   50
METERS

The famous usnu (administrative platform) is the best surviving Inca stepped pyramid

square. This is a form of font, where they killed and sacrificed young animals and (so they say) children, whose blood they used to offer to their gods. Some of the treasure that was buried in these terraces has been found by the Spaniards.''

Carvajal left a vivid description of this ceremonial. He wrote that the usnu was ''a platform surrounded by masonry, five estados high. It has a stone staircase, admirably made and cut in a theatrical manner. This is where the Inca used to go in person to be seen, and on top of it were two large stone seats, covered in gold at that time, where the Inca and his wife used to sit, as if on tribunes, and from which they worshipped the sun. When he was on this theater or throne, all his guard

The double-seated throne atop the usnu, the palace below

An offertory stone on the eastern edge of Vilcashuamán

protected its gates with much vigilance. He would sit there under a great canopy of plumage of a thousand colors, and the posts on which this awning rested were of gold. Twelve very aged captains of his own lineage used to carry the canopy. . . . The sacrifices they performed were as follows: to the creator of all things, whom they called Tiki Viracocha, the Inca would offer two small creatures, very clean, without mark or blemish and beautiful and selected. These were brought to him well prepared and adorned in their manner, with lovely clothes. He offered them, and killed them by cutting their throats. They then made a sacrifice to the sun of two other creatures, in the same manner; and then of two more creatures to the earth, which they called Pacha mama. They then offered a fat, white, chosen [llama] kid to the Lightning, which they called Catoylla or Illapa. They made these sacrifices, praying for health and good fortune for the Inca."

The majestic usnu still stands, and the stone block with the Inca's two seats is still at the top of the theatrical staircase. But the building is in a sorry state of disrepair. Spanish treasure seekers have dug into its terraces. A mass of vegetation has prized apart the interlocking Inca stones—I myself once spent two days cutting away the worst of these bushes with a machete. The outer wall has been ransacked for building blocks: it was largely intact in Angrand's and Wiener's drawings, but is now little more than a short stretch to the right of the monumental gate at the foot of the stairs. One detail has been revealed by the damage to the usnu. Its casing of dark granite masonry was arranged in tidy courses wherever it was visible. But the bases of the retaining walls have been exposed where the terraces have tumbled, and the hidden walling is of polygonal masonry—a sure sign that the Incas themselves valued coursed masonry above polygonal.

The walled enclosure of the usnu has the remains of a large Inca hall, known locally as the house of Topa Inca, on the side away from the square. In Wiener's plan he marks "unrecognizable ruins" and a "temple" a hundred meters farther west. We know from Cieza de León and other authors that the Incas had a large royal palace at Vilcashuamán. A close relative of the Inca ruled over this prosperous and strategic province. The local tribes had to supply levies of up to forty thousand people for his service, "and solely to guard the gates there were forty gatekeepers." There were also, according to Pedro de Carvajal, five hundred acclas working for the temple and a further five hundred mamaconas for the Inca. Cieza de León also described a vast depot of seven hundred storage huts at Vilcashuamán.

Ever since its conquest and foundation by Pachacuti and Topa Inca, Vilcashuamán was an important garrison city. It was mentioned as a valuable prize in the civil war between Huascar and Atahualpa on the eve of the Spanish Conquest. When Pizarro sent two Spaniards from Cajamarca to supervise the sack of Cuzco for Atahualpa's ransom, "the Indians carried them on their shoulders in litters. When the chiefs of this district [of Vilcashuamán] learned that the two Spaniards were going to Cuzco, they went out to the Tambo of Vilcas to pay homage to them and serve them." This subservience did not last for long. When Pizarro advanced toward Cuzco later in 1533, Atahualpa's troops planned to mount a resistance in Vilcas. They were frustrated by the speed of a force of Spanish cavalry under Hernando de Soto. Soto's men rode past the native sentries and entered Vilcashuamán early on 29 October. Atahualpa's men were away hunting. Diego de Trujillo described the action: "They had left their tents, their women and a few Indian men in Vilcas and we captured these, taking possession of everything that was there, at the hour of dawn which was when we entered Vilcas. We thought that there were no more troops than those who had been there. But at the hour of vespers, when the Indians had been informed [of our arrival] they came from the steepest direction and attacked us, and we them. Because of the roughness of the terrain, they gained on us rather than we on them. Some Spaniards distinguished themselves . . . by winning a height from the Indians and defending it strongly. On that day the Indians killed a white horse belonging to Alonso Tabuyo. We were forced to retreat to the square of Vilcas and all spent that night under arms. The Indians attacked next day with great spirit. They

were carrying banners made from the mane and tail of the white horse they had killed. We were forced to release the booty of theirs that we were holding: the women and Indians who were in charge of all their flocks. Then they withdrew." Although neither side won this battle, the native army had failed to stop a small force of Spanish horsemen. The Incas withdrew toward Cuzco. "Counting those who went, those who remained there, and the natives of the district, a vast quantity of Indians had assembled. We all agreed that there could have been twenty-five thousand Indian warriors." With the retreat of this army, the invading Spaniards were able to spend two days picking their way, unmolested, down the spectacular descent of almost two thousand meters (six thousand feet) to the hot gorge of the Pampas river far below.

Vilcashuamán had two brief moments of glory after the Conquest. Both were poignant reminders of the vanished grandeur of the Incas. In 1568 Manco Inca's son Sayri Tupac decided to leave his father's refuge of Vilcabamba and to live in Spanish-occupied Peru. He went down to Lima to meet the Spanish viceroy and then made a progress along the royal highway toward Cuzco. He paused at Vilcashuamán and there were emotional scenes as the natives paid homage and tried to relive their glorious past. A few years later a stern new viceroy, Francisco de Toledo, moved along this road and also paused at Vilcas. He outraged the native chiefs by usurping the privileges of an Inca ruler: "He reached Vilcas-huamán and mounted the steps to the throne and usnu of the Inca, and was received thus, like the Inca himself, by all the chief lords. And he ordered the oldest and most important chief to mount the usnu."

The region of Vilcas declined, like so much of Peru, after the Spanish Conquest. A report of 1586 admitted that "the Indians of this province [of Vilcas] were in far greater numbers than they are now. The natives say that the reason for their diminution was the excessive work they are forced to perform in the mercury and silver mines and the sugar mills. In addition, it is caused by the personal service they go to do in the city of Guamanga [Ayacucho] and on the cattle ranches and

*The view west from the usnu, toward the Pampas river. One gateway
remains from the walled enclosure around the palace courtyard*

other work in which they labor. Since these are outside their lands, and there are changes of climate in the places where they go to work, they are exposed to many diseases, from which the greater part of them have died."

Vilcashuamán is now a small village, remote on its hilltop, perched on the ruins of the great Inca city whose temples have been pillaged for building blocks, and surrounded by rolling, hilly country with few trees and little population.

TEMPLE OF VIRACOCHA, RAQCHI

THE INCAS' LEGENDARY CREATOR-GOD, VIRACOCHA, was said to have originated in Lake Titicaca. After creating the world, Viracocha and his followers moved northward, down the Vilcanota valley toward Cuzco. Spanish priests and missionaries were delighted by this legend. Viracocha corresponded admirably to the single creator-god of Christianity. The Viracocha of Inca legend, when transcribed by Spanish chroniclers, came to sound more and more like an apostle from the New Testament.

Juan de Betanzos, the Spanish officer who married an Inca princess, asked his Indian informants about Viracocha's appearance. They said that a stone statue of the god depicted him as "a man of tall stature who wore a white robe that fell to his feet and which he wore belted. He wore his hair short, with a form of crown on his head like a priest's. He went without a hat. In his hands he carried an object that now appears to them like the breviaries that priests carry. . . . They told me that he was called Kon Tiki Viracocha Pachayachachic, which means 'God, Creator of the World.'" Pedro de Cieza de León, an admirably dispassionate observer, actually went to see a famous statue of Viracocha at a place now called Raqchi. He effectively debunked his compatriots' idea that the statue showed Viracocha looking like Saint Bartholomew or one of the other apostles—not that this stopped later chroniclers from repeating the identification. Cieza wrote: "I went to see this idol [in 1549], for some Spaniards affirm that it might have been an apostle. I have heard many say that it held [rosary] beads in its hands but, unless I am blind, this is nonsense. For although I examined it carefully I could see no such thing. It simply had its hands above its hips, with the arms folded, and on its belt signs that must have signified that the robe it wore was fastened with buttons."

The Viracocha legend went on to say that the god moved through the land with his followers, creating all known living things. At Manta, in what is now southern Ecuador, Viracocha told his companions that he was leaving but would eventually return to them. "Having said this he went to sea with his two servants, moving across the water as if it were land, without sinking." Native Peruvians identified Europeans with Viracocha because of this legend. At the very outset of the Conquest, they hesitated to attack the Spaniards in case they might be the returning Viracocha—although they were soon disabused and learned that the conquistadores were mere brutal mortals. Throughout colonial times, however, Peruvian natives often addressed Spaniards as "Viracocha."

The famous statue of Viracocha that Cieza visited was beside the upper Vilcanota river at a place then known as Cacha. The statue has long since been destroyed; but remains of the Incas' largest temple still stand. They are behind the village of Raqchi, on the road between Titicaca and Cuzco but remote from any large city. The isolated location was chosen because it was here that Viracocha performed a celebrated miracle. While the god was moving northward down the Vilcanota he was insulted by the local people. To demonstrate his divinity, he summoned down fire from heaven. The hill behind Cacha was consumed by fire, which the god then proceeded to quench with his staff. The local people were suitably impressed and cowed. The scorched hillside, with volcanic pumice or tuff that Cieza described as being as light as cork, is still visible a few hundred meters above the temple.

The surviving central wall of the temple of Viracocha looks from a distance like a great aqueduct. It supported the largest known Inca roof

A row of round stone and adobe piers on each side of the central wall took some of the weight of the roof.
Openings in the central wall had lintels of small logs, with apertures above to relieve the weight of the adobe

This was a flow of lava from the volcano Quisma Chata.

The Viracocha temple was a vast rectangular hall with a pitched roof supported by a monumental central wall. Its scale is impressive. The plan measures 92 by 25.25 meters (302 by 83 feet) and the great dividing wall is 12 meters (over 39 feet) tall and 1.65 meters (some 5½ feet) thick. The roofed area was enormous for a people without the arch. It covered no less than 2,323 square meters (25,000 square feet). It is thus the largest surviving hall built by the Incas. The roof has vanished, but much of the central wall still stands, towering over the river valley like some gigantic Roman aqueduct.

Enough remains of the temple to deduce its original construction techniques. The central wall provides the clues. It consists of eleven rectangular "piers" supporting the solid upper part of the wall. The piers are built of fine Inca masonry —polygonal but arranged in rough courses—to a height of some 2.8 meters (over 9 feet). Above this, the piers and the wall they support are of adobe. The ten openings between the piers are 2.7 meters (almost 9 feet) wide and were once spanned by wooden lintels. The third pier from the southern end shows signs of these lintels in its adobes: there were five or possibly seven wooden beams, relatively thin poles 10 to 15 centimeters (4 to 6 inches) in diameter. Adobe is a heavy material; and the high, thick central wall would have weighed heavily on these delicate wooden lintels. Gasparini and Margolies have shown that the Incas solved the problem of the thrust by opening a large squarish window above each lintel. The sides of these windows slope inward and continue upward the trapezoidal incline of the doorways below. Above the windows are other small openings, which in turn relieve pressure on the lintels of the windows themselves. Earlier observers had always assumed that these upper openings indicated two or three stories in the temple. Careful observation by Gasparini showed that there was a system of beams supporting the enormous pitched roof; but he found no evidence of upper floors. The openings were simply to lessen the wall's weight load, and to spread light in the temple's gloomy interior.

Raqchi's only surviving circular column stands near one of the two gateways at the southern end of the temple

On either side of the eleven piers of the central wall were sturdy round columns. These are unique in Inca architecture. Round wooden poles were used to support roofs of kallanka halls at Huánuco and other towns; rectangular monoliths or masonry piers supported the open walls of masmas at and near Machu Picchu; and there were a few quadrilateral adobe columns in coastal Inca sites such as Tambo Colorado, and Incahuasi in the Cañete valley. But none of them compares with Raqchi's cylindrical columns. These begin, as does the central wall, with stone foundations. The highest surviving column rises to 6 meters (over 19½ feet), with the masonry to a height of 3.3 meters (almost 11 feet) topped by adobe. In the top of this column can be seen notches that once held beams: there are corresponding notches for the other ends of the beams in the central wall. Gasparini and Margolies argue convincingly that these beams were too weak to support an upper story. They must have been part of a frame of roof girders. The end walls of the temple were doubtless gabled to give further support to the roof.

Garcilaso de la Vega wrote a detailed but baffling description of the Viracocha temple. He said that it had four gates, but that only one gate on the eastern wall was open. This conflicts with evidence on the ground: from the ruins it is clear that the temple had two entrances on its southern, short wall and apparently none in the other walls. Garcilaso also described a labyrinth of stone partition walls within the temple. "These walls were spaced out at intervals of seven feet and each was three feet thick. There were twelve passages between these walls. . . . On entering the temple by the main gate, people turned right down the first passage until they came to the wall at the right-hand side of the temple; they then turned left down the second passage and went on till they came to the opposite wall. There they turned right again down the third passage, and by following the series of passages in the plan, went through the whole of the covered part of the temple, passage by passage, until they came to the twelfth and last, where there was a staircase up to the upper floor.

"Facing either end of each passage were embrasurelike windows that admitted sufficient light into the passages. Under each window there was a niche in the wall in which an attendant could sit without reducing the width of the passage. . . . Instead of a high altar there was a square chapel with walls

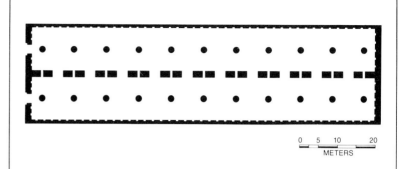

The plan of the great Viracocha temple at Raqchi, showing the central piers flanked by eleven pairs of circular columns

twelve feet long, covered in shining black flagstones fitted into one another and rising in a ceiling of four pitches. This was the most notable part of the whole structure. Within this chapel, there was a tabernacle in the thickness of the temple wall, and this contained the effigy of the Viracocha apparition."

It is possible to imagine Garcilaso's zigzag approach to the Viracocha statue, by tracing a path starting from the southern wall of the temple and moving right and left around the columns and through the openings in the central wall. This would provide the twelve passages of Garcilaso's description. It is also possible that a pilgrim or celebrant zigzagged inward along one side of the temple and returned in the same way on the far side. The stone sections of the central piers have trapezoidal windows cut with great care through the thickness of their masonry: these could have been some of Garcilaso's "embrasurelike windows." There are also square holes near the top of the masonry on the inner sides of the central openings: these clearly held some form of beam, possibly to support hanging curtains.

Raqchi's magnificent temple was too holy a shrine to escape the wrath of Christian zealots. Garcilaso lamented that "although the temple was so curious in its construction, it was destroyed by the Spaniards, like so many other notable works found in Peru, which they should have preserved at

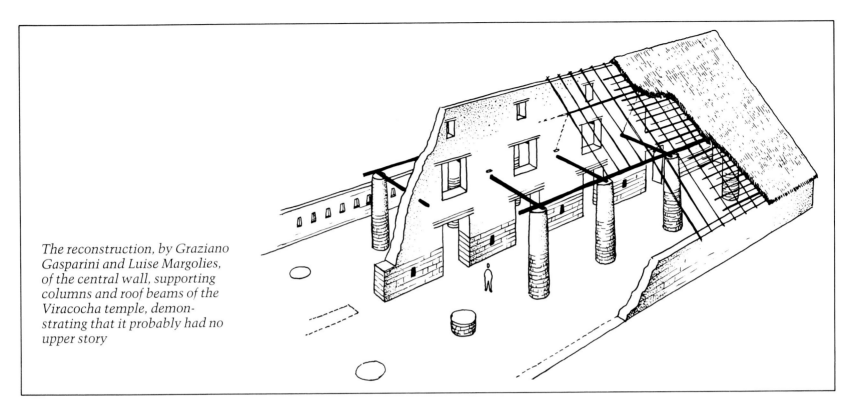

The reconstruction, by Graziano Gasparini and Luise Margolies, of the central wall, supporting columns and roof beams of the Viracocha temple, demonstrating that it probably had no upper story

their expense so that in future centuries people might see the glorious things they had won by strength of arms and good fortune. But they have deliberately razed them to the ground, as if from jealousy, so that today only the foundations of the building remain."

The Viracocha shrine at Raqchi consisted of more than the towering four-aisled basilica. The sacred precinct included the lava flows of Viracocha's miracle. A curtain wall 3.5 kilometers (over 2 miles) long runs along the crests of the surrounding hills and encloses an area of 80 hectares (198 acres).

Beside the temple is a series of five cancha-like courts, with twelve pairs of houses arranged along a straight avenue. All measurements of walls and angles at Raqchi are highly accurate, so that the view down this avenue is satisfyingly symmetrical. The enclosures are separated by pairs of back-to-back houses, similar to the ones in Ollantaytambo or at

Cusichaca downstream on the opposite bank of the Urubamba. These twinned houses echo the main temple in having stone in the lower part of their walls, with adobe for the upper walls and gables. They have rows of fine niches on their inner walls, as do pairs of ungabled houses on the south side of each court. The tidy compounds may have housed temple priests, or pilgrims arriving to worship at the shrine, or armies of soldiers and laborers passing along the strategic Vilcanota valley. South of the enclosures are some eighty circular structures, each roughly 8 meters (26 feet) in diameter. They were evidently storage qollqas but, as so often in Inca architecture, they are significantly different from similar structures elsewhere, by being wider, sunk below ground, and possibly unroofed. There are thus unanswered questions about Raqchi's magnificent Viracocha temple, despite the wealth of evidence in documents and in the strange ruins themselves.

The remote plain of Huánuco from the hill south of the town where lines of qollqas (storehouses) still stand.
Even from a distance, the usnu clearly dominates the central square. The kallankas are visible to the right

HUÁNUCO

WHEN FRANCISCO PIZARRO CAPTURED THE INCA ATAHUALPA at the outset of the Spanish Conquest, the Peruvian monarch told his captors that there was a province called Huánuco, ten days' march from where they were holding him at Cajamarca, and that it was rich in gold mines. Early in 1533, while the Inca's ransom was still being accumulated, Pizarro sent his brother Hernando to sack the coastal temple of Pachacamac and to explore the rich empire they planned to seize. During this reconnaissance, Hernando Pizarro climbed into the Andes to meet Atahualpa's most powerful general, Chalcuchima. Hernando persuaded Chalcuchima that his Inca wanted him to return to Cajamarca with the Spaniards. This Pizarro brother thus had the privilege of traveling along the main Inca highway in the company of the empire's greatest military commander. When they reached Huánuco, the largest provincial city in this part of central Peru, they were entertained for two days with a series of festivities.

Huánuco lies at an elevation of over 3,700 meters (12,150 feet) near the edge of a high, flat *puna* surrounded by mountains. (A puna is a cold, treeless, upland savannah carpeted in tough, pale-green ichu grass and watered by mountain streams, icy tarns and mossy bogs.) The ruins are near the headwaters of the Marañón, the river that becomes the main Amazon, above the pretty town of La Unión (formerly Aguamiro). The Incas built a stepped road that climbs for an amazing 963 meters (3,160 feet) from the river to Huánuco's puna (see plate, page 20). Miguel de Estete, who was with Hernando Pizarro on his reconnaissance noted that the road near Huánuco was paved with flagstones, and had "channels to carry water: they told us that this was done because of the snows that fall on this region at certain seasons of the year." Its altitude has saved Huánuco. The Spaniards tried to settle in the Inca city in 1539 and started to build blocks of European houses in the enormous central square. But the place was too remote, rainy and cold for Spaniards. Within a few years, the conquerors moved their settlement to a warmer, lower location eighty kilometers (fifty miles) to the east, and this new town is the place now called Huánuco. The old Inca city, known today as Huánuco Viejo (or Huánuco Pampa), has remained undisturbed on its high puna, hardly pillaged by later builders, scarcely occupied, and, because it is on firm ground, little buried by sediment. With remains of over thirty-five hundred structures covering two square kilometers (some five hundred acres), it is the largest undamaged Inca ruin, with all its stone buildings merely tumbled by the ravages of time and earthquakes.

The brief Spanish occupation of Huánuco was in response to a gallant and little-known chapter of native resistance. During Manco Inca's first rebellion, an Inca army attempted to invest and capture the Spaniards' coastal city of Lima. Their magnificently plumed phalanxes advanced bravely toward the new Spanish town. But at sea level, on the open coastal plain, they were no match for Spanish cavalry and they fell in their thousands, cut down by European horsemen and steel swords and lances.

One Inca general, Illa Tupac, survived this disaster and established himself as warlord of the region around Huánuco. He made a successful attack on a column led by Alonso de Alvarado, as it advanced on Abancay in 1537. In the following year he organized a revolt by tribes of the Conchucos region north of Huánuco. Thousands of natives swept down on the northern coastal town of Trujillo, killing any Spaniards they could catch. At the time of Manco Inca's second rebellion, in 1539, Illa Tupac was already in control of this strategic part of

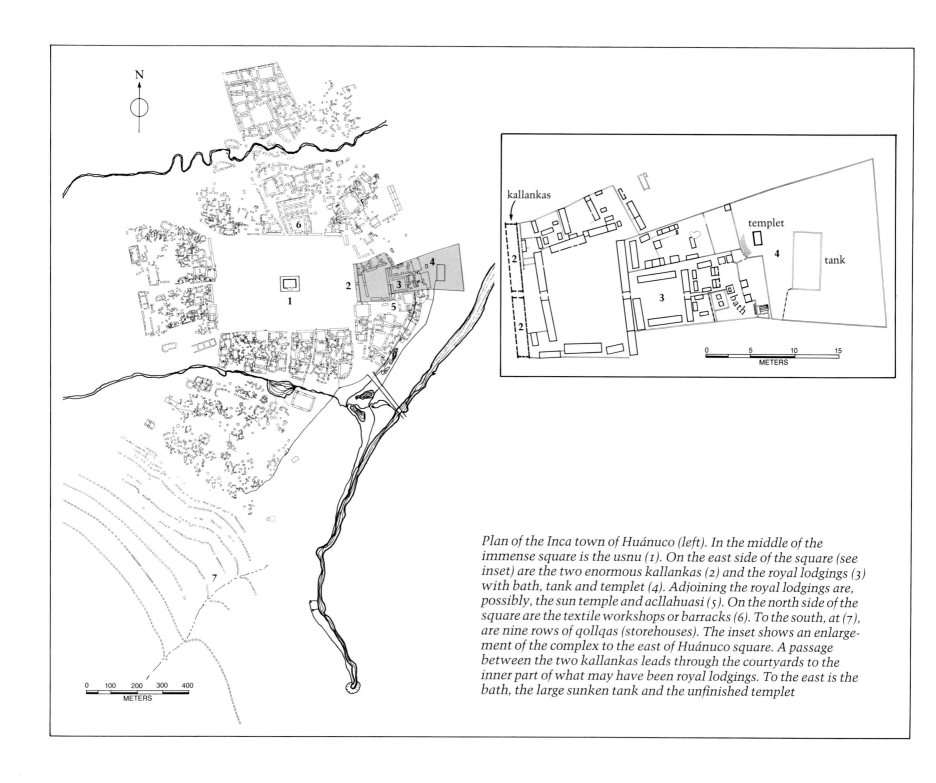

Plan of the Inca town of Huánuco (left). In the middle of the immense square is the usnu (1). On the east side of the square (see inset) are the two enormous kallankas (2) and the royal lodgings (3) with bath, tank and templet (4). Adjoining the royal lodgings are, possibly, the sun temple and acllahuasi (5). On the north side of the square are the textile workshops or barracks (6). To the south, at (7), are nine rows of qollqas (storehouses). The inset shows an enlargement of the complex to the east of Huánuco square. A passage between the two kallankas leads through the courtyards to the inner part of what may have been royal lodgings. To the east is the bath, the large sunken tank and the unfinished templet

the central Andes. Pizarro sent Alonso de Alvarado against him, but Illa Tupac's men surprised the Spaniards on a snow-covered puna north of Lake Junín. When Gonzalo Pizarro, the youngest of the Pizarro brothers, marched past here in mid-1539, "he had to fight the Indians of the province of Huánuco. These came out in battle against him, and placed him in such danger that the Marquis Pizarro had to send Francisco de Chaves to his rescue." This was the moment of Spanish occupation of Huánuco. Córdova Salinas wrote that "in 1539, because of the war that the rebel Illa Tupac was waging in this province, the Marquis Francisco Pizarro sent the illustrious captain [Alonso] Gómez de Alvarado, who founded it [as a Spanish municipality on 11 August]. It was later depopulated." The foundations of the few houses and a tiny Franciscan chapel built by the Spaniards can still be seen.

Illa Tupac is one of the unsung heroes of native resistance. His fate is uncertain. Pedro de Cieza de León said that he caused "much mischief" but was finally captured in 1542 "with great difficulty." But another chronicler said that he was still active in 1544. There is, however, no doubt about the conduct of Francisco de Chaves. His punitive expedition was a bloodbath. He swept through the province of Huánuco and the Conchucos, sacking towns, destroying fields, and hanging men, women and children indiscriminately. "The war was so cruel that the Indians feared they would all be killed, and prayed for peace." A few years later, after Chaves had died, a royal decree ordered that his estate make amends—for it was admitted that he had slaughtered six hundred children under three years of age and had burned or impaled many adults.

Spanish chroniclers were impressed by the magnificence of Huánuco. Cieza de Léon said that the area had been conquered by Pachacuti's son Topa Inca Yupanqui. This Inca ordered that each conquered province should have its imperial government, sun temple, acllahuasi, stores and barracks. At Huánuco he ordered the building of "the palace of such excellence that we can still see." This "admirably built royal palace was made of very large stones skillfully joined. . . . Beside it there was a temple to the sun with many vestals and priests. [Huánuco] was so important in the times of the Incas that there were always over thirty thousand Indians to serve it." Antonio Vázquez de Espinosa was struck by the mighty usnu that stands in the middle of the square. He described it as a "fortress all of hewn stone and two estados high, like a well-planned stronghold that could hold four thousand men." Two great kallankas along one side of the square were "halls so large that each could hold a horse race, with many doors: these must have been where important Indians or chiefs sent by the kings would have lodged. They now serve as stables for cattle." This author, who was in Peru at the start of the seventeenth century, was particularly struck by the line of stone gates, some with "royal arms" of carved pumas on their lintels, that led into the series of courtyards of what were presumably the royal lodgings. He also noted the walled enclosure nearby that may have been the convent of holy women.

The ruins of Huánuco were visited and described by some of the leading nineteenth-century travelers—the Frenchman Charles Wiener, the German Ernst Middendorf, the Austrian J. J. von Tschudi, the Peruvian-Italian Antonio Raimondi and the Englishman Reginald Enock. All of them, particularly Enock who was there in 1903, tried to deduce the original functions of the various labyrinths of fallen stones. Emilio Harth-Terré, an architect from Lima, made careful surveys and analyses of the buildings between 1934 and 1960. But the first attempt to excavate and restore Huánuco came only in the mid-1960s, when a strong team of American archaeologists under John Murra worked for a number of seasons at the remote site. The result is an admirable picture of an important provincial Inca city.

All the buildings of Huánuco radiate outward from the immense rectangular plaza, which was built on a scale to delight a modern totalitarian dictator. Its length is no less than 547 meters (1,800 feet, or almost a third of a mile), and its width is 370 meters (1,200 feet), so that this great space is twenty-four times the size of a standard Spanish city square. It is not a perfect rectangle; but important streets leave from its corners and the central usnu is at the meeting point of diagonals across the rectangle. Harth-Terré assumed that the Incas made the plaza so large to accommodate great herds of llamas, alpacas and guanacos. He imagined hundreds of animals being shorn, slaughtered or distributed on the city's broad grassy square. Various chronicles and colonial records speak of the famous herds of Huánuco and of the herdsmen who went from Huánuco to other parts of the Inca empire.

The square is dominated by the powerful mass of the stone-clad usnu. It is one of those buildings that epitomizes Inca architecture — massive, built of painstaking masonry, of a size and with design details whose purposes are not easily explained, and unadorned to a degree that is at once infuriating and impressive. The platform is long and squat. The central structure is some 30 by 50 meters (roughly 100 by 165 feet) in plan but rises only 4 meters (13 feet) above its terrace. Its core is solid earth, but it rises only for some 3 meters, allowing the retaining walls to form a parapet around the flat top of the terreplein. The walls are of the finest masonry, with courses of ashlars that diminish as they rise (see plate, page 37).

Daniel Shea directed the restoration of the usnu in 1965. His team of laborers diligently filled in a number of holes dug by treasure seekers who were convinced that there might be chambers or passages below this remarkable building. The depredations of these *huaqueros* (pothunters) were particularly bad on the mound's west side; but the Inca blocks had not been removed and it was possible to rebuild most of the wall and parapet.

The usnu is approached from the south by a broad monumental staircase, but this leads to two surprisingly narrow doorways through the parapet wall. Bold sculptures of crouching felines (or possibly monkeys) flank them. An elegant cornice projects outward around the entire building. Within the parapet are niches, two of which face the entrances. These may have been seats for attendants watching the doorways, or they could have served as steps for standing officials, who faced outward to address a crowd in the plaza below. A Spanish inquiry of 1562 into native customs has survived from the Huánuco region. In speaking about the uses of the city square

and about the powers of the Inca's provincial governor (*tocricoc*), it declared that "this official assembled in the square all the chiefs and leaders of that land and many other Indians and, in the presence of all, told them to observe how he administered justice." This confirmed the definition of *usnu* in one of the earliest Quechua dictionaries as "a judge's tribunal made of an erected stone."

The Huánuco usnu rests on a base of two low terraces. Shea's men cleaned and restored them, and noticed that they served an interesting optical purpose. The vast square slopes downward toward the east, presumably to drain off water from the heavy rains of this region. The usnu is at the point where the flat plaza starts to slope. The supporting terraces serve to counteract any optical illusion caused by this change of angle; without them the stone platform might look as though it were tilting in the opposite direction. The archaeologists also investigated two small buildings at the southeastern corner of the outer terrace. They concluded that these were built at the same time as the terraces, and not, as was popularly imagined, by the Spaniards during their brief occupation. A construction on top of the usnu itself, at its eastern end, probably *was* of post-Conquest date: John Rowe suggested that it might have been the remains of a *picota* — the ornamental pillar or gibbet that was the symbol of every Spanish municipality — since the walls of the usnu would have heightened the drop for any victim hanged from it.

The most important buildings of Huánuco are at the eastern end of the plaza. Two magnificent kallankas frame the entrance to a compound that was almost certainly the royal lodgings. Craig Morris was in charge of the restoration of the kallankas — those halls that Vázquez de Espinosa described as large enough to contain horse races. The interior of one is 84 meters long and the other 75 meters, while both are 9.7 meters wide (275 and 246 by 32 feet). Morris's team did an admirable job of rebuilding walls that had suffered from centuries of use as stabling for cattle. They cleared the original floor and discovered circles of stones that had once enclosed the bases of wooden pillars supporting the enormous thatched

The easternmost gateway of the royal compound

A line of gates each decorated with pairs of pumas

roofs. The various functions of these halls have already been discussed (page 36), but it is interesting to note that the kallankas of Huánuco formed the outer wall of the so-called Inca-huasi or Inca's palace. The alley between the halls looks directly through a succession of gateways in the palace compounds; and from the depths of the palace the sun sets over the usnu along this line of vision.

The royal palace of Huánuco corresponds admirably to Murúa's or Garcilaso's descriptions of an Inca's residence (page 41). Courtyard follows courtyard in the manner of the Turkish sultan's palace and harem of Topkapi, or the lodgings of the Chinese emperors in the Forbidden City of Peking. As Murúa explained, senior grades of officials were allowed to penetrate only as far as certain gates. The inner area was for the monarch alone, and it is within the innermost courtyards that we see the passage leading to an adjoining compound that may once have housed the chosen women. Cieza de León wrote that the "vestal virgins" were located alongside the Huánuco royal palace. The line of gates is built of fine ma-

sonry and adorned with crouching pumas in high relief. The walls and buildings of the courtyards are of more rustic stone-work, not because they were of later date, but probably because they were once plastered and painted. It is an interesting reminder of the Inca cleanliness that so impressed dirty European conquerors to find a stone bath in the inner courtyard as well as the remains of a shallow tank measuring 103 by 40 meters (338 by 130 feet).

The archaeologists in 1965, under Luis Barredo Murillo, cleared away the bushes that were destroying the gates and restored the Inca bath and its system of pipes and channels. They also restored a delightful building north of the axis of gates and the innermost courtyard. This "templet" or "tabernacle" has three double-jambed niches facing east. Emilio Harth-Terré noticed that the niches were aligned to catch the rays of the rising sun on the March and September equinoxes. During the cleaning in 1965 it was shown that this small temple was incomplete; work on it was presumably stopped by the Spanish Conquest.

A view south from the royal residence to the entrance gate

The buildings north of the central square were textile workshops

A plaza and a sunken bath east of the royal enclosure

The unfinished templet on the eastern edge of Huánuco

The complex of buildings immediately south of the Inca-huasi may well have been the temple of the sun, with the quarters of the chosen women discreetly hidden between the inner part of the temple and the inner quarters of the royal palace. The gates of the courts of the "temple" complex are aligned on an axis exactly parallel to that of the Inca-huasi. The second court has a well in its center that would correspond to the one in Cuzco's Coricancha. This could have been the font that received the daily sacrificial libations offered to the sun by the mamaconas. The first court has enough buildings to correspond to the temples of the lesser celestial deities: Venus and the Pleiads, thunder, the rainbow and the moon. At the far end of the second court are two "sentry boxes" which flank the gate leading on to the supposed quarters of the holy women. One aged chief declared to the Spanish inquiry of 1562 that "they used to place in Huánuco girls who were going to be beautiful, [to serve] as mamaconas. The Inca would give some of these, whom he did not keep for himself, to be wives of Indians whom he chose [to honor]."

This same chief also remarked that "they used to bring to the store at Huánuco, pots and pitchers and other pottery vessels." When American archaeologists excavated the buildings of the outer courts of the royal palace, they found tons of cooking pottery and an abundance of food remains. Their conclusion was that they had found a vast kitchen complex for the preparation of chicha and food for public banquets. Fasting was an important element of Inca religion—as it is in the Christian Lent and the Muslim īd; and it was normal to end a fast with an enormous *taqui* dance and banquet. Cieza de León described the Hatun Raymi (great feast) that marked the end of the harvest of potatoes, corn, *quinoa* and oca: "It was observed in many provinces and was the principal feast of the entire year. . . . It lasted fifteen or twenty days, during which there were great taquis or drinking feasts and other celebrations." There was sacrifice of many llamas, guinea pigs, pigeons and other animals. "The mamaconas came forth richly attired and with a great quantity of the chicha that they considered sacred. . . . After having eaten and drunk repeat-

edly and all being drunk, including the Inca and the high priest, joyful and warmed by the liquor, the men assembled a little after midday and began singing in a loud voice songs and ballads that had been composed by their forebears." Such feasts were a manifestation of Inca power. The Inca rulers organized them, "making the people joyful and giving them solemn banquets and drinking feasts, great taquis and other celebrations such as they use, completely different from ours. In these the Incas show their splendor, and all the feasting is at their expense." Garcilaso wrote that on the night before one regular festival, "the women of the sun busied themselves with the preparation of enormous quantities of a maize dough called zancu, of which they made little round loaves the size of an apple. . . . The flour for this bread . . . was ground and kneaded by the chosen virgins, the wives of the Sun, who also prepared the rest of the food for the feast. The banquet seemed a gift from the Sun to his children . . . and for that reason the virgins, as wives of the Sun, prepared it." It is easy to imagine such preparations and celebrations amid the once-splendid courts of Huánuco.

Another informant to the 1562 inquiry said that "in the time of the Inca they used to offer to the sun feathers from the [eastern forests] and colored seashells, and llamas and marrow fat, guinea pigs, chicha and coca. . . . And they gave all this of their own free will . . . for no one forced them." It is therefore no surprise to find that the important regional center of Huánuco had a magnificent battery of qollqas (storage huts). They are arranged in nine rows on the gentle slope of Chumipata hill, half a kilometer (a third of a mile) south of the city. The foundations of 497 qollqas can be counted, some circular and some rectangular. Craig Morris, who led the restoration, excavated 120 buildings and reroofed one of them with an imitation of its original conical thatch. The excavations revealed very few items of military equipment. But Morris calculated that the qollqas could have held a million bushels of potatoes, maize and other tribute foods.

On the northern side of the great square is a walled compound containing fifty rectangular buildings arranged in neat rows. These were low buildings, with rustic pirca walls and narrow doors. Harth-Terré assumed that they were "barracks" for levies of workers or soldiers, but excavation revealed over three hundred spindle whorls and numerous bone awls and other tools used to manipulate threads in looms. There were also a number of copper pins used by Andean women to fasten their cloaks. It thus became evident that these were workshops for textiles—for cloth was the fundamental item of tribute, royal patronage and trade in Inca Peru. This compound, rather than the enclosure alongside the royal palace, may therefore have been the acllahuasi housing the acllas or mamaconas engaged in making the Inca's cloth. In commenting on this textile factory compound, Murra and Morris quoted a sixteenth-century litigation recently discovered in a Bolivian archive. In it, a chief of Huancané on the north shore of Lake Titicaca recalled bitterly that "the Inca Huayna Capac settled one thousand weavers . . . and a hundred potters as mitimaes on our lands. Although their presence did us great damage, our ancestors did not dare resist the will of that Inca, because they were so afraid of the tyrant." The Huánuco compound, with its single entrance, could just as well have held such transplanted laborers as the beautiful chosen women of the acllahuasi.

North of the "barracks" or acllahuasi is a district that Harth-Terré called the herdsmen's ward because it contains a number of circular corrals. North of it, beyond the Ayararacra stream, is the best preserved of the residential wards. It is a fine example of Inca planning, with a series of canchas and a grid of streets grouped around a central square. Far off, at the southwestern corner of the square, on the road leading to the storehouses, is a notable group of houses arranged along four square courtyards. Harth-Terré called this complex the house of the chasquis (postal runners), although it was not on the main highway, which crossed the square from northwest to southeast.

From his work at Huánuco, Craig Morris was able to show six main characteristics of provincial highland Inca cities: They were often on new sites, settlements that appeared quickly in archaeological terms. Their official Inca ceramics differed markedly from the local wares of the surrounding districts. They were invariably on main roads, depending for defense on the mobility of Inca armies rather than fixed fortifications. This led to a preoccupation with storage and buildings for temporary lodging or nonresidential activities. They had royal palaces and temples, but no cemeteries. And many were rapidly depopulated after the fall of the Inca empire.

INGAPIRCA

THOUGH THE NORTHERN PART OF THE INCA EMPIRE was particularly rich and important, only a single Inca ruin survives in all of what is now Ecuador. This is an isolated temple complex known as Ingapirca. It is in rolling, bare and often misty hills of the Andes, at an altitude of 3,160 meters (10,370 feet). Although remote from any town, Ingapirca is only a short distance east of the main north-south highway, near modern Cañar. It is some thirty-five kilometers (twenty-two miles) due north of Cuenca, which was once the sumptuous Inca city of Tumibamba.

The most striking feature of Ingapirca is a platform faced with fine coursed masonry. The ashlars are gently rusticated with the joints countersunk in the finest Inca manner. This was clearly the work of master masons trained in Cuzco. The platform has straight sides and semicircular ends, a plan seen in no other Inca building. Graziano Gasparini noticed that the ends have diameters of 12.35 meters (40½ feet), while the entire platform is precisely three times this length. The plan thus consists of three circles in a line, with the triangular spaces between the circles filled in to give straight sides.

There could be some religious significance in the fact that the circular module is repeated three times. The platform is aligned roughly from east to west, and the three circles could correspond to the three positions of the sun: *anti* (or *punchao*) for dawn and the east, *inti* for the full overhead sun, and *cunti* for the western sunset. The Antisuyo and the Cuntisuyo (Condesuyo to the Spaniards) were the eastern and western quarters of the Inca empire. In this context it is worth recalling Cristóbal de Molina's account of the chanting at the Inti Raymi (sun festival) in Cuzco, which rose during the morning and fell in the afternoon, echoing in intensity the sun's path across the heavens. The three circles remind us of Garcilaso's description of the solar columns that were erected through-out the empire: "To ascertain the time of the equinoxes they had splendidly carved stone columns erected . . . before the temples of the sun. . . . These columns stood in the middle of great rings. . . . Across the middle of the ring, a line was drawn from east to west by a cord. . . . When the shadow fell exactly along the line from sunrise, and at midday the sun bathed all sides of the column and cast no shadow at all, they knew that that day was the equinox." Very possibly the terreplein of Ingapirca was such a solar observatory or temple, with its curving ends clad in coursed ashlars, so like the curving walls of the sun temples of Machu Picchu or of Cuzco itself.

A rectangular gabled building stands athwart the Ingapirca platform. It is of typical Inca design, with the crest of the roof supported by a solid wall that divides the building into two identical halves. This central wall occupies the diameter of the middle circle of the three circles that form the platform's plan. The building has good, coursed ashlars on the lower part of its four walls, with adobes in the triangular portions of the gables—almost as if it were originally planned as a hip-roofed building and the gables were added later. It is known locally as the "guardian's house" but was clearly far more important: it is difficult to imagine its being used for any purpose other than a religious one.

The platform is reasonably tall—its height varies from 3.15 to 4.10 meters (10 feet 4 inches to 13½ feet)—and it is approached by an elegant system of stairs in the middle of the south side. Five steps lead to a double-jambed trapezoidal gate in the outer casing of the platform. Inside this gate, the visitor faces the foundation of the central building, in which there is a trapezoidal niche. Identical staircases rise to right and left, to reach the eastern and western ends of the platform, which are otherwise separated by the dividing wall of the central building.

The temple platform of Ingapirca from the north

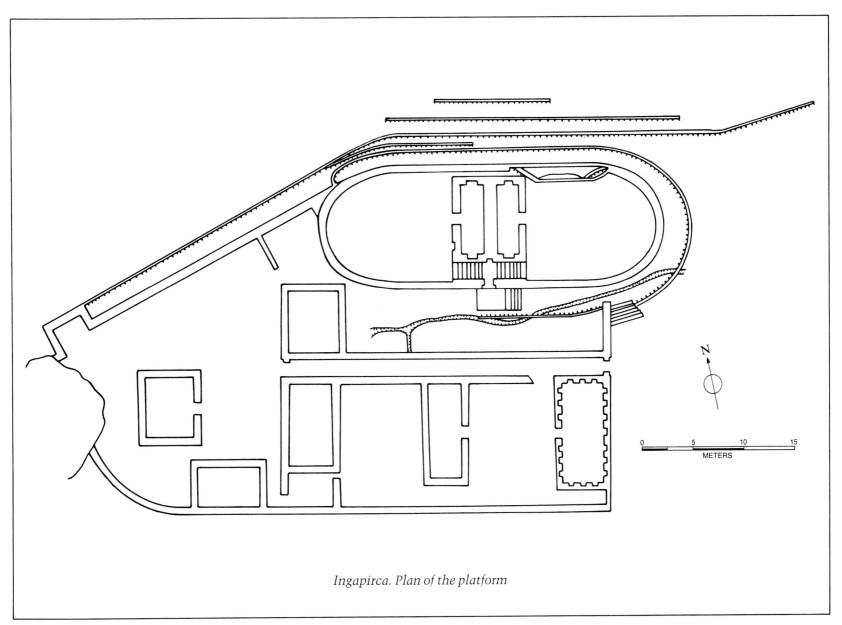

Ingapirca. Plan of the platform

The remainder of the Ingapirca complex is unremarkable, consisting of rectangular courts and buildings, some with niches, but all typically Inca. The site was visited by a number of earlier travelers. The best early plan was made in 1739 by Charles Marie de La Condamine, a member of a team sent by the kings of France and Spain to calculate the earth's circumference by surveys on the equator near Quito. (Their calculation of the length of the equator became the basis for the entire metric system of weights and measures.) Another plan was drawn by two Spanish government inspectors, Jorge

Juan and Antonio de Ulloa, a decade after La Condamine's. Humboldt visited the site in 1803 and pondered on the uniformity, quantity and geographical spread of Inca architecture. Ingapirca has recently been cleared and partially excavated by an archaeological team led by Gordon Hadden.

Ingapirca is in the territory of an ancient tribe called Cañari. There is no direct reference to the ruin in the chronicles, unless it was part of Hatun Cañar (Upper Cañar) where, according to Gaspar de Gallegos, "they say that in the time of Huayna Capac there were great towns of the Indians and that this was the main capital of the Cañari. This seems to be so, for there are still today [1582] great and very sumptuous buildings, among which is a very strong tower." The region was conquered by Pachacuti's son Topa Inca Yupanqui. That great Inca started to organize roads and towns on the Inca model, but it was his son Huayna Capac who developed the province. Huayna Capac loved this northern part of the empire and contemplated building a second capital at either Tumibamba (modern Cuenca) or at Quito. Pedro de Cieza de León marched through here in 1547 and was amazed by his first view of the Inca empire. He praised the magnificent storehouses, full of every sort of weapon, clothing, tool and foodstuff. "The temple of the sun was of stones put together with the subtlest skill, some of them large, black and rough, and others that seemed of jasper. . . . The fronts of many of the buildings are beautiful and highly decorative, some of them set with precious stones and emeralds and, inside, the walls of the temple of the sun and the palaces of the Inca lords were covered with sheets of the finest gold. . . . The roof of these buildings was of thatch so well laid that, barring a fire, it would last for ages. . . . Whatever I say, I cannot give an idea of the wealth the Incas possessed in these royal palaces, in which they took great pride, where many silversmiths were kept busy making the things I have described and many others. The woolen clothing in the storehouses was so numerous and so fine that, had it been kept and not lost, it would be worth a fortune. . . . These famous lodgings of Tumibamba, which were situated in the province of Cañari, were among the finest and richest to be found in all Peru, and the buildings the largest and best. Whatever the Indians said about these residences fell short of reality, to judge by the remains. . . . Today all is cast down and in ruins, but it can still be seen how great they were." The buildings that were ruins in Cieza's day are now vanished, swallowed up by the prosperous city of Cuenca. The German archaeologist Max Uhle excavated what he could find of their foundations in 1922; but the glorious temples and palaces are gone.

Tumibamba and the province of the Cañari were the scene of the first act in the destruction of the Inca empire. Hernando Pablos told how the Inca Huayna Capac, "a noble lord, well regarded and loved by all, and spirited in war," finished his conquests of what is now southern Colombia, and came to reside for ten years at Tumibamba because of its perfect climate. It was during those years that the Inca was informed about the arrival of a foreign ship off the coast of Ecuador. The ship was Pizarro's, from his second voyage, the reconnaissance of 1527–1528 during which he had his first sight of the mighty empire he was later to destroy. Shortly after the arrival of the first Europeans came their most deadly legacy. "At this time a terrible disease and epidemic occurred, in which an innumerable quantity of people died of a measles in which they all developed an incurable leprosy. This lord Huayna Capac died of it and they embalmed him and took him to Cuzco for burial. His death was greatly lamented among the natives." "They say that a great pestilence of smallpox struck, so contagious that over two hundred thousand people died of it in all the districts, for it was general." Smallpox was a European disease against which American natives had no hereditary immunity. It is now thought certain that this deadly disease swept across Colombia from the Caribbean, passing from tribe to tribe ahead of the invading Spaniards. It killed not only the Inca, but also his heir and most of his government. The result was a disputed succession between two of his surviving sons, Huascar in Cuzco and Atahualpa in Quito. The fatal war between them left the Inca empire divided, and vulnerable to the invasion that eventually destroyed it.

The temple building, looking south

NOTES

THE CATCHLINES FOR CITES TO QUOTATIONS consist of the *last* few words quoted. If the cite to a text quotation is a Spanish source, an additional cite to a published English translation may be given as an aid to readers who do not read Spanish.

Abbreviations used in the Notes are listed at the beginning of the Bibliography on page 216.

INCA ARCHITECTURE

PAGE

13   "appreciate them": B. Cobo, *Historia del Nuevo Mundo*, bk. 14, ch. 12, BAE (CONT) 92: 260.

13   "ninety years": *Noticia del Perú . . .* (ca. 1540), CLDRHP, 2 ser., 8 (1924): 47.

15   "everything efficiently": Cobo, bk. 12, ch. 12, BAE (CONT) 92:77–78.

16   "miraculous involved": Ibid., bk. 13, ch. 11, 92:166.

16   "he had founded": Ibid., bk. 12, ch. 4, 92:66.

18   "obedient to him": G. Diez de San Miguel, *Visita . . . a la provincia de Chucuito . . .*, 92–93.

21   "and appearance": J. de Betanzos, *Suma y narración de los Incas*, BAE (CONT) 209:47.

22   "of the gutter": P. Sancho, *Relación para S.M. . . .*, CLDRHP, 1 ser., 5:192.

23   "been involved!": Cobo, bk. 14, ch. 12, BAE (CONT) 92:261.

23   "obedient to him": Diez de San Miguel, 93.

26   "with the top": Cobo, bk. 14, ch. 12, BAE (CONT) 92:262.

26   Source of labor for Ollantaytambo: P. Sarmiento de Gamboa, *Historia índica*, ch. 40, Markham trans., 121.

26   "their empire": Cobo, bk. 13, ch. 19, BAE (CONT) 92:197.

28   "number of rooms": Ibid., bk. 14, ch. 3, 92:241–242.

28   "for that purpose": *Noticia del Perú*, 32.

28   "on their horses": F. de Jerez, *Verdadera relación . . .*, BAE (CONT) 26:332.

30   "overlapping tiles": E. G. Squier, *Peru*, 394–395.

30   Garcilaso's description of a thatched building: *Comentarios reales*, pt. 1, bk. 6, ch. 4, Livermore trans., 1:321.

30   "sheet of flame": *Relación del sitio del Cuzco . . .*, CLERC, 13:19.

30   "almost suffocated": C. de Molina (el Almagrista), *Relación de muchas cosas . . .*, CLDRHP, 1 ser., 1:175.

31   "the same fashion": Garcilaso, pt. 1, bk. 6, ch. 4, Livermore trans., 1:321.

36   "such vast halls": Garcilaso, pt. 1, bk. 6, ch. 4, Livermore trans., 1:320–321, and bk. 7, ch. 9, 1:424.

36   "with astonishment": Ibid., pt. 1, bk. 7, ch. 10, 1:426.

36   "very skillfully": P. de Cieza de León, *Crónica del Perú*, pt. 1, ch. 81, Onis–von Hagen edn., 101–102.

36   "anywhere on earth": Molina (el Almagrista), BAE (CONT) 209:69.

37   "or assemblies": Ibid., 68.

37   "from the square": Jerez, BAE (CONT) 26:330.

37   "into their midst": C. de Mena, *La conquista del Perú*, in A. Pogo, "The Anonymous *La Conquista del Perú*," *Proceedings of the American Academy of Arts and Sciences* (Boston), 64 (July 1930): 242.

37   "began to kill": P. Pizarro, *Relación del descubrimiento y conquista . . .*, BAE (CONT) 168:178.

37   "and lay feasts": Cieza, pt. 1, ch. 89, Onis–von Hagen edn., 127.

37   "in its honor": M. Cabello de Balboa, *Miscelánea Antártica*, pt. 3: *Historia del Perú*, ch. 21, 1951 edn., 365.

37   "animals and birds": Cieza, pt. 2, ch. 64, ed. Araníbar, 215.

37   "invoked their god": F. Guaman Poma, *Neuva corónica y buen gobierno*, ed. Métraux, 262.

37   "sacrifice of chicha": C. de Molina (of Cuzco), *Relación de las fábulas y ritos de los Incas*, ed. Morales, 46.

37   The usnu in Aucaypata square: Cobo, bk. 13, ch. 14, 4:39.

39   "for the Inca": Guaman Poma, pt. 1, ed. Bustíos Gálvez, 1:218–219.

39   "to the Spaniards": D. de Trujillo, *Relación del descubrimiento . . .*, 54. The rape was hinted at in Fernández de Oviedo and in Mena, but the more official report of Jerez mentioned only "a large, strong house surrounded by tapia [hardened mud] walls, with gates, in which were many women spinning and weaving clothing for Atahualpa's army" (BAE [CONT] 26:326).

39   Bingham's speculations: *Lost City of the Incas*, 183, 212.

41   "marvelous skill": M. de Murúa, *Historia general del Perú*, bk. 3, ch. 3, ed. Bayle, 2:165–166.

41   "and fruits": Garcilaso, pt. 1, bk. 6, ch. 2, Livermore trans., 1:315.

41   "space for mortar": Ibid., bk. 6, ch. 1, 1:313.

41   "his government": Guaman Poma, pt. 1, ed. Bustíos Gálvez, 1:245, 481.

42   "most remarkable": Sancho, *Relación*, CLDRHP, 1 ser., 5:192–193.

42   "rest was razed": Garcilaso, pt. 1, bk. 7, ch. 10, Livermore trans., 1:427.

42 "house or lodging": Ibid., pt. 2, bk. 1, ch. 32, 2:701.

44 "adobe houses": P. Pizarro, BAE (CONT) 168:214.

44 "and other metals": *Noticia del Perú*, 45.

44 "level and clear": P. Pizarro, BAE (CONT) 168:214.

44 The sacred pool: Cobo, bk. 13, ch. 13, 4:25. There is some confusion about which Inca ruler built which palace. Sarmiento wrote that Huayna Capac built Cassana and that Huascar built Amarucancha (chs. 58 and 63, Markham trans., 158, 170). P. Pizarro said that Cassana was Huayna Capac's (*Relación*, 192, 214) and Cobo agreed (bk. 13, ch. 13, BAE [CONT] 92:172). Cobo also said that Pachacuti lived in Condorcancha, north of the main square, but had a lodging in Cora-cora at the northern corner of the square.

44 "belongings and ornaments": Cobo, bk. 12, ch. 4, 3:155.

44 "and the Incas": Cristóbal de Castro and Diego Ortega Morejón, *Relación y declaración . . .* (1558), CLDRHP, 2 ser., 10:135–136.

44 "and drank there": P. Pizarro, BAE (CONT) 168:192.

46 "take his pleasure": Cieza, pt. 2, chs. 38, 40, ed. Araníbar, 131, 137; or Onis–von Hagen edn., 210, 215. Cieza wrote that Viracocha's palace was in the valley of Xaquixahuana, whereas other writers said that it was on a crag called Caquia Xaquixahuana. The name seems to be a corruption of the Quechua *qajya* (incomplete) or *qaqa qhawana* (rocky observatory).

46 The Yucay valley: The descendants of the first four Incas lived close to Cuzco, in the outlying wards of Membilla (Bimbilla) and Cayaucachi, so that those early Incas probably had land there (Cobo, bk. 12, ch. 4, 3:155; Sarmiento, ch. 14, Markham trans., 61). Inca Roca's panaca (lineage) was based at Rarapa (Cobo, bk. 12, ch. 9; Sarmiento, ch. 19, p. 72). It was Betanzos who clearly stated that Viracocha's fortress of Caquia Xaquixahuana was on a crag seven leagues from Cuzco and above the town of Calca in the Yucay valley (*Suma*, BAE [CONT] 209:17, 53–54). On the strength of this, Rowe supposed that it was the ruin now called Huchuy Cosco, which is in precisely this location ("Inca Culture at the Time of the Spanish Conquest," HSAI 2:204; "What Kind of Settlement," 68).

46 "magnificent buildings": Sarmiento, chs. 40, 41, Markham trans., 121, 124.

46 "their jurisdictions": Ibid., 124.

46 "he went hunting": Cobo, bk. 13, ch. 14, Pardo edn., 4:34, 36.

46 "his household": Sarmiento, ch. 54, Markham trans., 153. This Inca's ashes and his huauque (totem) effigy were kept at Calispuquio by his descendants. See Cobo, bk. 13, ch. 13, Pardo edn., 4:19.

46 "roofs are missing": Cobo, bk. 12, ch. 30, 3:287–288.

48 "or twelve years": Ibid.

48 "prior cooking": Guaman Poma, ed. Bustíos Gálvez, 1:251.

48 "each different province": Cobo, bk. 12, ch. 30, 3:287–288.

48 "these articles": Ibid.

48 "of foodstuffs": Ibid.

48 "so many items": Sancho, *Relación*, CLDRHP, 1 ser., 5:195; Estete, [Narrative of a Journey to Pachacamac], BAE (CONT) 26:47.

48 "leather chests": P. Pizarro, CDIHE 5:271–272.

48 Cieza on Vilcashuamán storehouses: Crónica, pt. 2, chs. 44, 84, 89, Onis–von Hagen edn., 68, 114, 127.

49 "various products": J. V. Murra and E. C. Morris, "Dynastic Oral Tradition . . . ," *World Archaeology* 7:273; E. C. Morris, "Master Design of the Inca," *Natural History* (Dec. 1976), 63.

49 "quantity of monuments": A. von Humboldt, *Vues des cordillères et monumens* [sic] *des peuples de l'Amérique*, (Paris, 1810), 114–115.

49 "the State": G. Gasparini and L. Margolies, *Arquitectura Inka*, 330.

50 "of the tyrant": litigation in the Bolivian National Archive, Sucre, quoted in Murra and Morris, "Dynastic Oral Tradition," 277.

50 "their sacrifices": *Relación de las costumbres antiguas de los naturales del Pirú*, BAE (CONT) 209:157.

ISLAND OF THE SUN

54 "and so it was": Sarmiento de Gamboa, *Historia índica*, ch. 7, Markham trans., 32–33. See also Molina (of Cuzco), *Relación*, 13–15; Betanzos, *Suma*, ch. 1, BAE (CONT) 109:9.

54 "for that age": Cobo, *Nuevo Mundo*, bk. 13, ch. 18, Pardo edn., 4:77. See also Garcilaso, *Comentarios reales*, pt. 1, bk. 3, ch. 25, Livermore trans., 1:189–190.

54 "teaching the people": Ibid., 190.

54 "his great majesty": Cobo, bk. 13, ch. 18, 4:78.

56 "have seen them": Ibid., 79.

56 "illume the world": Squier, *Peru*, 366.

58 "idolatrous shrine": Cobo, bk. 13, ch. 18, 4:82–83. Similar descriptions occur in the works of two of Cobo's contemporaries, Alonso Ramos Gavilán and Antonio de la Calancha (see the bibliography).

58 "in the island": Cobo, bk. 13, ch. 18, 4:83.

58 "rain was needed": Ibid., 84.

59 The two plans of Pilco Caima: Squier, 342; Gasparini and Margolies, *Arquitectura Inka*, 270. See also C. Wiener, *Pérou et Bolivie*, 441; A. F. Bandelier, *The Islands of Titicaca and Koati*, 176.

59 "shades of red": Squier, 345.

59 "beautiful in nature": Ibid., 346.

TAMBO-TOQO AND HUANACAURI HILL

61   "'you make offerings'": Sarmiento de Gamboa, *Historia índica*, ch. 12, BAE (CONT) 135:216, or Markham trans., 51–52. See also Cieza de León, *Crónica*, pt. 2, chs. 6–7, Onis–von Hagen edn., 32–33; Molina (of Cuzco), *Relación*, 64; Garcilaso, *Comentarios reales*, pt. 1, ch. 16, Livermore trans., 1:43; Betanzos, *Suma*, ch. 4, BAE (CONT) 209:13; Guaman Poma, *Nueva corónica*, ed. Bustíos Gálvez, 1:166, 188; *Informaciones que mandó levantar el Virrey Toledo*, CLERC 16:196.

61   "nobility and knighthood": Sarmiento, ch. 12, Markham trans., 52.

64   "the foster sons": Cobo, *Nuevo Mundo*, bk. 13, ch. 25, Pardo edn., 4:122; Molina (of Cuzco), 65–81; Molina (el Almagrista), *Relación*, BAE (CONT) 209:73–74; Garcilaso, pt. 1, bk. 6, ch. 24.

64   "wealth of treasure": Cieza, pt. 2, ch. 28, Onis–von Hagen edn., 150. See also J. de Santacruz Pachacuti, *Relación de antigüedades . . .*, BAE (CONT) 209:286.

64   "gold and silver": Guaman Poma, pt. 2, Dilke trans., 110. See also B. de Las Casas, *De las antiguas gentes del Perú*, ch. 16; J. H. Rowe, "An Introduction to the Archaeology of Cuzco," *Peabody Museum Papers* 27:41–43.

SACSAHUAMAN

65   "necessary food": Cieza de León, *Crónica*, pt. 2, ch. 51, Onis–von Hagen edn., 153. Two conquistadores who actually saw the contents of the Sacsahuaman storehouses gave other lists. Sancho wrote that "the entire fortress was an arsenal with stores of maces, spears, bows and arrows, axes, shields, vests of thickly padded cotton, and various other weapons. . . . There were many dyes—blues, yellows, browns and other colors—for painting; cloth; much tin, lead and other metals, much silver and a certain quantity of gold; and there were many mantles and quilted tunics for the soldiers" (Relación para S.M., CLDRHP, I ser., 5:194). P. Pizarro also stressed the stores of weapons, as well as the very tough cane helmets and litters for Inca nobles (*Relación*, BAE [CONT] 168:196–197).

65   "the world exists": Cieza, pt. 2, ch. 51, Onis–von Hagen edn., 153–154. Cobo (bk. 12, ch. 33, BAE [CONT] 92:132) said that 30,000 men at a time were employed.

65   "others laid them": Sarmiento de Gamboa, *Historia índica*, ch. 53, Markham trans., 152.

65   "roll downhill": Garcilaso, *Comentarios reales*, pt. 1, bk. 7, ch. 29, Livermore trans., 1:470.

67   "sight as this!": Sancho, *Relación*, 5:193.

67   "rather than men!": Garcilaso, pt. 1, bk. 7, ch. 27, BAE (CONT) 133:285.

67   Source of the stone for Sacsahuaman: C. Kalafatovich Valle, "Geología del grupo arqueológico de la fortaleza de Saccsayhuaman y sus vecinidades," *Saqsaywaman* 1:64–65; Gasparini and Margolies, *Arquitectura Inka*, 299–300.

67   "in their places": Garcilaso, pt. 1, bk. 7, ch. 28, BAE (CONT) 133:286; or Livermore trans., 1:467–468.

67   "level or uniform": J. de Acosta, *Historia natural y moral de las Indias*, bk. 6, ch. 14 BAE (CONT) 73:194, quoted in Garcilaso, pt. 1, bk. 7, ch. 27, Livermore trans., 1:465.

67   "approach obliquely": Sancho, *Relación*, CLDRHP, I ser., 5:194.

67   The archaeological work of 1968: The restorers were led by Luis A. Pardo and the architect Oscar Ladrón de Guevara Avilés. They were amazed to find the entire southern wall of Sacsahuaman buried under a century of deposits, with many of its stones tumbled into the Pucrumayo stream. They rebuilt a gate and called it Rumipuncu (stone gate). See their "Trabajos de limpieza y consolidación, estudio e investigatión," *Saqsaywaman* 1:30.

68   "joins alternating": Sancho, *Relación*, CLDRHP, I ser., 5:193.

68   "as above it": Garcilaso, pt. 1, bk. 7, ch. 29, Livermore trans., 1:469.

68   "top of a hill": Sancho, Relación, 5:193. In their descriptions both P. Pizarro and Cieza say that Sacsahuaman had only two towers (Pizarro, BAE [CONT] 168:196–197; Cieza, pt. 2, ch. 51, Onis–von Hagen edn., 154–155).

68   "see the ruins": Sarmiento, ch. 53, Markham trans., 152.

68   "of this land!": Cieza, pt. 2, ch. 51, Onis–von Hagen edn., 155.

68   "lost inside": Garcilaso, pt. 1, bk. 7, ch. 29, Livermore trans., 1:469. See also J. Ruiz de Arce, *Relación de servicios . . .*, BRAH 102:368.

68   "have mentioned": Garcilaso, 1:471. An anonymous chronicle called *Noticias cronológicas del Cusco*, written about 1740, said that the destruction of Sacsahuaman started in 1537; the ecclesiastical council of Cuzco, in a decision dated 6 October 1559, ordered stones from the temple-fortress to be brought down to build the cathedral; but on 13 May 1561 the civil cabildo, under Lieutenant Governor Licentiate Antonio de Gama, prohibited the removal of stones for house building, on pain of a fine of one hundred pesos de oro (V. Angles Vargas, *Historia del Cusco*, 1:122).

72   "of it remain": L. E. Valcárcel y Vizcarra, "Cuzco Archaeology," HSAI 2:178–179. See also his reports, "Sajsawaman redescubierto,' RMN, vols. 3–6 (1934–1937), and Squier, *Peru*, 473.

72   The geology of the Rodadero: Isaiah Bowman, *The Andes of Southern Peru* (New York, 1916); Arnold Heim, *Wunderland Peru, Naturerlebnisse* (1948), 195; G. C. Amstutz, "Der Rodadero bei Cusco als Beispiel eines geologischen Problems," *Leben und Umwelt*

74 "know what to do": Titu Cusi Yupanqui, *Relación de la conquista del Perú...*, CLDRHP, 1 ser., 2:67.

74 "so few of them": *Relación de los sucesos del Perú...*, GP 2:392.

74 "at breakneck speed": Titu Cusi Yupanqui, 68.

74 "was indeed brave": Francisco de Pancorvo's testimony in support of Francisca Pizarro's claim against the Crown, Cuzco, 7 October 1572, GP 2:153.

74 "in close combat": *Relación del sitio de Cuzco...*, CLERC 13:30.

74 "with determination": Ibid.

77 "became exhausted": Ibid., 31–32.

77 "stones and arrows": P. Pizarro, BAE (CONT) 168:204–205.

77 "top of the tower": Ibid.

77 "on his head": Ibid. The brave orejón is sometimes called Cahuide, but this was not a Quechua name and does not appear in any contemporary source.

77 "on his arm": Ibid.

77 "not been touched": *Relación del sitio del Cuzco*, 32.

77 "1,500 of them": Ibid., 33. Alonso Enríquez de Guzman said that three thousand were slaughtered during the capture of Sacsahuaman: *Libro de vida y costumbres...* (1543), trans. C. R. Markham, HAKL SOC, 1 ser., 29 (1862):98.

77 "heap of dead men": Titu Cusi Yupanqui, 70.

77 "died in it": Cédula of Charles V, Madrid, 19 July 1540, *Colección de documentos inéditos para la historia de Hispano-America*, 3 (1928):75.

CORICANCHA

78 The three-man mission to Coricancha: Mena, *La conquista del Perú*, ed. R. Porras Barrenechea, 92–93. It was once thought that Hernando de Soto was one of the three envoys, but they appear to have been Martín Bueno, Pedro Martín and someone from Zárate. Cieza de León named them; and Porras Barrenechea found a report by Martín Bueno about his journey, in a Spanish archive.

78 "evidently been secured": Jerez, *Conquista del Perú*, BAE (CONT) 26:343.

78 Cobo on Coricancha: *Historia del Nuevo Mundo*, bk. 13, ch. 12, Pardo edn., 4:9.

78 "excellent quality": Cieza de León, *Crónica*, pt. 1, ch. 92, Onis–von Hagen edn., 146.

78 "two handspans wide": Ibid. See also P. Pizarro, *Relación*, BAE

(CONT) 168:193; Garcilaso, *Comentarios reales*, pt. 1, bk. 3, ch. 21, Livermore trans., 1:181; Molina (el Almagrista), *Relación*, BAE (CONT) 209:75; Jerez, BAE (CONT) 26:343; A. Vázquez de Espinosa, *Compendio y descripción de las Indias Occidentales*, bk. 4, ch. 87, para. 1511, BAE (CONT) 231:371–372, or Clark trans., 561; Cobo, bk. 13, ch. 12, BAE (CONT) 92:169.

79 The sun idol: Betanzos, *Suma*, BAE (CONT) 209:33; P. Pizarro, BAE (CONT) 168:192.

79 "the present day": Molina (el Almagrista), BAE (CONT) 209:75. G. Fernández de Oviedo (*Historia*, bk. 47, ch. 9, BAE [CONT] 121:161) said that Rodrigo Orgóñez captured a sun image from the fugitive Inca Manco in 1537 and gave it to the puppet Inca Paullu, but this must have been an insignificant object as no other chroniclers mentioned it.

79 "many precious stones": Cieza, pt. 1, ch. 92, Onis–von Hagen edn., 146. See also Cobo, bk. 13, ch. 12, BAE (CONT) 92:168–169; Acosta, *Historia natural*, bk. 5, ch. 12, BAE (CONT) 73:153; Guaman Poma, *Nueva corónica*, ed. Métraux, 258, 264; Santacruz Pachacuti, *Relación*, CLDRHP, 2 ser., 9:159–161; *Relación de las costumbres antiguas*, BAE (CONT) 209:158.

79 "we went in": Trujillo, *Relación*, Barrenechea edn., 63–64.

79 "food was consumed": P. Pizarro, BAE (CONT) 168:192–193.

79 "made love to them": Cobo, bk. 13, ch. 12, BAE (CONT) 92:169.

79 "who were many": P. Pizarro, BAE (CONT) 168:193, or Means trans., 255. Garcilaso said that no women were allowed to enter Coricancha; but other chroniclers mention their presence. Women attended all Inca rulers. Juan Ruiz de Arce, one of the first conquistadores, also described the role of women in these ceremonies, although he may have confused the ritual attending the Inca mummies in the Hatun-cancha and the acllahuasi with that for the sun in Coricancha (*Relación de servicios*, in BRAH 102:371–372.

80 "on those occasions": P. Pizarro, BAE (CONT) 168:193. See also Molina (el Almagrista), BAE (CONT) 209:75; Cobo, bk. 13, ch. 12, BAE (CONT) 92:169; Vázquez de Espinosa, bk. 4, ch. 76, 563. Cieza (pt. 1, ch. 92, Onis–von Hagen edn., 147) added that there were golden llamas and herdsmen as well as golden maize. Garcilaso (pt. 1, bk. 3, ch. 24, Livermore trans., 1:188) let his fertile imagination run riot, with the garden full of golden plants, trees, animals, reptiles, birds and butterflies.

80 "four-year-old boy": Jerez, BAE (CONT) 26:345–346.

80 "magnificent specimens": Cieza, pt. 1, ch. 94, Onis–von Hagen edn., 255. For details of these objects, see a document called *Relación del oro del Perú que recibieron de Hernando Pizarro que trujó la nao de que era maestre Pedro Bernal en febrero de 1534*, in

Rafael Loredo, *Los repartos* (Lima, 1958), 42–43. The correspondence with the King about the treasures is published in Enrique Torres Saldamando, ed., *Libro primero de cabildos de Lima*, 3 (Paris, 1900):127–130.

80   "those distant lands": Dürer's journal for 27 Aug. 1520 in *Albrecht Dürer's Tagebuch der Reise in die Niederlande*, ed. Friedrich Leitschuh (Leipzig, 1884), 58.

80   "form of a pyramid": Garcilaso, pt. 1, bk. 3, ch. 21, Livermore trans., 1:181.

80   "turned to stone": Cobo, bk. 13, ch. 16, Pardo edn., 4:58.

80   The stone font: R. de Lizárraga, *Descripción y población*, ch. 80, BAE (CONT) 216:61.

82   "kept in that place": Garcilaso, pt. 2, bk. 8, ch. 11, BAE (CONT) 135:146.

82   Sayri Tupac anecdote: Ambrosio Morales, *Documentos para la historia del Cuzco. Las tumbas de los Incas Sayri Tupac, D. Felipe Tupac Amaru . . . y de la coya doña María Cusihuarcay*, in *Revista del Instituto Americano de Arte*, Cuzco, 3 (1944):13–21.

82   "ancient edifice": Squier, *Peru*, 439.

82   "underground passages": Kubler, *Cuzco: Reconstruction of the Town and Restoration of Its Monuments* (Paris, 1952), 8. M. Uhle, "El Templo del Sol de los Incas en Cuzco," *XXIII International Congress of Americanists, Proceedings* (1930), 291–295; J. H. Rowe, "An Introduction to the Archaeology of Cuzco," *Peabody Museum Papers* 27.

84   John H. Rowe's plan of Coricancha: J. H. Rowe, "An Introduction to the Archaeology of Cuzco," *Peabody Museum Papers* 27. Rowe's plan is reproduced in *Arquitectura Inka*, Gasparini and Margolies, 232.

84   "of the square": Garcilaso, pt. 1, bk. 3, ch. 21, Livermore trans., 1:181. For comment on the restoration of Coricancha, see Gasparini and Margolies, *Arquitectura Inka*, 230–238; O. Ladrón de Guevara Avilés, *La restauración del Ccoricancha y Templo de Santo Domingo* (1966).

86   "to the festivity": Garcilaso, pt. 1, bk. 3, ch. 22, Livermore trans., 1:184.

86   "of the universe": Betanzos, BAE (CONT) 209:31.

PISAC

89   "town of the Cuyos": Sarmiento de Gamboa, *Historia índica*, ch. 34, Markham trans., 107.

89   "all his glory": Squier, *Peru*, 529. See also Garcilaso, *Comentarios reales*, pt. 1, bk. 2, ch. 22, Livermore trans., 1:116; Cieza de León, *Crónica*, pt. 2, ch. 26, Onis–von Hagen edn., 172; Acosta, *Historia*

natural, bk. 6, ch. 3, BAE (CONT) 73:184. The French traveler Charles Wiener also visited Pisac at about the same time as Squier, but left a more boastful account, claiming that he was the first white man to have discovered it. He made a drawing of the "fortress" in which it looks like a grandiose castle with the agricultural terraces as battlements (*Pérou et Bolivie*, 374).

91   "his perilous way": Squier, 529.

91   *ennuyé* garrison": Ibid., 530. The best modern descriptions of Pisac are by V. Angles Vargas, in his *P'isaq, metropoli Inka* and *Historia del Cusco*, 1:152–188. For a description of the adobe buildings of Pisac, see E. Moorhead's "Highland Inca Architecture in Adobe," *Ñawpa Pacha* 16:70–83.

MORAY

95   "they are filled": Garcilaso, *Comentarios reales*, pt. 1, bk. 5, ch. 1, Livermore trans., 1:241; Cobo, *Historia del Nuevo Mundo*, bk. 14, ch. 8, Pardo edn., 4:220; Sarmiento de Gamboa, *Historia índica*, ch. 30, Markham trans., 98; Guaman Poma, *Nueva corónica*, pt. 3, Dilke trans., 191.

95   "hot and humid": H. de Santillán, *Relación del origen . . . y gobierno de los Incas*, BAE (CONT) 209:144.

OLLANTAYTAMBO

99   "ford was defended": *Relación del sitio del Cuzco*, CLERC 13:47.

99   "masses of masonry": P. Pizarro, *Relación*, BAE (CONT) 168:209.

99   "on all fours": Ibid.

99   "well-armed warriors": *Relación del sitio del Cuzco*, 47, 48.

99   "hillsides and plains": *Relación de los sucesos del Perú*, GP 2:397.

99   "hear the shouting": *Relación del sitio del Cuzco*, 48.

99   "have been killed": P. Pizarro, 209.

99   "by either side": *Relación del sitio del Cuzco*, 49. See also *Relación de los sucesos*, 396–397.

99   "control of his army": A. de Herrera y Tordesillas, *Historia general . . .*, dec. V, bk. 8, ch. 6, ed. Ballasteros and Gómez, 11:216.

100   "could not skirmish": *Relación del sitio del Cuzco*, 49.

100   "the horses' tails": Ibid., 50.

100   "with great spirit": P. Pizarro, 209.

100   "nothing else": *Relación del sitio del Cuzco*, 51.

100   "shrines and altars": Cieza de León, *Crónica del Perú*, pt. 4 (*La guerra de las Salinas*), ch. 21, Markham trans., 87.

103   "we have yet seen": Squier, *Peru*, 492–493. See also Wiener, *Pérou et Bolivie*, 332–333.

103   "carried it away": Cieza, pt. 1, ch. 94, Onis–von Hagen edn., 255.

109   Rugendas' sketch: it is in the Staatlische graphische Sammlung in Munich, according to H. Ubbelohde-Doering (*Auf den Königstrassen der Inka*, Brown trans., 252).

110   "which was not his": Sarmiento de Gamboa, *Historia índica*, chs. 32, 35, Markham trans., 103, 107–108. P. Gutiérrez de Santa Clara said that Tampu Apu was one of the four *ayllus* (noble clans) of Cuzco, and Santacruz Pachacuti described Apu Tampu as a pre-Inca chief who received the royal scepter (*Relación de antigüedades*, BAE [CONT] 209:283). In the Inca origin myth, the cave of Tampu-toqo probably referred to this tribe. The spring above Cuzco called Tambo Machay may have meant "cave of the Tampus," according to L. E. Valcárcel y Vizcarra (*Machu Picchu . . .*, 25–26).

110   "people who were there": Sarmiento de Gamboa, ch. 40, BAE (CONT) 135:245; or Markham trans., 121–122.

MACHU PICCHU

119   "incredible height": Bingham, *Inca Land*, 314.

119   "toward the east": Wiener, *Pérou et Bolivie*, 345. Wiener also wrote that the only written record he could find of these places was a reference to Huaina-pata, which meant roughly the same as Huayna Picchu, on p. 26 of a book called *El brillante porvenir del Cuzco* by Friar Julián Bovo de Revello (Cuzco, 1848).

122   "exquisitely fitted together": Bingham, *Inca Land*, 320.

122   "beautifully constructed houses": Bingham, *Lost City of the Incas*, 149.

126   "ridge was explored": Ibid., 174.

131   "the lower ward": Cobo, *Historia del Nuevo Mundo*, bk. 12, ch. 24, Pardo edn., 3:257.

131   "entertainments they devised": Ibid., 258.

131   "in many folds": Kubler, "Machu Picchu," 53.

133   "and dense jungles": Cobo, bk. 12, ch. 12, Pardo edn., 3:185. P. Sarmiento de Gamboa said that Pachacuti defeated his brother Urco and killed him downstream of Ollantaytambo (*Historia índica*, ch. 33). He also said that Pachacuti's uncle was called Vicchu (Picchu?) because he defeated a tribe of that name (ibid., ch. 23).

142   "to be employed": Bingham, *Lost City*, 170.

149   "means 'to tie'": Garcilaso, *Comentarios reales*, pt. 1, bk. 2, ch. 22, Livermore trans., 1:116.

149   "of their foods": Guaman Poma, *Nueva corónica*, pt. 1, Bustíos Gálvez edn., 1:165, or Dilke trans., 60.

149   "annual timepiece": Sarmiento, ch. 30, BAE (CONT) 135:235–236, or Markham trans., 98–99. Garcilaso said that there were eight sucana columns on either side of Cuzco (pt. 1, bk. 2, ch. 22); Cieza de León said that there were many of these ruined observatory towers around Cuzco (*Crónica*, pt. 2, ch. 26); Acosta said that there were twelve pillars, one for each month (*Historia natural*, bk. 6, ch. 3, BAE [CONT] 73:184).

149   "all his full light": Garcilaso, pt. 1, bk. 2, ch. 30, Livermore trans., 1:117.

149   The sun festival: Molina (el Almagrista), *Relación de muchas cosas . . .* , CLDRHP, 1 ser., 1:160, trans. J. Hemming, *The Conquest of the Incas*, 172–173.

154   "here centuries ago": Bingham, *Lost City*, 160.

154   "were not mortars": V. Angles Vargas, *Machupijchu*, 428.

155   "devour them alive": Guaman Poma, pt. 1, Bustíos Gálvez edn., 1:221. The most important descriptions of Inca punishments were in Cobo, *Nuevo Mundo*, bk. 12, ch. 26; Cieza, pt. 2, ch. 26, Onis-von Hagen edn., 171–172; H. de Santillán, *Relación del origen . . . y gobierno de los Incas*, CLDRHP, 2 ser., 9:68; Las Casas, *De las antiguas gentes del Perú*, CLERC 21:158, 204, 211; Murúa, *Historia general del Perú*, bk. 3, ch. 20, ed. Bayle, 211–212; Acosta, bk. 6, ch. 18, BAE (CONT) 73:197–198; B. Valera, *Relación de las costumbres antiguas de los naturales del Perú*, in Jiménez de la Espada, ed., *Tres relaciones de antigüedades peruanas*, 198–205. The laws and punishments are summarized by Rowe, "Inca Culture at the Time of the Spanish Conquest," 271–272, and by S. F. Moore, *Power and Property in Inca Peru*, 165–174.

155   "obtain confession": Guaman Poma, 222.

155   "until they died": Cobo, bk. 12, ch. 26, Pardo edn., 3:272.

156   "to the departed": Bingham, *Lost City*, 159.

160   "third Suticttoco": Santacruz Pachacuti Yamqui, *Antigüedades deste reyno del Perú*, BAE (CONT) 209:286; Bingham, *Lost City*, 209.

SAIHUITE

165   "gave true answers": Molina (of Cuzco), *Relación de las fábulas y ritos de los Incas*, ed. Morales, 30–31.

165   "through the stone": P. J. de Arriaga, *Extirpación de la idolatría del Pirú*, ch. 3, BAE (CONT) 209:205.

165   "an inch or two thick": Sancho, *Relación*, CLDRHP, 1 ser., 5:157; Santillán, *Relación*, BAE (CONT) 209:111. Cieza de León also mentioned this oracle of Apurímac and said that a quantity of gold was found near it (*Crónica*, pt. 2, ch. 28, ed. Araníbar, 98; or Onis-von Hagen edn., 152).

165   "whom she had served": P. Pizarro, *Relación*, BAE (CONT) 168:190–191.

167   "topographical synthesis": Wiener, *Pérou et Bolivie*, 289. See also Squier, *Peru*, 555.

TARAHUASI

178   "groups of four": Ruiz de Arce, *Relación de servicios*, BRAH 102: 367.

178   "with greater fury": Sancho, *Relación*, CLDRHP, 1 ser., 5:159.

180   "'sport with you!'": Trujillo, *Relación*, 62.

180   "a common Indian": Molina (el Almagrista), *Relación*, 156.

180   "'you burned alive!'": Sancho, *Relación*, 164.

VILCASHUAMÁN

181   "river in Chile": Vazquez de Espinosa, *Compendio*, bk. 4, ch. 70, para. 1476, BAE (CONT) 231:365; or Clark trans., 546. Cieza de León also noted this central location (*Crónica*, pt. 1, ch. 89, Onis–von Hagen edn., 126). See also Pedro de Ribera and Antonio de Chaves, *Relación de la ciudad de Guamanga y sus términos* (1586), RGI, in BAE (CONT) 183:181.

181   "all of cut stone": Pedro de Carvajal, *Descripción fecha de la provincia de Vilcas Guaman . . .* (1586), RGI, in BAE (CONT) 183:218. Cieza wrote that Vilcas had a population of 40,000 (pt. 1, ch. 89, Onis–von Hagen edn., 126), and there is confirmation of this figure in earlier royal decrees: "Ordenanza para el tratamiento de indios," Valladolid, November 1536, in Richard Konetzke, ed., *Colección de documentos para la historia de la formación social de Hispano-América*, 1 (Madrid, 1953):180–181; and a royal instruction to Bishop Tomás de Berlanga, 1535, in Angel de Altolaguirre, ed., *Colección de documentos inéditos relativos al descubrimiento, conquista y organización de las antiguas posesiones españoles de Ultramar*, 10 (Madrid, 1897):466–467.

181   "in the building": Cieza, pt. 2, ch. 48, Araníbar edn., 159.

181   "vows faithfully": Ibid., pt. 1, ch. 89, Onis–von Hagen edn., 127. Vázquez de Espinosa, who preached in the churches near here in the early seventeenth century, also mentioned the two staircases of thirty steps each.

181   "temple and buried": Cieza, 127.

181   "they already had": Carvajal, 218.

181   "is founded here": Ibid.

182   "judge what it was": Cieza, 127. Angrand left his valuable sketchbooks to the Bibliothèque Nationale, but some of his notes are in Ernest Desjardins, *Le Pérou avant la conquête des espagnoles* (Paris, 1858). His drawing of Vilcas is reproduced in Gasparini and Margolies, *Arquitectura Inka*, 121, and in Angrand, *Imagen del Perú en el siglo XIX* (Lima, 1972), 261–262. Wiener also made a good plan of the terraces (*Pérou et Bolivie*, 265).

182   "for this purpose": Carvajal, 218. There is another stepped usnu at

Curamba, between Andahuaylas and Abancay, which was also sketched by Angrand in 1847 (*Imagen del Perú*, 263).

184   "by the Spaniards": Cieza, pt. 1, ch. 89 (Buenos Aires, 1945, edn., 237). H. de Onis, whose translation is normally so elegant, mistranslated this passage (Onis–von Hagen edn., 126–127).

185   "fortune for the Inca": Carvajal, 218–219.

186   "forty gatekeepers": Cieza, pt. 1, ch. 89, Onis–von Hagen edn., 127.

186   "and serve them": Luis Monzó, Pedro González and Juan de Arbe, *Descripción de la tierra del repartimiento de San Francisco de Atunrucana y Laramati . . .* (1586), RGI in BAE (CONT) 183:227.

186   "They then withdrew": Trujillo, *Relación*, 60–61.

186   "Indian warriors": Ruiz de Arce, *Relación de servicios*, 366.

186   "mount the usnu": Guaman Poma, *Nueva corónica*, quoted in R. Levillier, *Don Francisco de Toledo, supremo organizador del Perú: su vida, su obra (1515–1582)*, 1 (Madrid, 1935):440; loosely translated by Dilke in *Letter to a King*, 125. Viceroy Toledo held an inquiry into native taxation and the legitimacy of Inca rule, at Vilcas Tambo in 1571. The respondents confirmed that their region had been conquered by Topa Inca Yupanqui.

187   "them have died": Carvajal, 205.

TEMPLE OF VIRACOCHA, RAQCHI

188   Viracocha's appearance: Betanzos, *Suma y narración*, ch. 2, BAE (CONT) 209:11; Cieza de León, *Crónica*, pt. 2, ch. 5, Araníbar edn., 9–11; Sarmiento de Gamboa, *Historia índica*, ch. 7, Markham trans., 35.

188   "without sinking": Sarmiento de Gamboa, ch. 7, Markham trans., 36. Sarmiento wrote that Viracocha means sea foam, and other chroniclers repeated his definition. Cieza said that this was wrong, and that the Spaniards were called Viracocha because of the three envoys who reached Cuzco to loot Coricancha for Atahualpa's ransom: the inhabitants of Cuzco had been praying to Viracocha for deliverance from Atahualpa's army, so that the curious strangers were taken to be messengers from the god. Garcilaso also refuted the common definition, even though *vira* meant tallow, or possibly foam, and *cocha* meant sea or lake. He preferred to follow the Jesuit Blás Valera in translating Viracocha as "the Will and Power of God" (*Comentarios reales*, bk. 5, ch. 21, Livermore trans., 1:288). Two words of the Inca god's titles have recently achieved fame as the name of Thor Heyerdahl's raft *Kon Tiki*.

191   Solution to the thrust problem: Gasparini and Margolies, 254–255.

192   Garcilaso's description of the temple: bk. 5, ch. 22, BAE (CONT) 133:179–180; or Livermore trans., 1:290–291. See also Gasparini

and Margolies, *Arquitectura Inka*, 249–263; Squier, *Peru*, 403–414; Bingham, *Inca Land*, 129; Moorehead, "Highland Inca Architecture in Adobe," 86–89.

193   "building remain": Garcilaso, bk. 5, ch. 22, BAE (CONT) 133:180–181.

HUÁNUCO

195   "seasons of the year": Estete, quoted in Jerez, *Verdadera relación*, BAE (CONT) 26:342; or in Oviedo, *Historia general*, bk. 43, ch. 12, BAE (CONT) 121:76. The remark about Huánuco's gold is in ibid., ch. 9, 61.

197   "to his rescue": A. de Zárate, *Historia del descubrimiento y conquista del Perú*, bk. 4, ch. 1, BAE (CONT) 26:493.

197   "later depopulated": D. de Córdova Salinas, *Crónica franciscana de las provincias del Perú* (1651), bk. 1, ch. 15, Gómez Canedo edn. Washington, D.C., 1957).

197   "great difficulty": Cieza de León, *Crónica*, pt. 4 (*La guerra de Chupas*), ch. 82, Markham trans., 293.

197   "prayed for peace": Ibid., ch. 17, 50.

197   "can still see": Ibid., pt. 2, ch. 57, Araníbar edn., 188.

197   "Indians to serve it": Ibid., pt. 1, ch. 80, Onis–von Hagen edn., 109. The figure of 30,000 for Huánuco's population was repeated by J. López de Velasco, *Geografía . . .*, BAE (CONT) 248:240; by A. Vázquez de Espinosa, *Compendio*, bk. 4, ch. 51, para. 1361, BAE (CONT) 231:329; and by Garcilaso, pt. 1, bk. 8, ch. 4, Livermore trans., 1:484. The surviving ruins do not look as though they could have housed so large a population.

197   "four thousand men": Vázquez de Espinosa, bk. 4, ch. 51, para. 1361, BAE (CONT) 231:329, or Clark trans., 486.

197   "stables for cattle": Ibid.

198   The herds in the plaza: E. Harth-Terré, "El pueblo de Huánuco Viejo," 4–5.

198   "administered justice": I. Ortiz de Zúñiga, *Visita . . . a Huánuco*, in *Revista del Archivo Nacional* (1956), 43, 301. See also D. Shea, "El conjunto arquitectónico central en la plaza de Huánuco Viejo," CIAH 1:109–111; J. V. Murra and G. J. Hadden, "Informe presentado al Patronato Nacional de Arqueología . . . ," CIAH 1:131–133.

198   "an erected stone": Diego González Holguín, *Vocabulario de la lengua general . . . llamada lengua qqechua* (1608) (Lima, 1952), 358.

201   "chose [to honor]": Declaration by Chief Diego Xauxa, in I. Ortiz de Zúñiga, Murra edn., 1:37.

201   "pottery vessels": Ibid.

201   "by their forebears": Cieza de León, pt. 2, ch. 30, ed. Araníbar, 103–104; or Onis–von Hagen edn., 181–183.

201   "at their expense": Ibid., ch. 29, ed. Araníbar, 101; or Onis–von Hagen edn., 191.

201   "prepared it": Garcilaso, *Comentarios reales*, pt. 1, bk. 6, ch. 20, BAE (CONT) 133:219–220; or Livermore trans., 1:357–358.

201   "no one forced them": Declaration by Chief Diego Xauxa, in Í. Ortiz de Zúñiga, Murra edn., 1:41.

202   "of the tyrant": Litigation by the lords of Guancané, in the National Archive of Sucre, quoted in J. V. Murra and C. Morris, "Dynastic oral tradition . . . ," 277.

202   Morris on provincial cities: *Establecimientos estatales en el Tawantinsuyu* (Spanish trans. of his "State Settlements in Tawantisuyu"), 127–141.

INGAPIRCA

203   "was the equinox": Garcilaso, *Comentarios reales*, pt. 1, bk. 2, ch. 30, Livermore trans., 1:117. Gasparini and Margolies quote from Fernando Cabieses' manuscript on Machu Picchu, in which he mentions many aspects of the Inca religion that appear in units of three. An obvious example is the three mouths of the cave of Tambo-toqo. Some of the other groups of three are not strictly correct (for instance, his inclusion of Huanacauri as the third element in the Inca "pantheon," or naming only three celestial bodies), and he omits an obvious example in the divisions of the Cuzco ceque lines into groups of three, which repeat the names Collana, Payan and Cayao.

206   "very strong tower": Gaspar de Gallegos, *Relación de . . . Sant Francisco Pueleusi del Azogue* (1582), RGI in BAE (CONT) 184:275.

206   "great they were": Cieza de León, *Crónica*, pt. 1, ch. 44, Onis–von Hagen edn., 69–70, 73.

206   "spirited in war": Hernando Pablos, *Relación . . . de Cuenca*, RGI in BAE (CONT) 184:267.

206   "among the natives": Ibid. Cieza de León tells about the news of Pizarro's arrival (pt. 1, ch. 64, Onis–von Hagen edn., 72–73).

206   "it was general": Cieza de León, pt. 2, ch. 69, 231. The epidemic was also reported by M. de Murúa, *Historia*, ed. Ballesteros-Gaibrois, 1:103–104; M. Cabello de Balboa, *Miscelánea austral*, pt. 3, CLDRHP, 2 ser., 2:128; P. Sarmiento de Gamboa, *Historia índica*, ch. 62, Markham trans., 167–168; B. Cobo, *Nuevo Mundo*, bk. 12, ch. 17, BAE (CONT) 92:93; and others.

BIBLIOGRAPHY

ABBREVIATIONS USED IN THE NOTES AND BIBLIOGRAPHY

AA   *American Anthropologist*

BAE   *Biblioteca de autores españoles desde la formación del lenguaje hasta nuestros días.* Ed. Manuel Rivadeneira. 71 vols. Madrid, 1846–1880.

BAE (CONT)   *Continuación.* Ed. M. Meléndez Pelayo. Madrid, 1905–.

BRAH   *Boletín de la Real Academia de la Historia,* Madrid

CDIHE   *Colección de documentos inéditos para la historia de España.* Ed. M. Fernández de Navarrete and others. 112 vols. Madrid, 1842–1895.

CIAH   *Cuadernos de Investigación, Antropología,* Huánuco

CLDRHP   *Colección de libros y documentos referentes a la historia del Perú.* Ed. Carlos A. Romero and Horacio H. Urteaga. First series, 12 vols., Lima, 1916–1919. Second series, 10 vols., Lima, 1920–1934.

CLERC   *Colección de libros españoles raros ó curiosos.* 25 vols. Madrid, 1871–1896.

GP   *Gobernantes del Perú, cartas y papeles, siglo XVI . . .* Ed. Roberto Levillier. 14 vols. Madrid, 1921–1926.

HAKL SOC   The Hakluyt Society. First series, 100 vols., Cambridge, 1847–1898. Second series, Cambridge, 1899–.

HSAI   *Handbook of South American Indians.* Ed. Julian H. Steward. Smithsonian Institution, Bureau of American Ethnology Bulletin 143. Washington, D.C., 1946–1963.

RGI   *Relaciones geográficas de Indias.* Ed. M. Jiménez de la Espada. 4 vols. Madrid, 1881. In BAE (CONT), vols. 183–185 (1965).

RH   *Revista histórica,* Instituto Histórico del Perú, Lima. 1906–.

RIAC   *Revista del Instituto Arqueológico del Cuzco*

RMN   *Revista del Museo Nacional,* Lima. 1932–.

RSAC   *Revista de la Sección de Arqueología,* University of Cuzco

RU   *Revista Universitaria,* Cuzco. 1912–.

EARLY WORKS

THE YEAR A WORK was completed is given in parenthesis after its title if it was not published at the time.

Acosta, José de. *Historia natural y moral de las Indias.* Seville, 1590; Mexico, 1940; BAE (CONT) 73 (1954). Trans. C. R. Markham, HAKL SOC, 1 ser., 60–61 (1880).

Arriaga, Pablo José de. *Extirpación de la idolatría del Pirú* (Lima, 1621). BAE (CONT) 209:191–277.

Betanzos, Juan de. *Suma y narración de los Incas* (1551). In M. Jiménez de la Espada, Biblioteca Hispano-Ultramarina 5 (Madrid, 1890); CLDRHP, 2 ser., 8 (1924); BAE (CONT) 209 (1968):1–55.

Cabello de Balboa, Miguel. *Miscelánea Antártica,* pt. 3: *Historia del Perú* (1586). Paris, 1840; CLDRHP, 2 ser., 2 (1920); Quito, 1945; Lima: Instituto de Etnología, 1951.

Calancha, Antonio de la. *Corónica moralizada del orden de San Agustín en el Perú.* Barcelona, 1638.

Cieza de León, Pedro de. *Parte primera de la crónica del Perú.* Seville, 1553. Many Spanish editions. Trans. C. R. Markham, *The Travels of Pedro de Cieza de León,* HAKL SOC, 1 ser., 33 (1864).

——. *Segunda parte de la crónica del Perú, que trata del señorío de los Incas Yupanquis* (1554). Ed. Carlos Araníbar. Lima, 1967. Many other editions. Trans. C. R. Markham, HAKL SOC, 1 ser., 68 (1883).

——. *The Incas of Pedro de Cieza de León* [combination of pts. 1 and 2]. Trans. Harriet de Onis; ed. Victor W. von Hagen. Norman, Okla., 1959.

——. *Tercera parte: Descubrimiento y conquista* (ca. 1554). Ed. Rafael Loredo. In *Mercurio Peruano* 27 (1946), 32 (1951), 34 (1953), 36–39 (1955–1958).

——. *La crónica del Perú,* pt. 4: *La guerra de las Salinas, La guerra de Chupas, La guerra de Quito.* Many Spanish editions. Trans. C. R. Markham; *The War of Las Salinas,* HAKL SOC, 2 ser., 54 (1923); *The War of Chupas,* HAKL SOC, 2 ser., 42 (1918); *The War of Quito,* HAKL SOC, 2 ser., 31 (1913).

Cobo, Bernabé. *Historia de la fundación de Lima* (1639). BAE (CONT) 92 (1956).

——. *Historia del Nuevo Mundo* (1653). Ed. Luis A. Pardo. 4 vols. Cuzco, 1956; BAE (CONT) 91–92 (1956).

Cuzco. Actos de los libros de cabildos de Cuzco, años 1545 a 1548. In *Revista del Archivo Histórico del Cuzco* 9, no. 9, (1958):5–13, 37–305.

——. Acta de fundación del Cuzco (23 Mar. 1534). In R. Porras Barrenechea,

"Dos documentos esenciales sobre Francisco Pizarro y la conquista del Perú . . . el acta perdida de fundación del Cuzco." RH 17 (1948):88–95; CDIHE 26: 221–232.

Diez de San Miguel, Garci. *Visita hecha a la provincia de Chucuito en el año 1567*. Ed. Waldemar Espinoza Soriano. Lima, 1964.

Estete, Miguel de. [Narrative of a Journey to Pachacamac], in Francisco de Jerez, *Verdadera relación de la conquista del Perú*. Seville, 1534; BAE (CONT) 26 (1947):338–343. Trans. C. R. Markham, *Reports on the Discovery of Peru*, HAKL SOC, 1 ser., 47 (1872):74–94.

Garcilaso de la Vega ("El Inca"). *Primera parte de los comentarios reales* (Lisbon, 1609); *Segunda parte de los comentarios reales de los Incas: Historia general del Perú* (Córdoba, 1617). BAE (CONT) 134–135 (1960). Pt. 1 trans. C. R. Markham, HAKL SOC, 41 (1869), 45 (1871). Both parts trans. Harold V. Livermore, 2 vols., London and Austin, 1966.

Guaman Poma de Ayala, Felipe. *Nueva corónica y buen gobierno* (? 1580–1620). In *Travaux et mémoires de l'Institut d'Ethnologie* 23, ed. Alfred Métraux, Paris, 1936. Ed. L. F. Bustíos Gálvez, 3 vols., Lima, 1956–1966. Partly trans. Christopher Dilke, *Letter to a King*, London, 1978.

Gutiérrez de Santa Clara, Pedro. *Historia de las guerras civiles del Perú y de otros sucesos de las Indias* (? 1600). BAE (CONT) 165–167 (1963–1964).

Herrera y Tordesillas, Antonio de. *Historia general de los hechos de los castellanos en las islas i tierrafirme del Mar Océano*. 4 vols. Madrid, 1601–1615. Ed. Antonio Ballesteros and Miguel Gómez del Campillo, 17 vols., Madrid, 1934–1956.

Jerez, Francisco de. *Verdadera relación de la conquista del Perú y provincia del Cuzco*. Seville, 1534. Many editions, including CLDRHP, 1 ser., 5 (1917):1–121; BAE (CONT) 26 (1947):320–346. Trans. C. R. Markham in *Reports on the Discovery of Peru*, HAKL SOC, 1 ser., 47 (1872):1–109.

Lizárraga, Reginaldo de. *Descripción breve de toda la tierra del Perú, Tucumán, Río de la Plata, y Chile* (ca. 1605). BAE (CONT) 216 (1968):1–213.

López de Velasco, Juan. *Geografía y descripción universal de las Indias* (1571–1574). Ed. Justo Zaragoza. Madrid, 1894. BAE (CONT) 248 (1971).

Mena, Cristóbal de (attributed to). *La conquista del Perú, llamada la Nueva Castilla*. Seville, April 1534. Ed. R. Porras Barrenechea, in *Las relaciones primitivas de la conquista del Perú* (Lima, 1967), 79–101. Trans. Joseph H. Sinclair, *The Conquest of Peru, as recorded by a member of the Pizarro expedition*, with a facsimile of the 1534 edition (New York, 1929).

Molina, Cristóbal de (el Almagrista or of Santiago). *Relación de muchas cosas acaesidas en el Perú . . . en la conquista y población destos reinos* (ca. 1553). Paris, 1840; CLDRHP, 1 ser., 1 (1916):111–190; ed. F. A. Loayza (Lima, 1943); BAE (CONT) 209 (1968):56–96.

Molina, Cristóbal de (of Cuzco). *Relación de las fábulas y ritos de los Incas* (1573). CLDRHP, 1 ser., 1 (1916):1–103; ed. Ernesto Morales, Buenos Aires, 1959. Trans. C. R. Markham, *The Fables and Rites of the Incas*, HAKL SOC, 2 ser., 48 (1873).

Montesinos, Fernando de. *Memorias antiguas historiales y políticas del Perú* (1630). CLERC 16 (1882). Trans. P. A. Means, HAKL SOC, 2 ser., 48 (1920).

Murúa, Martín de. *Historia general del Perú, origen y descendencia de los Incas* (1590–1611). Ed. Manuel Ballesteros Gaibrois. 2 vols. Madrid, 1962, 1964 (Wellington MS); CLDRHP, 2 ser., 4, 5 (1922–1925); ed. Constantino Bayle, 2 vols., Madrid, 1946 (Loyola MS).

Ortiz de Zúñiga, Íñigo. *Visita a la provincia de León de Huánuco en 1562*. Ed. John V. Murra. 2 vols. Huánuco, Peru, 1967.

Oviedo y Valdés, Gonzalo Fernández de. *La historia general y natural de las Indias* (Seville, 1535; including section on Peru: Salamanca, 1547). Valladolid, 1557. Ed. Juan Pérez de Tudela Bueso, BAE (CONT) 117–121 (1959).

Pizarro, Hernando. [Letter to the Oidores of Santo Domingo, Panama, 23 November 1533]. In Gonzalo Fernández de Oviedo y Valdés, *La historia general y natural de las Indias*, bk. 46, ch. 16, BAE (CONT) 121 (1959): 84–90. Trans. C. R. Markham in *Reports on the Discovery of Peru*, HAKL SOC 47 (1872):113–127.

Pizarro, Pedro. *Relación del descubrimiento y conquista de los reinos del Perú* (1571). BAE (CONT) 168 (1965):159–242. Trans. P. A. Means as *Relation of the Discovery and Conquest of the Kingdoms of Peru*, Cortes Society, New York, 1921.

Poma de Ayala. *See* Guaman Poma de Ayala.

Ramos Gavilán, Alonso. *Historia del célebre santuario de Nuestra Señora de Copacabana*. Lima, 1621.

Relación de las cosas del Perú desde 1543 hasta la muerte de Gonzalo Pizarro (ca. 1550; attributed to Juan Polo de Ondegardo, Rodrigo Lozano or Agustín de Zárate). BAE (CONT) 168 (1965):243–332.

Relación de las costumbres antiguas de los naturales del Pirú. BAE (CONT) 209 (1968):151–189.

Relación del sitio del Cuzco y principio de las guerras civiles del Perú hasta la muerte de Diego de Almagro (1539; often attributed to Vicente de Valverde, but more probably by Diego de Silva). CLERC 13 (1879): 1–195; CLDRHP, 2 ser., 10 (1934).

Ruiz de Arce, Juan. *Relación de servicios; Advertencias que hizó el fundador del vínculo y mayorazgo a los sucesores en él* (ca. 1545). BRAH 102 (1933):327–384.

Sancho, Pedro. *Testimonio de la acta de repartición del rescate de Atahualpa* (1533). Trans. C. R. Markham, HAKL SOC, 1 ser., 97 (1872): 131–143.

——. *Relación para S.M. de lo sucedido en la conquista y pacificación de estas provincias de la Neuva Castilla y de la calidad de la tierra* (1543). CLDRHP, 1 ser., 5 (1917):122–202. Trans. P. A. Means, New York: Cortes Society, 1917. (The original MS is lost but was translated in Giambattista Ramusio, *Delle navigationi e viaggi* 3 [1559], from which subsequent texts are derived.)

Santacruz Pachacuti Yamqui, Joan de. *Relación de antigüedades deste reyno del Pirú* (ca. 1615). Ed. M. Jiménez de la Espada in *Tres relaciones de antigüedadas peruanas* (Madrid, 1879); CLDRHP, 2 ser., 9 (1927). BAE (CONT) 209 (1968):279–319. Trans. C. R. Markham, HAKL SOC, 1 ser., 48 (1873):67–120.

Santillán, Hernando de. *Relación del origen, descendencia, política y gobierno de los Incas* (ca. 1563). Ed. M. Jiménez de la Espada in *Tres relaciones de antigüedadas peruanas* (Madrid, 1879), 1–133; CLDRHP, 2 ser., 9 (1927):1–117; BAE (CONT) 209 (1968):97–150.

Sarmiento de Gamboa, Pedro. *Historia índica* (1572). Ed. Richard Peitschmann (Berlin, 1906); BAE (CONT) 135 (1960):189–279. Trans. C. R. Markham, *History of the Incas*, HAKL SOC, 2 ser., 22 (1907).

Titu Cusi Yupanqui [Inca Diego de Castro]. *Relación de la conquista del Perú y hechos del Inca Manco II; Instrucción para el muy Ille. Señor Ldo. Lope García de Castro, Gouernador que fue destos rreynos del Pirú* (1570). CLDRHP, 1 ser., 2 (1916).

Trujillo, Diego de. *Relación del descubrimiento del reyno del Perú* (1571). Ed. R. Porras Barrenechea. Seville, 1948.

Vázquez de Espinosa, Antonio. *Compendio y descripción de las Indias Occidentales* (1628). BAE (CONT) 231 (1969). Trans. Charles Upson Clark; Smithsonian Collections, 102 no. 2646 (1942).

Zárate, Agustín de. *Historia del descubrimiento y conquista del Perú*. Antwerp, 1555; Seville, 1577; BAE (CONT) 26 (1947):459–574. Trans. T. Nicholas, London, 1581; J. M. Cohen, Harmondsworth, Middx., 1968.

MODERN WORKS

Agurto Calvo, Santiago. *Cuzco: la traza urbana de la ciudad inca*. UNESCO Per 39 Project. Cuzco, 1980.

Alcina Franch, José. *Manuel de arqueología americana*. Madrid, 1965.

——. "Excavaciones en Chinchero (Cuzco): Informe preliminar." *XXXVIII Internationalen Amerikanistenkongress* (Stuttgart, 1968), *Verhandlungen* 1 (Munich, 1969):421–428.

——. "Excavaciones en Chinchero (Cuzco): Temporadas 1968 y 1969." *Revista Española de Antropología Americana*, Madrid, 5 (1970):99–121.

——. "El sistema urbanístico de Chinchero." RMN 37 (1971):124–134.

——. and Manuel Ballesteros Gaibrois. *La arqueología en Chinchero*. Madrid, 1976.

Altieri, Andrés Radamés. "El templo de Viracocha en Cacha (Perú)." *Revista Geográfica Americana*, Buenos Aires, 2, no. 4 (1934):350–356.

Angles Vargas, Víctor. *P'isaq, metrópoli Inka*. Lima, 1970.

——. *Machupijchu, enigmática ciudad inka*. Lima, 1972.

——. *Historia del Cusco*. Lima, 1978. Vol. 1.

Ballesteros Gaibrois, Manuel. *Sencilla historia de Chinchero*. Cuzco, 1971.

Bandelier, Adolf Francis. "The Aboriginal Ruins of Sillustani, Peru." AA, n.s. 7 (1905):49–68.

——. *The Islands of Titicaca and Koati*. New York, 1910.

Baudin, Louis. *L'Empire socialiste des Inka. Travaux et mémoires de l'Institut d'Ethnologie* 5. Paris; 1928. Trans. Katherine Woods, *A Socialist Empire: The Incas of Peru*, Princeton, N.J., 1961.

——. *La Vie quotidienne au temps des derniers Incas*. Paris, 1955. Trans. Winifred Bradford, *Daily Life in Peru*, London, 1961.

Bayon, Damián, "Las vistas antiguas del Cuzco en la Bibloteca Nacional de París." *XXXVIII Internationalen Amerikanistenkongress* (Stuttgart, 1968), *Verhandlungen* 4 (Munich, 1972):239–246.

Bedoya Maruri, Ángel Nicanor. *La arqueología en la región internadina del Ecuador*. Puebla, Mexico, 1974.

Bennett, Wendell Clark. "Machu Picchu: The Most Famous Inca Ruin." *Natural History*, New York, 35 (1935):64–76.

——. *Ancient Arts of the Andes*. New York, 1954.

——. and Junius B. Bird. *Andean Culture History*. American Museum of Natural History, Handbook 15. New York, 1949.

Bingham, Hiram. "The Ruins of Choqquequirau." AA 12, no. 4 (October 1910):505–525.

——. "Vitcos, the Last Inca Capital." *Proceedings of the American Antiquarian Society*, Worcester, Mass., April 1912, 135–196.

——. *Inca Land*. London, 1922.

——. *Machu Picchu, Citadel of the Incas*. New Haven, Conn., 1930.

——. *Lost City of the Incas*. London, 1951.

Bonavia, Duccio. "Factores ecológicos que han intervenido en las transformación urbana a través de los últimos siglos de la época precolombina." *XXXIX Congreso Internacional de Americanistas (Lima), Actas y Memorias* 2 (1972).

——. and Rogger Ravines, *Pueblos y culturas de la Sierra Central del Perú*. Lima, 1972.

Brundage, Burr Cartwright. *Empire of the Inca*. Norman, Okla. 1963.

Buschiazzo, Mario J. "El templo y convento de Santo Domingo del Cuzco." *Revista de Arquitectura*, Buenos Aires, 22, no. 191 (1936).

Buse, Hermann. *Machu Picchu. Antología*. Lima, 1963.

——. *Epoca prehistórica*. In *Historia marítima del Perú*, tomo 2 (vols. 1–2). Lima, 1976.

Bushnell, Geoffrey H. S. *Peru*. Rev. ed. London and New York, 1963.

Busto Duthurburu, José Antonio del. *Perú incaico*. Lima, 1980.

Cabieses, Fernando. *Los dioses vinieron del mar*. Lima, 1972.

——. "Machu Picchu, apuntes etnohistóricos." MS, Lima, 1974.

Chávez Ballón, Manuel. "El sitio de Raqchi en San Pedro de Cacha." *Revista Peruana de Cultura*, Lima, 1963, 105–111.

——. "Ciudades Incas: Cuzco, capital del imperio." *Wayka*, Cuzco, 3 (1970):1–14.

Cornejo Bouroncle, Jorge. "Huakaypata, la Plaza Mayor del viejo Cuzco." RU 35, nos. 90–91 (1946):85–116.

Covarrubias Pozo, Jesús M. *Primer libro de actas de cabildos de la ciudad del Cuzco y fundación del hospital de naturales*. Cuzco, 1960.

——. *Extracto y versión paleográfica del Segundo Libro de actas de Cabildo, Justicia y Regimiento de la ciudad del Cuzco*. Cuzco, 1963.

Donkin, Robin A. *Agricultural Terracing in the Aboriginal New World*. Viking Fund Publications in Anthropology 56, Tucson, Ariz., 1979.

Enock, C. Reginald. "The Ruins of Huánuco Viejo or Old Huánuco." *Geographical Journal*, London, 26 (1905):153–179; also in *Boletín de la Sociedad Geográfica de Lima* 3 (1904):317–324.

——. *The Andes and the Amazon*. London, 1913.

Espinoza Soriano, Waldemar. *La destrucción del imperio de los Incas*. Lima, 1973.

——, ed. *See* Diez de San Miguel in "Early Sources" section.

Fejos, Paul. *Archaeological Explorations in the Cordillera Vilcabamba, Southeastern Peru*. Viking Fund Publications in Anthropology 3. New York, 1944.

Franco Inojosa, José María, and Alejandro Gonzales. "Los trabajos arqueológicos en el Departamento del Cusco. Informe . . . sobre las ruinas incaicas de Tarawasi (Limatambo)." RMN 6 (1937):66–80.

——, and Luis A. Llanos. "Trabajos arqueológicos en el Departamento del Cusco. Sajsawaman: excavación en el edificio sur de Muyumarca." RMN 9, no. 1 (1940):22–32.

Frost, Peter. *Exploring Cuzco*. Lima, 1979.

García, José Uriel. *La ciudad de los Incas: estudios arqueológicos*. Cuzco, 1922.

——. *Guía histórica-artística del Cuzco*. Lima, 1925.

——. "Machu Picchu." *Cuadernos Americanos*, Mexico, 4 (1961).

García Rosell, César. *Los monumentos arqueológicos del Perú*. Lima, 1942.

Gasparini, Graziano, and Luise Margolies. *Arquitectura Inka*. Caracas, 1977. Trans. Patricia Lyon, *Inca Architecture*, Bloomington, Ind., 1980.

Gregory, Herbert E. "The Rodadero: A Fault Plane of Unusual Aspect." *American Journal of Science*, N.Y., 37, no. 220 (Apr. 1914):289–298.

Guillén, Víctor M. "El gran templo de Huiraccocha." RU 2 (1937):82–97.

Gutiérrez, Miguel F. "Monolitos y petroglitos de Say-hui-te antes de Concacha." RIAC 4, nos. 6–7 (1939):91–96.

Hagen, Victor Wolfgang von. *A Guide to Ollantaytambo*. New York, 1949; Lima, 1958.

——. *Highway of the Sun*. New York and Boston, 1955; London, 1956.

——. *The Royal Road of the Inca*. London, 1976.

——, ed. *The Incas of Pedro de Cieza de León*. Trans. Harriet de Onis. Norman, Okla., 1959.

Hardoy, Jorge Enrique. *Ciudades precolombinas*. Buenos Aires, 1964.

——. *Urban Planning in Pre-Columbian America*. London, 1968.

Harth-Terré, Emilio. "Incahuasi—ruinas incaicas del valle de Lunahuana." RMN 2 (1933):99–125.

——. "El pueblo de Huánuco Viejo." *Arquitecto Peruano*, Lima, 320–321 (1964):1–20.

Hemming, John Henry. *The Conquest of the Incas*. London and New York, 1970.

——. *Machu Picchu*. New York, 1981.

Horkheimer, Hans. "Guía bibliográfica de los principales sitios arqueológicos del Perú." *Boletín Bibliográfico de la Biblioteca Central de la Universidad Nacional Mayor de San Marcos*, Lima, 20, nos. 3–4 (1950):181–234.

——. *El Perú prehispánico*. Lima, 1950.

——, and Federico Kauffmann Doig. *La cultura Inca*. Lima, 1965.

Kalafatovich Valle, Carlos. "Geología del grupo arqueólogico de la fortaleza de Saccsayhuaman y sus vecinidades." *Saqsaywaman, Revista del Patronato Departamental de Arqueología del Cuzo* 1 (July 1970):61–68.

——. "Geología de la ciudadela incaica de Machupicchu y sus alrededores." RU, 1963.

Kauffmann Doig, Federico. *Arqueología peruana*. Lima, 1971.

——. *Guía de las ruinas de Pachacamac*. Lima, 1961.

Kendall, Ann. *Everyday Life of the Incas*. London and New York, 1973.

——. "Aspects of Inca Architecture." 2 vols. Doctoral dissertation, University of London, 1974.

——. "Architecture and Planning at the Inca Sites in the Cusichaca Area." *Baessler-Archiv, Neue Folge*, Berlin, 22 (1974):73–137.

Kosok, Paul. *Life, Land and Water in Ancient Peru*. New York, 1965.

Kubler, George Alexander. *Reconstruction of Cuzco and Restoration of Its Monuments*. Paris, 1953.

——. "Machu Picchu." *Perspecta* 6 (1960):49–54.

——. *The Art and Architecture of Ancient America*. Harmondsworth, Middx., 1962.

Ladrón de Guevara Avilés, Oscar. "La restauración del Ccoricancha y templo de Santo Domingo." RIAC 21 (June 1967).

Lanning, Edward P. *Peru Before the Incas*. Englewood Cliffs, N.J., 1967.

Lara, Jesús. *Inkallajta Inkaraqay*. La Paz, 1967.

Lavallée, Danielle. "Estructura y organización del habitat en los Andes Centrales durante el período Intermedio Tardío." RMN 39 (1973):91–116.

Lehmann-Nitsche, Robert. "Coricancha, el Templo del Sol en el Cuzco y las imágenes de su altar mayor." *Revista del Museo de La Plata*, La Plata, Argentina 31 (1928):1–260.

Leicht, Hermann. *Arte y cultura preincaicos*. Madrid, 1963.

Llanos, Luis A. "Informe sobre Ollantaytambo." RMN 5, no. 2 (1936):123–156.

Lumbreras, Luis Guillermo. *De los pueblos, las culturas y las artes del antiguo Perú*. Lima, 1969.

Martínez Martínez, Valentín. *Monografía de Ollantaytambo*. Lima, 1966.

Mason, J. Alden. *The Ancient Civilizations of Peru*. Harmondsworth, Middx., 1957.

Menzel, Dorothy. "The Inca Occupation of the South Coast of Peru." *Southwestern Journal of Anthropology* 15, no. 2 (1959):125–142.

Mesa, José de, and Teresa Gisbert. "La arquitectura incaica en Bolivia." *Boletín del Centro de Investigaciones Históricas y Estéticas*, Caracas, 13 (1972):129–168.

Middendorf, Ernst W. *Peru, Beobachtungen und Studien über das Land und seine Bewohner*. 3 vols. Berlin, 1893–1895.

Moore, Sally Falk. *Power and Property in Inca Peru*. New York, 1958.

Moorehead, Elizabeth L. "Highland Inca Architecture in Adobe." *Ñawpa Pacha*, Berkeley, Calif., 16 (1978):65–94.

Morris E. Craig. "El tampu real de Tunsucancha." CIAH 1 (1966):95–107.

——. "Storage in Tawantinsuyu." Doctoral dissertation, University of Chicago, 1967.

——. "Master Design of the Inca." *Natural History*, New York, Dec. 1976: 60–66.

——. "The Identification of Function in Inca Architecture and Ceramics." *XXXIX Congreso Internacional de Americanistas* (Lima), *Actas y Memorias* 3 (1971):135–144.

——. "State Settlements in Tawantinsuyu: A Strategy of Compulsory Urbanism." In M. P. Leone, ed., *Contemporary Archaeology: A Guide to Theory and Contributions*, Carbondale, Ill., 1972. Spanish trans. in RMN 39 (1973).

——, and Donald E. Thompson. "Huánuco Viejo: An Inca Administrative Center." *American Antiquity* 35, no. 3 (1970):344–362.

Murra, John V. "Rite and Crop in the Inca State." In Stanley Diamond, ed., *Culture in History: Essays in Honor of Paul Radin* (New York, 1960), 394–407.

——. "Cloth and Its Function in the Inca State." AA 64, no. 4 (1962): 710–728.

——. *Formaciones económicas y políticas del mundo andino*. Lima, 1975.

——, and G. J. Hadden. "Informe presentado el Patronato Nacional de Arqueología sobre la labor de limpieza y consolidación de Huánuco Viejo (20 de julio a 23 de noviembre 1965)." CIAH 1 (1966):129–144.

——, and E. Craig Morris. "Dynastic Oral Tradition, Administrative Records and Archaeology in the Andes." *World Archaeology*, London, 7, no. 3 (Feb. 1976):267–279.

——, ed. *See* Ortiz de Zúñiga in "Early Sources" section.

Nordenskiöld, Erland. "Incallajta, una ciudad fortaleza edificada por Tupaj Yupanki Inka." *Yoner*, Stockholm, 2 (1915).

Núñez del Prado, Oscar. "Chinchero, un pueblo andino del sur." RU 38 (1949):177–230.

Pardo, Luis A. *La metropoli de los Incas*. Cuzco, 1932.

——. *Ruinas precolombinas del Cuzco*. Cuzco, 1937.

——. "Exposición de las ruinas del santuario de Huiraccocha." RIAC 2, no. 2 (1937):3–32.

——. "La ciudadela de Sacsaihuaman." RIAC 2, no. 3 (1938):3–18.

——. *Machupijchu, una joya arquitectónica de los Incas*. Cuzco, 1944.

——. "Los grandes monolitos de Sayhuiti." RSAC 1 (1945):6–28.

——. "Ollantaitampu, una ciudad megalítica." RSAC 2 (1946):43–73.

——. "La metropoli de Paccaritampu: el adoratorio de Tamputtocco . . ." RSAC 2 (1946):3–46.

——. *Historia y arqueología del Cuzco*. 2 vols. Cuzco, 1957.

——. "La fortaleza de Saccsayhuaman." *Saqsaywaman: Revista del Patronato Departamental de Arqueología del Cuzco* 1 (July 1970):89–157.

——. *El imperio de Vilcabamba*. Cuzco, 1972.

——, and Oscar Ladrón de Guevara Avilés. "Trabajos de limpieza y consolidación, estudio e investigación." *Saqsaywaman* 1 (July 1970):21–42.

Porras Barrenechea, Raul. *Antología del Cuzco*. Lima, 1961.

Raimondi, Antonio. "Ruinas de Huánuco Viejo." *Boletín de la Sociedad Geográfica de Lima* 11 (1901):397–400.

——. *El Perú*. 6 vols. Lima, 1874–1913.

Regal Alberto. *Los puentes del Inca en el antiguo Perú*. Lima, 1972.

——. *Los trabajos hidráulicos del Inca en el antiguo Perú*. Lima, 1970.

Rivero, Mariano E., and Johann Jakop von Tschudi. *Antigüedades peruanas*. 2 vols. Vienna, 1851. Trans. Francis L. Hawks, *Peruvian Antiquities*, New York, 1854.

Robertson, Donald. *Pre-Columbian Architecture*. New York, 1963.

Rostworowski de Diez Canseco, María. *Pesos y medidas en el Perú prehispánico*. Lima, 1960.

——. "Neuvos datos sobre tenencia de tierras reales en el Incario." RMN 30 (1962):130–159.

——. "Nuevos aportes para el estudio de la medición de tierras en el Virreynato e Incario." RMN 28 (1964).

——. "Las tierras reales y su mano de obra en el Tahuantinsuyu." *XXXVI Congreso Internacional de Americanistas, Actas, y Memorias* (Seville, 1966), 31–34.

Rowe, John Howland. "An Introduction to the Archaeology of Cuzco." *Papers of the Peabody Museum of American Archaeology and Ethnology*, Cambridge, Mass., 27, no. 2 (1944).

——. "Inca Culture at the Time of the Spanish Conquest." HSAI 2:183–330.

——. 'What Kind of Settlement Was Inca Cuzco?" *Ñawpa Pacha*, Berkeley, Calif., 5 (1967):59–76.

——. "Urban Settlements in Ancient Peru." In John H. Rowe and Dorothy Menzel, eds., *Peruvian Archaeology: Selected Readings* (Palo Alto, Calif., 1967):293–319.

——. "La arqueología del Cuzco como historia cultural." *Revista del Museo e Instituto Histórico del Cuzco* 32, año 10, nos. 16–17 (1967).

Rozas L., Edgar Alberto. *Cuzco, ciudad monumental*. Cuzco, 1962.

Sasser, Elizabeth Skidmore. *Architecture of Ancient Peru*. Lubbock, Tex., 1969.

Shea, Daniel. "El conjunto arquitectónico central en la plaza de Huánuco Viejo." CIAH I (1966):108–116.

Squier, Ephraim George. *Peru: Incidents of Travel and Exploration in the Land of the Incas*. London, 1877.

Thompson, Donald E. "Incaic Installations at Huánuco and Pumpu." *XXXVII Congreso Internacional de Americanistas* (Buenos Aires), *Actas y Memorias* I (1968).

——. "An Archaeological Evaluation of Ethnohistorical Evidence of Inca Culture." In Betty S. Meggers, ed., *Anthropological Archaeology in the Americas* (Washington, D.C., 1968).

——. "Huánuco, Peru: A Survey of a Province of the Inca Empire." *Archaeology*, Brattleboro, Vt., 21, no. 3 (1968).

——. "Una evaluación arqueológica de las evidencias etnohistóricas sobre la cultura incaica." In Rogger Ravines, ed., *100 años de arqueología en el Perú* (Lima, 1970):565–582.

——. "Peasant Inca Villages in the Huánuco Region." *XXXVIII Internationalen Amerikanisten Kongress* (Stuttgart, 1968), *Verhandlungen* 4 (Munich, 1972):61–66.

——, and John V. Murra. "Puentes incaicos en la región de Huánuco Pampa." CIAH I (1966). Trans. "The Inca Bridges in the Huánuco Region," AA 31, no. 5 (1966).

Ubbelohde-Doering, Heinrich. *The Art of Ancient Peru*. New York, 1952.

——. *Auf den Königstrassen der Inka*. Trans. Margaret Brown, *On the Royal Highways of the Incas*. London, 1967.

Uhle, Max. "El Templo del Sol de los Incas en Cuzco." *XXIII International Congress of Americanists* (New York, 1928), *Proceedings* (New York, 1930), 291–295.

——. *Las ruinas de Tomebamba*. 2 vols. Quito, 1923.

——. "Fortalezas incaicas: Incallacta-Machupicchu." *Revista Chilena de Historia y Geografía*, Santiago, 21 (1917):154–170.

Valcárcel y Vizcarra, Luis Eduardo. *Cuzco, capital arqueológico de Sudamérica, 1534–1934*. Lima, 1934.

——. "Los trabajos arqueológicos del Cuzco." RMN 3(1934):3–36, 181–191, 209–234; 4:1–24, 161–205, 209–233; 5:123–156; 6:67–80, 201–231.

——. "Cuzco Archeology." HSAI 2:177–182.

——. *Machu Picchu, el más famoso monumento arqueológico del Perú*. Buenos Aires, 1964.

——. *Historia del Perú antiguo*. 3 vols. Buenos Aires, 1964.

Velarde y Bergmann, Hector. *Arquitectura peruana*. Mexico, 1946.

Vidal, Humberto. *Visión del Cuzco*. Cuzco, 1958.

Wachtel, Nathan. *La vision des vaincus: les Indiens du Pérou devant la conquête espagnole, 1530–1570*. Paris, 1971. Trans. Ben and Siân Reynolds, *The Vision of the Vanquished: The Spanish Conquest of Peru through Indian Eyes, 1530–1570*, Hassocks, Sussex, 1977.

Wiener, Charles. *Pérou et Bolivie: récit de voyage*. Paris, 1880.

Zuidema, Rainer Tom. *The Ceque System of Cuzco*. Leiden: International Archives of Ethnography 50 (1964).

——. "La relación entre el patrón de poblamiento prehispánico y los principios derivados de la estructura social incaica." *XXXVII Congreso Internacional de Americanistas* (Buenos Aires), *Actas y Memorias* I (1968):45–55.

GLOSSARY

aclla (ajlla, aqlla): beautiful young woman chosen to serve the Inca

acllahuasi (ajllahuasi, aqllawasi): house of the chosen women

amaru: snake

anti: dawn; the east

Atahualpa (Atawallpa)

Aucaypata (Huacaypata, Waqaypata)

ayllu: clan, lineage

cancha (kancha): enclosed compound and courtyard

Carmenca (Karminqa)

Cassana (Casana, Qasana)

Ccorihuayrachina (Qoriwayrachina)

ceque: radiating line of shrines

chaca (chaka): bridge

chasqui: courier, postal runner

chicha: maize beer

Choquequirau (Choqek'irau, Choqquequirau)

chullpa: burial tower

Coati (Koati)

Colcampata (Qollqanpata)

Cora Cora (Qoraqora)

Coricancha (Qoricancha, Qorikancha)

cunti: sunset; the west

Cusipata (Kusipata)

Cuzco (Cusco)

hatun: large, great

Hatun Rumiyoc (Jatun-rumiyoc)

huaca (waka, waqa): shrine

huaman (waman): falcon

Huanacauri (Huanacaure, Wanakauri)

Huanka (Wanka)

Huari (Wari)

Huascar (Washkar)

huasi (wasi): house, building

huatana: hitching post

huauque: totem

Huayna Capac (Huaina Capac, Wayna Qhapaq)

Huayna Picchu (Wayna Pijchu)

Huchuy Cosco (Uchuy Cosco, Huch'uy Qosqo)

ichu: tough mountain grass used for thatch

illapa: thunder

inca (inka): emperor; tribe living around Cuzco

Incahuasi (Inka-wasi)

Incallacta (Inkallaqta)

inti: sun

inti-huatana (hitching post of the sun, gnomon)

kallanka: long rectangular hall with many doors

Kenko (Qenqo, Q'enqo)

Limatambo (see Rimac-tampu)

llacta (llaqta): town

llautu: woolen braid

Machu Picchu (Machupijchu)

mamacona (mamacuna, mamakuna): holy woman

Mañay Raqay (Maniaraki)

Manco Capac (Manko Qhapaq)

marca (marka): tower, fortified settlement

masma: open-sided building

Mauca Llacta (Mauq'a Llaqta)

mita (mit'a): labor service for the state

mitimaes (mitmaq, mijmaq): tribute payers resettled as colonists

Muyuc Marca (Muyu Marca, Muyucmarca, Muyuc Marka)

ñusta: princess, royal lady

Ollantaytambo (Ollantay Tanpu)

Paccaritambo (Pacarectambo, Paqareq Tanpu, Paqarejtanpu, Paqari-tambo, Paqari-tampu)

pacha: land, time

Pachacamac (Pachakama)

Pachacuti (Pachakuteq, Pachacutec, Pachakuti, Pachakutej, Pacakoti)

pampa: plain

panaca (panaqa): clan, lineage

pata: platform, plateau, terrace

Paucar Marca (Paucarmarka)

Paucartambo (Pauqar Tanpu)

phutu: niche

Pilco Caima (Pilco Kaima, Pilco Kayma)

pirca: walling of fieldstone in clay

pirua (pirwa): storehouse

Pisac (Pisaq)

Puca Pucara (Pukapukara)

pucará (pukará): fort

pucyu (puquio, pucjiu): spring, well

Puma Orco (Puma Orqo)

puna: high-altitude savannah

punchao: sun idol; dawn; the east

puncu (punku): gate

pururauca: a venerated rock

qollqa (collca): storehouse

quilla (killa): moon

quipu (khipu, qhipu): knotted string record

Quishuar-cancha (Kiswar Kancha)

racay (raqay): hall, shed

Raqchi (Racche, Racchi, Rajch'i)

rimac (corrupted to lima): oracle

Rimac-Tampu (Rimaq Tanpu, Limatambo)

rumi: rock, stone

Rumicolca (Rumiqollqa)

Runcu Raccay (Runku Raqay, Runturaqay)

Sacsahuaman (Sacsaihuaman, Sacsayhuaman, Saqsaywaman, Sajsawaman)

Saihuite (Saywite, Sayhuite)

Sallac Marca (Sayac Marka, Sayaqmarka)

suyo (suyu): quarter, region of the Inca empire

Tahuantinsuyo (Tawantinsuyu)

tambo (tampu, tanpu): inn, posthouse

Tambo Machay (Tanpumach'ay, Tampumachai)

Tambo-toqo (Tamputoco, Tanput'oqo)

tapia: compacted-mud walling

Tarahuasi (Tarawasi)

Tiahuanaco (Tiahuanacu, Tiwanaku)

Tumibamba (Tomebamba, Tumipampa)

urco: hill

usnu (ushnu, usno): administrative/religious platform

Vilcabamba (Willkapanpa)

Vilcanota (Willcamayu)

Vilcashuamán (Willka[s] Waman)

Viracocha (Wiracocha, Huiracocha, Wiraqocha)

Vitcos (Vitcus)

Xaquixahuana (K'aq-ya Qhawana, Jaquijahuana)

INDEX